SPORT examined

Paul Beashel
Andy Sibson
John Taylor

Published in 2004 by:
Nelson Thornes Ltd
Delta Place
27 Bath Road
CHELTENHAM
GL53 7TH
United Kingdom

04 05 06 07 08 / 10 9 8 7 6 5 4 3 2 1

A catalogue record for this book is available from the British Library

ISBN 0 7487 7722 9

Illustrations by David Burroughs, David Eaton, Keith Howard, Tony Morris, Gary Rees, Oxford Designers & Illustrators and Pantek Arts Ltd
Page make-up by Pantek Arts Ltd, Maidstone, Kent

Printed in Great Britain by Scotprint

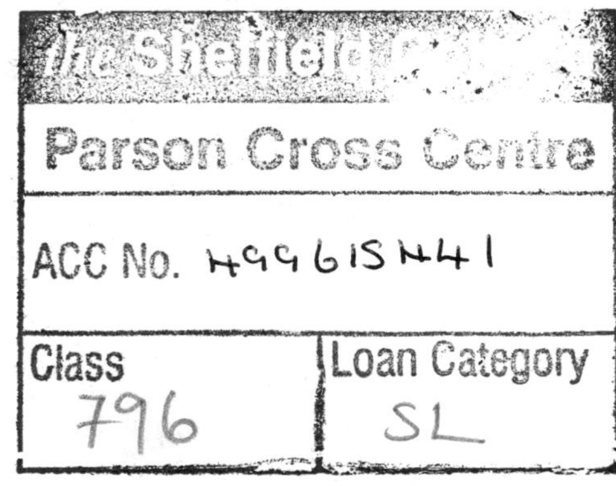

CONTENTS

ACKNOWLEDGEMENTS

Photo credits

All photos supplied by Getty Images, apart from the following:

- p.1 (top), p.7, p.22 (right), p.24, p.39, p.44, p.57 (bottom left), p.58 (left), p.86, p.144, p.153 (bottom), p.174, p.184, p.248, p.249, p.250, p.251, p.252 photographed by Simon Punter.
- p.8 photographed by Paul Beashel.
- p.15 and p.16 Stromotion photos by Dartfish.
- p.17, p.51, p.121 (top left) Photodisc 10 (NT).
- p.33 (right), p.57 (top), p.121 (right), p.209 Photodisc 51 (NT).
- p.35 (top) photographed by Colin Habberton.
- p.42, p.282 (bottom), p.319 (top), p.324, p.325 (bottom) Supersport Photographs/Eileen Langsley.
- p.73 Corbis Images/Duomo.
- p.77, p.266, p.279 (top), p.282 (top), p.283, p.286 (second row, second from right), p.311, p.321 (top), p.321 (bottom left), p.325 (top), p.326 Actionplus Sports Images.
- p.82 Offside Sports Photography.
- p.138, p.277 Photofusion Picture Library.
- p.216 Associated Press.
- p.243 Michael Cole/Camerawork.
- p.253 Alamy Images.
- p.279 (bottom) TopGolf Game Centre, Watford, www.topgolf.co.uk.
- p.286 (second row, second from left) Rex Features Limited.
- p.286 (bottom row, second from right) Sue Sharp.
- p.299 Kobal Picture Library.
- p.322 Topfoto.
- p.333 Topham Picture Point.

Picture research by Getty Images and Sue Sharp.

Dear Student,

Welcome to the world of sport. We are very pleased that you have decided to study physical education and sport. Over the next two years you will acquire a wealth of knowledge about your own body and how it stands up to the stresses and strains of modern sport. We are sure that you are already aware that sport makes many physical demands. However, our bodies are extremely adaptable. With a well planned and sustained training programme you will certainly improve your sporting performance.

A thorough and wide-ranging knowledge of the workings of the body is essential for an understanding of sporting performance. Nevertheless your own performance will not improve merely by reading books about sport or by watching sport on television. It is on the games field, in the gym or in the swimming pool that your sporting knowledge is applied and becomes of real value.

We know that you will get a great deal of fun and enjoyment from your course as you improve your sporting skills. You will also have the opportunity to gain a valuable GCSE in Physical Education. For us and for thousands of people around the world, sport is a daily inspiration and a challenge. We hope that you too will continue to enjoy sport for the rest of your life, and we wish you every success on this course.

Paul Beashel
Andy Sibson
John Taylor

Coursework support

Your Personal Training Programme (AQA 'A') or Performance Improvement Programme (AQA 'B' Short Course)*

As part of your GCSE course you are required to produce a **Personal Training Programme** or **PTP**. The programme should include a minimum of five training sessions. This gives you an opportunity to show how much you know about fitness and training.

What is a Personal Training Programme?

A Personal Training Programme is a training programme designed specifically for an individual sportsperson. It is prepared using knowledge about the individual's needs, the needs of the sport for which he or she is training and an understanding of the basic principles of fitness and training.

Your programme must be designed to improve your levels of:

- flexibility
- stamina
- maximum strength
- muscular power
- muscular endurance.

Most importantly, it needs to be specific to you and to your sport.

What do I need to include in my PTP?

- **Introduction**: You need to begin with an introduction which explains what a PTP is and which sport you are designing it for. You should include information about your age, gender and any medical conditions or injuries that need to be taken into account.
- **Seasonal factors**: A pre-season training programme is very different from a programme planned for the mid-season. You must make it clear which season your programme is intended for.
- **Types of fitness**: In this section you should define each type of fitness, so that the reader can see that you understand each one.
- **Effects of exercise on the body**: You should show that you understand the effects of exercise on the body. Your explanation should include details about:
  - the difference between aerobic and anaerobic exercise
  - oxygen debt
  - the effect of lactic acid in the muscles
  - the difference between inhaled and exhaled air

* The term 'Personal Training Programme' or 'PTP' is used throughout this section to refer to both a Personal Training Programme and a Performance Improvement Programme.

- the effect of exercise on breathing and heart rates.

- **Effects of training**: You should include a description of the effects that you expect to see from completing the PTP. You will need to list the long-term effects of exercise on the muscular system, the respiratory system and the circulatory system (see pages Chapters 7, 8 and 9). You should include details about:
  - how muscles change in size, strength and endurance
  - changes to vital capacity and tidal volume
  - changes to stroke volume, cardiac output, resting heart rate, recovery rate and blood composition.

- **SPORT principles of training**: In the next section you should explain each of the SPORT principles of training (see pages 186–188) and show how they apply to your PTP. For example:

  'I am planning to use cycling, running and swimming to increase my level of stamina. This will help to avoid tedium.'

  When writing about specificity, you should describe your individual needs and compare your levels of fitness with those required for your sport. This will produce a list of priorities. For example:

  'I need to work very hard on improving my stamina, but my flexibility levels are high, so I just need to maintain them.'

- **FITT principles of training**: You then need to explain the FITT principles and show how you will incorporate them in your PTP. You need to consider the types of fitness you wish to improve and relate them to the types of training that will lead to improvement. Make clear statements. For example:

  'Plyometric training will improve my muscular power.'

  You will also need to be scientific when explaining the intensity of your training. For example:

  'To improve my stamina I will train at 70% MHR for the first two weeks. By the sixth week I will be training at 75–80% MHR. This shows progression.'

  This section should also include information about the use of heart rate and recovery rate to monitor activity and fitness levels.

- **Phases of a training session**: You need to show your understanding of the phases of a training session. You can do this by describing the three phases (see page 195), but you need to mention that skill is not included in your PTP. However, you can use activities that are specific to your sport and you should provide examples of these. For example:

  'I will complete three sets of 15 blocking movements in volleyball to improve my muscular endurance.'

  In this section you should describe your warm-up and warm-down exercises in detail. Remember that you will be expected to lead a warm-up during your PE lessons, so you must understand every aspect of it. You do not need to write out a detailed warm-up for every session – just explain that the warm-up and warm-down is similar for each session.

  If you are planning a flexibility programme you should describe it in some detail here.

Safety issues

When planning the exercises in your training programme you must describe the way in which apparatus and equipment will be moved. You need to explain how to lift, carry and place equipment safely in your plans and when leading a session.

Training sessions

You need to outline at least five training sessions, taking into account all the issues described above. It is likely that you will train three times a week. This takes into account the principle of reversibility – which you will have explained in the FITT section when describing the frequency of training.

You must be sure that the exercises are set at your level of fitness. You can show progression by making the exercises more demanding by the end of the programme.

Example of one-week PTP

Week 1 Session 1	Venue: school field and gymnasium
Warm-up	See description
Cardiovascular endurance	20-minute run at 70% MHR
Flexibility	15 minutes active stretching of major muscle groups
Muscular strength	–
Power	Five sets of 10 reps plyometrics using two gymnastic box tops
Muscular endurance	Circuit of biceps, triceps, abdominals, shuttle exercises (2 x 30 seconds on each)
Warm-down	See description
Date/notes	

Week 1 Session 2	Venue: local leisure centre
Warm-up	See description
Cardiovascular endurance	25-minute swim at 70% MHR
Flexibility	15 minutes active stretching of major muscle groups
Muscular strength	Weight training in fitness centre. Heavy weights, low reps
Power	–
Muscular endurance	–
Warm-down	See description
Date/notes	

Week 1 Session 3	Venue: school field and gymnasium
Warm-up	See description
Cardiovascular endurance	25-minute run at 70% MHR
Flexibility	15 minutes active stretching of major muscle groups
Muscular strength	–
Power	Five sets of 10 reps plyometrics using two gymnastic box tops
Muscular endurance	Circuit of biceps, triceps, abdominals, shuttle exercises (2 x 40 seconds on each)
Warm-down	See description
Date/notes	

In the examples above, the athlete is avoiding tedium by training in two different environments. Maximum strength training is only taking place in the fitness centre, where swimming is the chosen exercise to improve cardiovascular endurance. But your PTP must be designed for you. If you have access to a fitness centre, you may choose to do all your training there. If not, you may have to plan to use the school gymnasium, fields or local park.

As each session is completed you should add the date and notes about how it went, or any changes you made.

Monitoring and evaluation

Once you have prepared your PTP, you actually have to do the work! As you complete each session you should note any changes, but be aware that if your programme is only five sessions in length you are unlikely to see significant gains in fitness.

At the end of the programme you need to evaluate the PTP as a whole. A good way of doing this is to retake the fitness tests that you completed for your Fitness Match. It is important to use the actual scores that you achieved before and after completing your PTP. You may find, for example, that your stamina level has increased significantly from the low end to the high end of 'above average' in the norm tables. If you only look at the tables you will think that there has been no improvement.

Your evaluation should consider:

- if your fitness levels have improved – and by how much
- any changes to your heart rate at rest and when exercising
- changes to your recovery rate
- noticeable effects on your muscles
- good and bad points about your exercise programme and how you might improve it.

Analytical Investigation (AQA 'B')

As part of your GCSE course for AQA 'B' you are required to produce an **Analytical Investigation (AI)**. This is worth 20% of the overall mark. The investigation gives you an opportunity to show how much you know about your chosen sport. By following the guidance in this section you can ensure that your investigation meets all of the examination requirements.

AQA suggest a number of contexts in which you can analyse your chosen sport. You can choose from any of the roles they describe and investigate any relevant areas of the sport.

The AQA suggestions are:

Context	Suggested investigations
As a choreographer	■ Improving solo dance performance through structured observation and feedback ■ Analysis of warm-up activities and their effect on flexibility in dance.
As a coach	■ A six-session series to improve the passing skills of the Year 7 netball squad ■ Does the ability to throw a ball transfer to the ability to throw a javelin?
As a leader	■ The impact of the captain on team performance ■ An analysis of the strengths and weaknesses of my leadership skills on the Duke of Edinburgh award expedition.
As an official	■ The similarities and differences in my officiating at basketball and soccer activities ■ The use of video analysis to improve my officiating skills in a selected activity.
As an organiser	■ The effects of the JSLA course on my organisational skills in Physical Education lessons ■ A review of my Year 8 inter-form basketball tournament in rally and knockout format.
As a performer	■ A study of the effects of improving my leg strength on jump shooting in basketball ■ The effect of selected flexibility exercises on my hurdling technique ■ A conditioning programme leading to performance improvement as measured by the bleep test.

(Source: AQA Specification 'B' Physical Education: Teachers Guide)

Once you have selected your context and topic, the next step is to plan the investigation. It should be presented in five sections to ensure that the work is clear and that everything is included. Your preparation should match the five sections. These are:

1 Audit

2 Planning

3 Implementation

4 Analysis

5 Evaluation.

1 Audit

This is the introduction to the investigation, in which you describe the skill or performance that you are studying. You should explain the improvements that you hope to secure in your area of focus. If you are looking at skills or fitness levels, you should complete a pre-test to give a baseline for comparison. You will find a number of fitness tests on pages 39–64. You may need to devise your own skills test, although there are many available in books and on the Internet.

2 Planning

In this section you clearly state the aims of your work. You will explain, in precise terms, what you expect to achieve by the end of your investigation. You should also describe the environment in which the investigation will take place – for example, a sports hall, fitness suite or swimming pool. Who will be involved? What equipment can you use? How long will the investigation last? How many sessions will it comprise? What will happen in each session?

If you are planning a Personal Training Programme (PTP) you should refer to the guidance given above. If you are analysing a performance you will find practical support on pages 1–30.

3 Implementation

Here you describe the investigation as it proceeds. You might keep a diary describing each session from your point of view and noting any problems or successes as they arise. At the end of the programme, if you are investigating skills or fitness levels, you should retake the tests used at the audit stage and record the results.

4 Analysis

This is a key section. You can demonstrate your understanding of the issues by linking test results and observations from the period of investigation or training with your original aims. Begin by presenting your results and observations. Then list each of your aims and describe how they have been affected by your programme.

5 Evaluation

How effective was your investigation? Did it meet its aims? What were its strengths? What were its weaknesses? If you did it again, what would you do differently? In this concluding section you should answer all these questions. You will receive marks for showing that you are able to constructively criticise your own work. This is not a negative process and you should not simply look for faults. Highlight the successes of your investigation, but show that you can also see ways to improve it.

SYLLABUS STRUCTURE

This book has been written to match precisely the requirements of the AQA GCSE Physical Education syllabus A and also syllabus B. At the start of each chapter we have set out the necessary key words, together with a summary of the syllabus requirements. We have explained clearly the different requirements of the two syllabuses. The text is based on the knowledge that is required by both syllabuses. However, we have indicated those sections that are required only for syllabus A or syllabus B. At the end of each chapter there is a set of AQA examination-style questions which include some questions common to both syllabuses and some appropriate for syllabus A and B separately.

Syllabuses A and B

Analysis of performance

The ability to observe and accurately analyse sporting performance is at the heart of this course. This section helps you develop these skills. You will also learn how to take training sessions and improve your leadership skills. You will be expected to demonstrate all of these skills as part of your GCSE assessment.

Factors affecting performance and participation in physical activities

The main part of this book is split into a number of sections and chapters. Here you will learn about the many factors that determine whether or not you choose to take part in sport and how you develop your ability. You will analyse the way in which your attitude in sport is influenced by the people around you, including your family, friends, teachers and also by the media. Local and national sports organisations and their facilities in your area will also affect your sporting choices.

You will need a sound knowledge of how your body works to understand sporting performance and so the important body systems for sport are explained. You will learn what is meant by the various types of fitness, the principles and different methods of training, your diet, health and hygiene.

Sport is not only exciting it is also potentially dangerous. You will need to know how to assess the risks in a wide range of sporting activities in order to prevent accidents and injuries. You must also be able to recognise the basic signs and symptoms of the most common sporting injuries and conditions.

Syllabus A and Syllabus B (short course) only

Personal training programme

You will be given helpful guidance and support to enable you to plan, perform and evaluate a health related exercise programme.

Syllabus B only

Analytical investigation

You will be give clear guidance and support to complete your analytical investigation.

The world of sport covers a wide variety of activities. Enjoyment is the main reason why we take part in sport and physical recreation. We do not know in which sports you will specialise. Therefore we have designed our book to give you the knowledge, principles and skills that are the basis of sporting performance. We know that we all learn in different ways, so we have included many different types of activities throughout the book. We hope that not only will you enjoy them but that they will stimulate you and lead you to success in your AQA Physical Education examination.

1 Analysis of performance

All of us involved in sport want to improve our **performance**. We train hard and practise our skills so that in competition we can produce our very best. To improve our performance we must first be able to **analyse** it. Learning the skills of analysing sporting action will help us to improve our own performance. We can also learn to analyse the performance of others and so work towards becoming a coach. This takes time, effort and experience.

Assessing analysis of performance

In this part of your GCSE course, you will be assessed on your ability to analyse your own and others' performance and to suggest ways to improve. Although you should have a good understanding of all sports and events you can select one sport for assessment purposes. You must be able to demonstrate your knowledge and understanding in five areas of coaching and leadership. These are:

- rules, regulations and terminology
- observation and analysis
- evaluation of performance compared with the Perfect Model
- planning strategies, tactics, practices and training to improve performance
- understanding the principles and roles of sports leadership.

activity

Analysing performance

Watch a group of your classmates playing a small sided game, for example, indoor hockey or netball. Try to decide who is the most effective player. Now explain why his or her performance is so effective. Is the player fitter? Faster-thinking? Harder-working? More skilful?

You can use the checklist on Worksheet 1 to help.

KEYWORDS

Analyse: to examine in detail and to explain

Arousal: level of alertness

Data: facts or information

Drill: training by repeating a technique or skill

Evaluate: to decide what is good and what needs to improve

Feedback: information about the outcome of a performance

Game plan: a set of tactics for use in a particular game

Motivation: determination to achieve

Observe: to watch carefully

Perfect Model: a mental image of the correct technique

Performance: how well a task is completed

Skill: the learned ability to choose and perform the right techniques at the right time

Strategy: long-term plan for success in sport

Tactics: methods used to put strategies into a game

Technique: basic movements in sport.

Key to Exam Success

For your GCSE you will need to know:

- the rules and regulations of your chosen sport and how to apply them as a player, coach, referee or judge. You should be able to use technical terms when describing your sport
- how to observe and analyse a performance and how to give feedback to the performer
- how to evaluate a performance, how to compare it with the Perfect Model and how to provide comprehensive and detailed feedback
- how to plan strategies, tactics, practices and training to improve performance with evidence from your own Personal Training Programme (PTP)
- the importance of leadership in sport and the different roles of sports leadership.

“ KEY THOUGHT ”

‘Preparation is the key to success in sport.’

Rules, regulations and terminology

activity

What would happen if...?

Imagine if these sports changed their laws:

- cricket – no lbw law
- football – no offside law
- hockey – the ball is allowed to touch the feet during play
- athletics – no lanes for the 200m
- tennis – no second service.

Discuss how each sport might change as a result of these new laws.

Think about your favourite sport. Have any rule changes been made in recent years? You may need to research the official rules.

Why do you need to know the rules and regulations?

You will often be asked to referee, umpire or score during PE lessons. GCSE assessment includes your ability to apply the rules and regulations, also called laws, as an official in charge of a match. When refereeing you must think about the rules of the activity and how to make sure that the players obey them. Every time you are asked to referee you should take the opportunity to practise, as you will then improve. As an official you need to show the players that you understand the rules thoroughly. They also want to see you make confident decisions and to control the game fairly but firmly.

Your teacher will assess your knowledge and understanding of the rules of your chosen sport. You will need to demonstrate this knowledge by refereeing or umpiring a game or a match. You will also be asked questions about the rules and basic tactics. You should take a pride in knowing the rules and also playing and refereeing fairly at all times. Ultimate Frisbee has included this idea in the official rules of the game. There is no referee. All players – even at the world championships – referee the game as they play!

Why do you need to keep up to date with the rules of your sport?

You should also keep up to date with rule changes. Every governing body reviews the rules of its sport on a regular basis. It may change the rules to make the game safer; for example, in rugby union, players must now stay on their feet at rucks. Rule changes may also be introduced to speed up the game; for example, in volleyball, teams now score a point every time they win a rally, not just when they win from their own serve. Often changes affect the way that the game is played and coached. In 1992 FIFA changed the rules so that goalkeepers could not pick up a ball that was passed to them by their own team. This stopped teams wasting time or using the goalkeeper as a 'safety' player. Defenders had to change their tactics as a result. Attackers began to run down back passes instead of leaving the goalkeeper to pick up the ball. The pace of the game increased and now we see many goalkeepers making mistakes.

Sports quiz

Choose a sport. It would be good if this is your Analysis of Performance assessment sport. Research the rules and produce a ten-question quiz to test participants' knowledge of the rules. Look for some obscure rules or situations to baffle your friends. If you like, create your quiz on a computer in order to make it more interactive. DataPower and Powerpoint programs could be used.

Why do coaches modify rules?

Sometimes coaches and teachers modify the rules of the game in training to develop skills or to create a new challenge. In some football games, players may only be allowed to control the ball with one or two touches in order to encourage movement and passing. Some rules will complicate the game too much for beginners; for example, in PE lessons the three-second and other time rules are rarely used in basketball, and in hockey lessons young players do not have to worry about offside. Some sports have different rules for junior games: for example, high fives netball, which is a five-a-side game with players rotating positions and roles.

What is terminology?

When you talk about your sport you will often use technical terms such as 'lbw' or 'offside'. These technical terms are called terminology. You probably know a lot of sports terminology already, but if you are going to coach effectively you need to know which terms to use to describe your sport.

Look at this example of terminology from badminton:

> 'You may play a forehand or a backhand shot. It may be a clear, a drive, a drop shot, a hairpin drop shot or a smash.'

You should be able to describe each shot and suggest to a player when he or she could use it as a tactic. Once everybody knows the terminology it is much easier to talk about the sport. Terminology includes examples of techniques, skills, strategies, tactics and rules.

Observation and analysis

The first stage in coaching is observing and analysing a performance. We have to watch a sportsperson in action and try to break down the movement into parts. If we watched a long jump we would need to look at the run-up, the take-off, the action in the air and the landing. Only when we have completed this part can we go on to evaluate the performance and explain to the performer how improvement can be made. At this second stage we can compare the jump in our mind with what we would like to see and then suggest to the athlete how he or she could do better.

Many coaches today use technology to help them to analyse performance. However, most of the time you will have to carry out live observation. That is to say, you must watch a player performing and then make decisions about the quality of the performance. This requires

activity

Terminology test

Are there any special terms in your chosen sport? Think about equipment, rules, techniques and strategies. Produce a list of terms on small cards, then pass the cards amongst your class. Each person has to explain the term to the rest of the class. If they do not know the answer you will have to make sure that you can explain it.

a lot of planning and practice. You can use a four-step approach to learn how to **observe** and **analyse**.

The four-step approach

The four-step approach begins with observing a simple activity involving one person. It builds up to a complex situation with many players in action.

Step 1
Observe and analyse a single technique – for example, a forward roll. In this situation you can control the environment, decide when the roll takes place and where you should stand to watch.

Step 2
Observe and analyse a single technique in action – for example, a forehand drive in tennis. This is a technique that requires a feed, that is someone to throw the ball for the player to hit. You are still in control of most of the situation, but the feed will vary and the player has to move to play the shot. There is much more to look at and to analyse.

Step 3
Observe an individual competitive performance – for example, a player in a badminton match. You can decide where to stand to observe the player, but you cannot decide which shots will be played. You will have to concentrate on just a few parts of the performance or you will get very confused. You will now be observing skill and tactics.

Step 4
Observe a competitive team performance – for example, a basketball team playing a match. In this situation you must focus on one or two aspects of performance and observe them carefully. Both team skill and team tactics can be observed.

Step 1: How do you analyse a specific technique?

You must know what the very best technique looks like. We call this the **Perfect Model**. You can then compare what you are seeing with the Perfect Model in your head. To build up this image you might use books, photographs, video footage or an expert performer. Your PE teacher, or one of your group, may be able to demonstrate during a lesson.

Before observing the technique you must break it down into a number of simple parts. You can then concentrate on each part in turn as the performer repeats the technique. Making a list of the different parts of the technique will help you to analyse in detail.

For example, if we were looking at a forward roll, we would look at the starting position, especially the hands and the head, the shape of the body during the roll and the finishing position, particularly of the arms. We would compare each part of the movement with the same part from our image of the Perfect Model.

You must decide where to stand to get the best view before observing any performance. You could view from either side, from the front or from behind, and also in some cases from above or below. The position you choose will depend on the specific technique that you are observing, the nature of the sport and on your knowledge of the sport. An experienced javelin coach will first note whether the athlete is right- or left-

handed and will then view the run-up and throw from a number of different positions. Safety would also be an important consideration for the coach in this event.

Step 2: Analysing a technique in action

When observing a technique in action you should use a help sheet to list the points you will be looking for before you begin.

Here is an example of a technique to analyse the overhead clear in badminton.

You might want to look separately at:

- movement into position
- foot placement and body position under the shuttlecock
- arm and racket preparation
- hitting action and follow-through.

Before observing this technique you must decide who is going to feed the shuttle to the player. A feeder in this context means another player or coach who throws, kicks or places the ball or shuttle in the best position so that the technique can be practised. If the feed is not accurate, the player will not be able to play the shot that you wish to see. Top coaches in sports such as volleyball have to pass tests to make sure that they can feed a ball accurately to the right place for each technique to be practised. When practising, the feeder has a very important role and should be told exactly how and where to feed. He or she must take the job very seriously.

Using ICT

Observation and analysis are much easier if you can slow down the action and study it in detail. Using ICT can help you to do this. There are many CD-ROMS and DVDs available which show footage of different sports. The web has examples too. If you have the facilities, you can make your own video using editing software. The simplest way of slowing down the action is to use a digital video camera and to watch the technique on the camera LCD screen.

Step 3: How do you analyse a competitive individual performance?

A performer will use a range of techniques and skills very rapidly during competition. Your analysis must focus on these and also consider a number of other factors, such as fitness, tactics and strategies. Better performers will know both their own and their competitors' strengths and weaknesses. As a result they will be able to develop a plan or **strategy** in order to win. To achieve their strategy they will decide which particular **tactics** they can use during the competition. For example, suppose that a 1,500-metre runner knows that she has a much faster finish than the other competitors in a race. Her strategy is to have the race run at as slow a pace as possible in order that she has enough energy left for her sprint finish. Her tactic will probably be to take the lead and then try to keep the pace as slow as possible. Her opponents may have other ideas and she may have to rethink her tactics as the race progresses.

In planning your observation you should think about your performer's plan, performance and evaluation.

The plan

What overall strategy does the performer have and what tactics are they attempting to use? When you know these you can look at how effective they are within the game. If they are not effective you must look for reasons.

The performance

This includes the techniques and skills in action. By looking at these you can see if poor performance or technique is preventing your player from being skilful and carrying out his or her tactics.

The fitness level of your player is also a vital factor. Tired people perform less well. You must look carefully at fitness levels. If in doubt, ask the performer how he or she feels.

The evaluation

Good decision-making within the game is essential. If your performer is

activity

Where to stand

Choose a technique from a sport of your choice and consider where you should stand to observe it. Is it best to stay in one place? Do you need to observe from a number of different angles to get an overall picture – for example, from the side, the front and from behind? Are you better placed at ground level or should you observe from above?

activity

Observing a technique in action

Select a technique from a sport that requires a feeder. Write down a list of the parts of the technique that you wish to observe. Decide who is to feed and give precise instructions to the feeder. Then observe the technique in action and analyse the performance.

activity

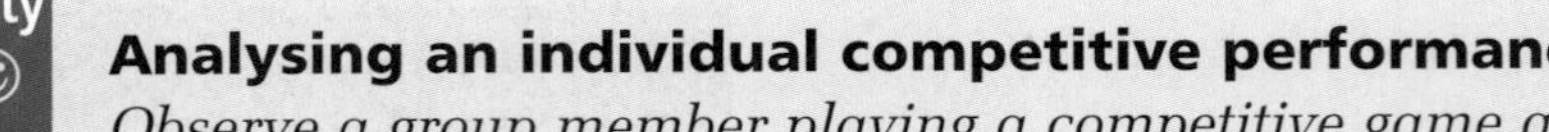

Analysing an individual competitive performance

Observe a group member playing a competitive game and assess his or her performance. Use the three factors, the plan, the performance and the evaluation, to focus your observation. Discuss your findings with the player and suggest ways to improve.

anticipating the opponent's moves and selecting successful moves then his or her performance will be good. You must analyse the decisions made by your player. This is especially important if your player is losing and needs your help as a coach to select better tactics.

Step 4: How do you analyse a competitive team performance?

In a team game you can observe either an individual player within the team or the performance of the team as a whole.

Individual performance

If you are focusing on an individual player you should not only look at his or her individual competitive performance, but at his or her contribution to the team effort. This will differ according to the sport, but might include running off the ball to support in attack, supporting in defence by covering others and getting back to mark opponents. The attitude of the player should also be assessed – for example, whether he or she encourages or criticises others – as this can play an important part in team games.

Using data to analyse performance

Choose a sport and decide on the data to be gathered in order to analyse team performance. This may be the number of successful passes, tackles, attacks, etc. Have at least two observers for each team or player. Observe a team or player for a period of time and note everything that happens on a checklist. The checklist below can be used for football or hockey but you will need to adapt it to suit other sports. You may also wish to observe a particular player using a similar checklist.

Team performance

You can also observe and analyse the team performance as a whole. A team will have an overall strategy and a chosen set of tactics. You will need to decide which aspect of the performance will be your focus; top teams have a number of assistant coaches who only look at attack or defence. If you try to look at everything you will find that there are too many things happening for you to analyse easily.

The example below from football shows how **data** could be gathered on a number of aspects of a team performance:

Date:	Period of observation (minutes):	Tally total
Aspects observed	Record each incident with a tally mark	
Pass completed		
Possession lost		
Successful tackle		
Unsuccessful tackle		
Shot off target		
Shot on target		

How do you analyse a strategy?

A **strategy** is a plan for success in sport. A team of talented individuals will need to work together on their tactics and strategies to ensure success. Without a strategy team performance will suffer.

You can gather data to analyse the effectiveness of a strategy. Coaches and players have to select strategies in many sports. Sometimes the strategies are very different:

- A tennis player might stay at the baseline throughout a match or serve and volley – that is, run to the net to cut off shots from their opponent.
- Badminton pairs will often play 'front and back', with one player taking the short shots whist the other takes those to the rear of the court. Others choose to play side-to-side, with each player covering one side of the court from the net to the baseline.
- Basketball teams might use a 'man-to-man' defence or 'zone' defence.
- Some athletes in middle distance events will run as fast as they can from the start and hope to 'hang on' to their lead. Others will pace themselves then speed up and sprint to the finish.
- Throwers and jumpers often complete their first attempt at less than 100% effort to make sure that they do not produce a foul. Others try their hardest each time, but sometimes 'no-jump' or 'no-throw' throughout the competition.

Wise coaches will ensure that players are able to switch strategies and/or tactics to suit specific situations.

Analysing a strategy

Consider this example from football and then decide how you could observe, gather data and advise the managers.

Mickey and **Johanne** are two experienced football managers in a local league.

Mickey believes that his team will be more successful in getting the ball into the opposition penalty area if his goalkeeper always plays the ball out to a full back to restart play. He thinks that his players will keep possession and create scoring opportunities for his strikers in the opposition penalty area.

Johanne has told his goalkeeper always to kick the ball as far up the pitch as possible. He thinks that this will lead to more scoring opportunities in the opposition penalty area.

Neither manager has any facts to back up their beliefs.

Can you find some facts to support one of the managers?

You could gather data by observing a number of live football matches on TV. You will need to decide what to look for, and create a rota of observers so that each match has at least two people watching the entire 90 minutes. Once you have collected enough information you will know which is the best strategy.

You might wish to send the results to your local club to help their manager!

Evaluation of performance compared with the Perfect Model

We have seen that the first stage in coaching is observing and analysing performance. The second stage is to evaluate the performance and to provide feedback to the performer.

- **Evaluating** a performance means deciding what is good and what needs improvement.
- Providing **feedback** means giving information about the performance to the performer.

Giving feedback is a very important stage as the performer needs to know how to improve. The coach must be careful to provide accurate feedback in a positive way. Providing incorrect advice or giving

feedback in a thoughtless manner can damage the performer's confidence. A good coach will always allow the performer the opportunity to comment on his or her performance. You can use the coaching model on the right to guide your observation, analysis, evaluation and feedback.

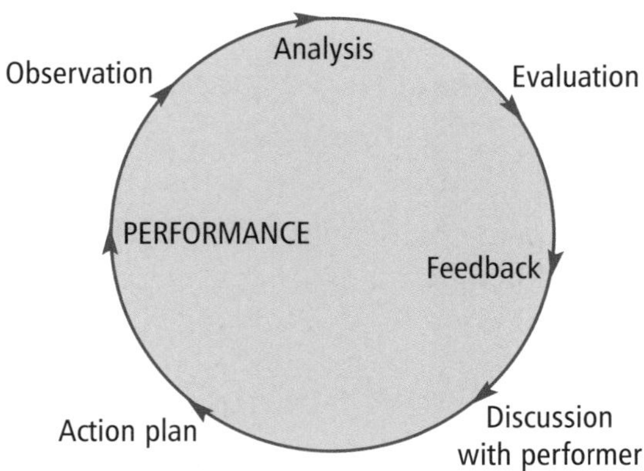

Back to basics

For this activity you need to put yourself in the position of a complete beginner. Attempt a simple technique in your chosen sport – for example, a set shot in basketball or netball, a serve in tennis or badminton, or a penalty kick in football – but use your non-preferred hand or foot. Do you have to think about the action? Are you able to perform it as quickly? How different was it? What expectations do you have of yourself when playing like this?

Coach the basics

Try coaching a group member to perform a simple technique with the non-preferred hand or foot. How easy is it to correct errors?

Evaluating a performance

When you evaluate a performance you should be clear about the standard of performance that you are expecting. Players can be at the beginner, intermediate or advanced level. It is important that coaches and players understand the level at which the players are performing. A lack of understanding can lead to unreasonable expectations of novice players. This in turn can create pressure and tension, which affects performance and slows the learning process.

The Perfect Model

We have seen earlier (page 7) that in order to analyse a particular technique we need to have a clear picture in our mind of what the technique looks like when performed very well. We call this mental image the Perfect Model. When we watch the performances of either ourselves (by means of video) or others, we compare these performances with our mental image of the Perfect Model. We gain our mental image of the Perfect Model by watching good performers in competitive action, either live or on video. Video footage is particularly useful if we are able to slow it down or freeze-frame it. This helps us to see exactly what is happening and helps us to understand why the movements we have in our mind are particularly effective.

Strengths and weaknesses

Whenever you observe a performance you should look for strengths and weaknesses. When giving feedback it is important to tell the performer about the good things you have seen before talking about the weaknesses.

Feedback

Feedback is essential for skill learning. We would find it very difficult to improve without knowledge of how well we are doing. However, when we are coaching we must take care to give the right kind of feedback at the right time if we are to get the best from our performers. The feedback given will mainly depend upon the ability and experience of the performers.

How much feedback?

Beginners only need a small amount of verbal or visual feedback, that is comments or demonstrations. They find

it difficult to use their own internal feelings about their performance and they cannot handle a great deal of detailed information. As performers become more experienced they get the 'feel' of successful movements and they can rely more on internal feedback, backed up by their coach's observations.

When is feedback given?

Comments should be made at key moments, but not after every attempt. Sportspeople will usually be trying to do the right thing and will know when they have made a mistake. Coaches should always allow a little time for performers to consider their performance. They should also check that performers have understood what was expected of them. It could be that they did not understand earlier instructions, or they might have been trying to achieve something different. Above all, feedback needs to motivate as well as correct the performer.

Using technology and data to improve performance

There are a number of different types of aid that coaches can use to help improve performance. These are:

- technical information
- video recordings of player performance
- statistical analysis
- fitness monitoring and analysis equipment
- interactive white boards.

You may have the opportunity to try some of these during your GCSE course. They can provide a lot of evidence to support your feedback to performers. Further information about the use of new technology in sport can be found on pages 242–244.

activity

Which is the Perfect Model?

Working in pairs, look at the two long jumpers in the photographs below and on page 15. One is the Perfect Model. The other is also a very good performer. Discuss the strengths and weaknesses of each performer with your partner. What do they both have in common? Look at the take off, action in the air and landing.

Planning strategies, tactics, practices and training to improve performance

After observing, analysing and evaluating performance, you must plan to improve performance. You have looked at performances, compared them with the Perfect Model and decided what needs to be done to improve them. Now you have to consider how you can ensure that this improvement takes place. You must be able to plan practices and training sessions to improve fitness, techniques and skills.

You will also need to show that you understand the strategies and tactics of your sport. Chapter 11, Principles of Training, shows you how to construct an exercise programme and how to organise a training session. Your Personal Training Programme (PTP) will include research into training methods. In this section you will learn about the practical side of coaching.

activity

Looking at arousal

Work in groups of about 12. Each player in turn attempts three free shots in netball or basketball under normal conditions. They then repeat it with a supportive audience, a totally silent audience and a hostile audience. The rest of the group provide the audience.

Discuss the results. Did the audience affect performance? How did the performer feel about each type of audience?

How do coaches plan to improve performance?

It is vital that coaches know their players so that they can plan programmes that match the player's level of ability and experience. Analysis of performance plays a large part in enabling a coach to prepare training sessions. It provides specific information which enables him or her to select activities and drills to suit the needs of the players. A good coach will also understand the personality of each player and will know how best to motivate each individual in the team.

Motivation and arousal

In sport the level of motivation is called **arousal**. If your arousal level is not high enough, you may feel bored and you will perform badly. If your arousal gets too high you may become anxious and worried. This creates tension, which causes your performance to become less effective. Coaches must look very carefully at the personality of different players and the nature of the sport before deciding on the level of motivation needed. For example, most snooker players need support to remain calm and focused before a major competition. Increasing their level of arousal is likely to lead to poor performance.

Inverted U theory

Performance: high, low
Arousal: low, moderate, high

How do coaches improve different types of skill?

We can put skills in sport into two different groups.

- **closed** skills are skills not affected by the sporting environment.
- **open** skills are skills that are affected by the whole sporting environment such as other players and the weather.

Closed skills

Closed skills are relatively easy to train. In gymnastics and archery, for example, competition is very similar to training. Closed skills are also found within 'open' games, for example, bowling the ball in cricket, taking penalties in football or taking a free throw in basketball. In all these activities the coach has to try to create the pressure that a player may feel within a competitive situation if the player is to be fully match-prepared. This can be done by:

- setting 'closed' drills when the player is tired
- creating pressure by rewarding success or punishing failure (in the sporting sense, of doing an extra run)
- simulating the match with recorded crowd noise
- creating pressure by having team mates talking at, and trying to put off, the performer.

Open skills

Open skills are performed within open activities where it is difficult to predict what will happen next. Most sports are open in this sense, including invasion games and racket sports. Coaches need to provide their performers with as wide a variety of experiences as possible so that they can practise their skills in many different situations. To help them perform skilfully and develop tactical understanding, the coach needs to allow them to make their own decisions during game play. The best coaches know when to advise and when to let their players take control for themselves.

Putting skills into action

Tactical skill is the ability to choose the right plan of action when taking part in sport. Different types of sport require us to use different strategies and tactics. In order to develop our tactical skill we need to understand the needs of our sport.

What are strategies and tactics in sport?

- **Strategies** are plans that we think out in advance of the sporting competition. They are methods of putting us in the best position to defeat our opponents.
- **Tactics** are what we use to put our strategies into action. Tactics can also be worked out in advance, but they will often need to be adapted to the real situation during competition. Tactics involve planning and team work.

Strategies and tactics will be very different for different types of games. For example, an invasion game like rugby involves large numbers of players, a variety of set plays as well as an opportunity for individuals to respond to many different situations. It gives many choices to players, such as kicking, passing or running with the ball. By contrast, in a judo competition there is only one opponent to worry about and there are a limited number of attacking moves to make or defend.

Beginners are not able to cope with complex strategies. They will need simple tactics such as 'Pass the ball to a player who is free'. More skilful players are able to give time and attention to strategies and tactics.

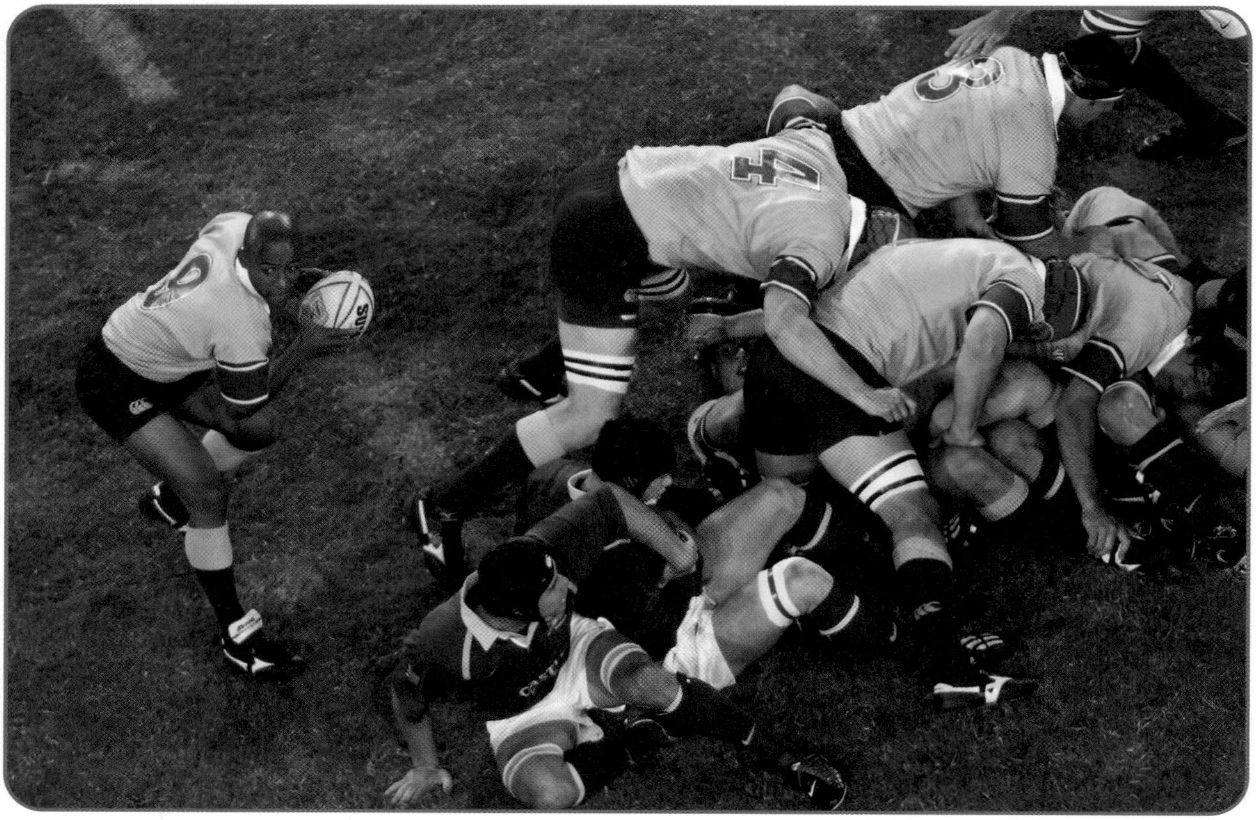

What sort of strategies and tactics are used in sport?

Strategies and tactics become more important as the level of competition increases.

When developing a strategy the coach will focus on:

- teamwork
- the game plan
- team formation
- restarts and set plays.

Teamwork

A successful team will have good teamwork. This means that all members of the team understand the agreed strategy. They also put the tactics for each game into practice by working as a unit. Managers, coaches and captains have important roles to play in teamwork. The motivation to work hard for each other has to be developed through training and team-building activities. A coach will also try to make sure that all the players are in their best positions during the game. For example, a tall, powerful footballer is likely to be in the centre of defence or attack, not expected to play in the middle of the midfield area where a quicker, more mobile player is required.

Game plan

In some matches and competitions, players and teams talk of a **game plan**. This is the set of tactics for use in a particular game. The game plan will be based on their own strengths and the weaknesses of the opposition.

Team formation

Teams can use different formations; that is, the players can take up different positions on the field of play. Some sports have rules limiting where the players can move during the game. In netball these restrictions present certain problems to be solved. In basketball there are few restrictions on the positions of players, so teams can be more flexible. Everyone discusses the formations in football. Some teams choose to have four defenders, four midfield players and two attackers (4:4:2). Others play with three central defenders, five midfielders and two attackers (3:5:2). Attack-minded teams or teams trying to score an equaliser in a cup-tie might play 4:3:3 or even 2:5:3.

Restarts and set plays

All games have restarts. In net games these are the serves. In invasion games they are free hits, throw-ins, corners, scrums, etc. These restarts give the team an opportunity to have free possession of the ball. At these times many teams use set plays which are practised during training.

How to develop strategies and tactics

To develop a strategy you will need to know:

- your own strengths and weaknesses
- the strengths and weaknesses of the opposition
- your level of fitness
- the importance of the competition
- any important environmental factors.

In a net game such as tennis, you might have considered all the factors above and decided your strategy. Let us say it is to move your opponent around the court in order to get her out of position and to tire her, allowing you to play a winning shot or to force an error. The tactic you use to achieve this might be to serve wide on both sides of the court and to come in to the net quickly.

In the game you might find that your tactics are not working because your opponent is returning your serve very well. In this case you will have to decide whether or not to continue with the same tactic or change it. If you change it you might stay at the baseline, but try to play disguised drop shots to draw the opponent forward and then lob or pass the ball beyond her. Alternatively, you might notice that her backhand is weak so you could decide to play most of your shots to her backhand side. Your tactics must be flexible to respond to the situations you meet during each game.

activity

Changing tactics

Working in groups, consider the following situations and make suggestions for strategies and tactics to help the individual player or improve team performance. You must explain to the whole group how you think your tactic or strategy will make a difference.

1 Your basketball team is losing heavily at half time. One player of average height but excellent all-round court movement has scored most of the opposition's points. Your zone defence has been unable to cope with him.

2 Your hockey team is winning 1–0 with 15 minutes remaining in the match. The opposition are playing almost entirely in your half. Your defenders are tired and keep hitting the ball away, but the opposition regain possession very quickly.

3 You are a middle distance runner. Both you and your rival have personal best times of 5 minutes for the mile (4 laps of the track). You plan to race at 75 seconds per lap and then out-sprint your rival to the finish. You begin the race and stay at the shoulder of the leader. However, after the first lap your rival speeds up to a pace of 65 seconds per lap.

Training to improve performance

The objective of every training session must be to improve performance. Your analysis of performance will provide a focus for your training sessions. Each session must be well planned. The coach must guide the players through techniques and into skills. They must also develop strategies and tactics in preparation for competition. The players' fitness will have to be maintained or improved. Training must include three essential phases:

- Warm up
- Main activity including skills training, fitness training, game and tactical development
- Warm down.

Warm up and warm down

These are an essential part of any training session. They must be linked closely to the sporting activity. Full details are given on pages 195–196.

Skills training

Skills practices in sport are often called **drills**. They are used to teach techniques and skills. A drill is a movement or number of movements that are repeated until they can be performed easily. You might practise techniques individually even if you are training for a team game. Small groups, or units, might also practise their skills separately from the rest of the team. An example might be the defenders working on defending crosses in hockey.

A series of techniques are often linked into a skilled movement that mirrors the game situation. This is a very important aspect of training because skill practices should always reflect the reality of the game situation.

How to design a drill

If a drill is to work it must be prepared carefully. Before the coach begins to lead the drill, every aspect of it must be planned and all equipment must be in place. This checklist can be used to ensure that no detail is missed when you plan your drills. By answering all the questions you will have prepared well.

- What is the drill trying to teach or improve?
- How many players are involved? What do they each do (feeder, performer, coach, ball collector)?
- What equipment is needed (bibs, balls, cones, goals, rackets, nets, posts, etc.)?
- What does the drill look like? Draw a diagram and write a key.
- What instructions will need to be given to explain the drill? Write them out.

activity

Design a drill

Training sessions often involve identifying areas for improvement and then practising skills or techniques. With your teacher, decide on a technique that could be developed and design a drill to teach this technique to your group. You must plan the drill in enough detail for someone else to be able to teach it.

- How many times do the players repeat the drill?
- What happens after the first player has completed the drill? Where does he or she go next?
- How do the players know if they have been successful?

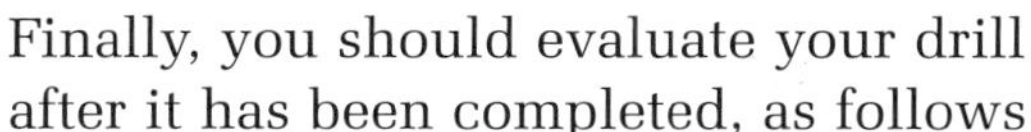

Finally, you should evaluate your drill after it has been completed, as follows:

- Did it achieve what you set out to do?
- Were all the players able to follow your instructions?
- How would you change it if you did it again?

Types of skill training

Once a technique has been taught and learned, skill training can take one of four different forms, depending on the amount of opposition required.

Unopposed

We can learn techniques more easily if there is no opposition. In basketball, the shooter can practise the jump shot unopposed at first, and opposition can be introduced gradually as technique improves. In volleyball, team organisation often takes some time to learn. This is best practised with the coach feeding the ball rather than within the game itself, when the team will be under pressure from the opposition.

Passive opposition

Opposition is essential for some techniques to be learned. However, in the early stages of learning it is often best for opposition to be static or minimal.

Learning how to tackle in rugby is far easier if the player with the ball stands still! This is known as passive opposition. It is much easier to learn how to keep control of a ball whilst dribbling in and out of a line of opponents when the opponents are not trying to steal it from you. Passive opposition drills are often used with beginners.

Active opposition

In order to make practices more realistic, the opposition must be real but limited in order for the techniques and skills to be learned. A common example of active opposition in football and hockey is the 3 *v* 1 possession drill in a grid square, where the player in the middle has to try to get the ball.

Pressure training

Pressure training is a method for putting a technique or skill under stress. It should only be used when a performer has developed the technique or skill to a high level. Pressure can be applied in a number of different ways:

- You might make the performer work very hard for a period of time. This combines skill and fitness work. As the performer tires, the skill level will drop. The practice will increase fitness levels and help the performer to play when tired. For example, in football, practice in heading the ball can be alternated with sprinting.
- Pressure can also be applied by forcing the performer to react very quickly. In basketball the jump shooter could receive the ball from a player who is between him and the basket. As he receives it, the player runs at the shooter and attempts to block the shot. The pressure to receive the ball, prepare and execute the shot in a short period of time is similar to the game situation. It will lead to improvement within the game.

activity

Designing practices

Choose a technique or skill from the sport of your choice. Describe how you would set up a number of drills to improve performance using the techniques outlined above. Then try them out with your group. You may find that some of your group cope well with all types of practice. Others will find that their performance drops off as the pressure increases.

How are games used to develop strategies and tactics?

Skills need to be transferred from the practice situation into the game situation. Practice games also let coaches try out strategies and practise tactics.

- **Modified** games give each player plenty of action and lots of time with the ball – for example, five-a-side hockey.
- **Conditioned** games have rule changes that focus on a particular skill or tactic. For example, two-touch football can develop good control and passing, but it also encourages support for the player with the ball.

  Conditioning the game can extend to providing areas of the pitch where the player with the ball cannot be tackled. If these are down both wings the teams are encouraged to play the ball wide because they can then keep possession until they wish to cross the ball. Once the habit of looking to create width in attack has been learned, the players will try to introduce it into normal games.

The use of games within training sessions also helps coaches to assess players' strengths, find out weaknesses and plan future sessions.

How do we plan and use fitness training?

Players must take responsibility for their own personal fitness. This includes eating and drinking sensibly, avoiding smoking and recreational drugs and getting plenty of rest. Nevertheless fitness training should be part of all training sessions. Further details can be found on pages 39–65. It can be part of the skills practices in the form of pressure drills, but should not exhaust players so much that they cannot concentrate on their skills. Regular fitness testing provides valuable feedback to coaches and players.

Understanding the principles and roles of sports leadership

When you analyse a team performance you look to see who influences the game. Players who influence those around them are leaders. Coaches, officials and others involved in sport can also be leaders. Your teacher will assess your own leadership ability, based upon your work during the GCSE course. It will include how well you demonstrate leadership through refereeing, organising and playing sport. You must always remember that good leadership has a direct impact on performance. If a game is refereed poorly, or a practice is disorganised, the players involved will not play to the best of their ability.

activity

Organising a club tournament

Imagine that you have to organise a tournament for your club involving players or teams from the surrounding area. Make a list of all the things that need to be done before the day of the tournament. Then list all the jobs that will have to be done on the day. Do not forget the clearing up afterwards! You will not be able to do everything, so divide all the jobs between a number of people. You can give them job titles, such as secretary, referee coordinator, referee, scorer, equipment organiser, equipment helper, etc.

What makes a good leader in sport?

A good leader in sport is likely to have one or more of the following qualities:

- outstanding ability in the sport
- great enthusiasm
- sound judgement
- good motivational powers
- ability to read the game or sporting situation.

Captains of cricket teams have a lot of responsibility for making tactical decisions during games. When fielding they must decide who is to bowl and where the fielders are to be placed.

activity

Follow the leader

Observe a competitive team performance. Look for leadership on the pitch. Give examples of when leadership is shown. Is it always the same players? Is it always the high-profile or popular ones, or can you find an unsung hero who leads well, but whose contribution is often overlooked?

Captains in other sports do not usually make as many crucial decisions, but they must set an example to the players in their team and motivate them. This is very important when a team is losing.

Motivators on the pitch are players who perform reliably under pressure. The other players look to them for inspiration. Some players drift in and out of games. They may be highly skilful but are not good leaders. Sometimes the most skilful players, or the most popular players, are given the captaincy of a team. However, the real leaders in the team may be doing an excellent job without being recognised.

What makes a good organiser in sport?

Sport needs organisers. Whether you are playing in a Sunday league netball team, or representing your country in the Commonwealth Games, you depend on many people to ensure that the event goes ahead smoothly. Sports organisers are needed at all levels in both professional and amateur sport and they carry out a wide range of roles. Some help to plan the event or take responsibility for the finance, while others will officiate. All these people are essential, although their work often goes unnoticed.

activity

Officials and sport

Do you know how many officials are required to control a game or event in your chosen sport? Research the answer and complete a checklist with details of each official and the roles they have.

Officials and sport

An official's central task, whether an umpire in tennis or a referee in rugby, is to enable sportspeople to take part in sport fairly and safely. Administrators organise events, but officials control the sporting action.

Officials must:

- have excellent knowledge of the sport and its rules
- apply rules firmly and fairly
- be patient, good with people and have a sense of humour!
- look after the safety of all those involved
- be in good physical condition.

Officials deserve respect and should not be taken for granted. Without them, organised sport would not exist.

Health, fitness and factors affecting performance

2 Health

Health and fitness mean more than just the absence of illness. If we are healthy and fit, then the physical, mental and social aspects of our lives are working together. We also know that following a healthy lifestyle when we are young will slow the ageing process and reduce the risk of an early death from disease.

activity

Lifestyle and health

Look at the pictures and descriptions below and decide what in the lifestyles of these people makes them healthy and unhealthy.

Phil is a 45-year-old married man with a wife and two young children. He has been unemployed for two years and is often depressed. His wife has a part-time job but does not earn very much. He watches a lot of television and likes fast food and beer. He supports his local football team but his regular exercise is limited to walking his children to and from school each day. He is overweight and would find running for a bus quite stressful, even though he is a non-smoker.

Sylvia is a 63-year-old widow who lives alone with her cat. She walks half a mile to the shops and back each day and most weekends she joins the local Ramblers on one of their walks. She likes the occasional glass of wine but watches her weight carefully. She smokes 20 cigarettes a day. She enjoys being with her many grandchildren and rarely needs to visit her doctor.

John is 16 and spends most of his spare time on his computer, often working until the early hours. He not only plays games but also uses the Internet to keep up to date with his music and his friends. For PE at school he chooses archery and weightlifting but he does not participate in any lunchtime or after-school sport. His mother ensures he eats sensibly at home and she prepares sandwiches and fruit for his lunch every day.

Sarah, now 26, is confined to a wheelchair as a result of a road accident five years ago. Before her accident she was an outstanding hockey player and she now plays wheelchair basketball for her county. This involves regular training sessions including fitness work in the gym. She drives her own specially adapted car and has a boyfriend who plays rugby for a local team.

Try to decide, from the descriptions above, who has the most healthy lifestyle and why.

What advice would you give to the person above who you consider has the most unhealthy lifestyle?

KEYWORDS

Activity: 'moving sufficiently to raise the heart rate above resting rate for reasonably sustained periods of time' (AQA)

Exercise: 'physical activity or exertion for health and fitness' (AQA)

Fitness: 'sufficient bodily function to carry out a specific task safely' (AQA)

Health: 'a state of mental, physical and social well-being' (AQA)

Training: physical activity to improve fitness.

Key to Exam Success

For your GCSE you will need to know:

- the definition of health
- how health, fitness and exercise relate to each other
- the short- and long-term effects of physical activity on the body systems
- how physical activity affects the unfit performer, the average performer and the trained athlete
-  the physical, mental and social benefits of physical activity
-  how to describe and evaluate health-promoting physical activity programmes for different age groups

“ KEY THOUGHTS ”

'Good health is the starting point for success.'

What is health?

Health is defined as 'a state of mental, physical and social well-being' (AQA). It is 'not merely the absence of disease or infirmity'.

Good health means that our mental state is sound, our body is working well and we are at ease socially. We are able to lead a full and active life, combining work, duties, recreation and social activities on a regular basis without becoming exhausted. We all need to lead a healthy lifestyle.

Good health comes from:

- eating sensibly
- taking regular physical exercise
- getting regular rest and sleep
- limiting our alcohol intake
- not smoking or taking social drugs
- improving our ability to cope with stress.

Good health needs physical, mental and social well-being.

Physical well-being

- Our cardiovascular system (heart and circulation) and our respiratory system (lungs) work well for normal activities and also emergencies.
- Our muscular system is strong enough to meet the needs of our daily life.
- Our body shape gives us confidence.
- We are able to resist and recover from illness.

Mental well-being

- We are able to cope with the stress and tensions of everyday life by relaxing and developing leisure interests.
- We are able to control our emotions, bringing stability to our behaviour.

Social well-being

- We need the company of other people in order to develop friendships and good personal relationships.
- We improve our own self-esteem and feel good about ourselves when we feel that other people value us.

Heredity

Heredity may affect our health. For example, problems such as high blood pressure and heart disease may run in families. If our grandparents and parents live a long and healthy life then we are likely to do the same, but we should not assume that this will be the case. We should all adopt healthy lifestyles to ensure good health.

What is exercise?

Exercise is physical activity that we do for health or to increase fitness. We should all exercise every day to keep healthy. Some people are sedentary. This means that their jobs and lifestyles involve very little exercise. With a few changes to their routines they can improve their exercise levels and health.

They might:

- walk, or run, upstairs at home, at work or in shopping centres instead of using escalators and lifts
- walk to school, work or the shops instead of taking the bus or going in a car
- use a bicycle instead of motorised transport
- stretch a little each day – even when sitting at a desk.

AQA B only

Physical activity programmes for health are not the same as intensive training regimes. Many local authorities have information boards in parks and public places to encourage people to walk for heart health. Regular walks are very effective in reducing the risk of heart disease in middle-aged and older people.

Children benefit from active play. Pre-school movement centres provide an ideal way for youngsters to develop healthy bodies.

It is well known that low-intensity, enjoyable activities are the best way to encourage regular participation in exercise for health.

The immediate effects of exercise on our body systems

We start to exercise.

↓

Our muscles work harder and use up more oxygen.

↓

The amount of carbon dioxide in our blood increases.

↓

Our brain detects this increase and releases adrenaline.

↓

Action by our heart

Our heart beats faster and stronger
(increased heart rate and stroke volume)

↓

More blood pumped to our lungs
(increased cardiac output)

- to collect oxygen
- to remove carbon dioxide.

↓

More blood pumped to our muscles
(increased cardiac output)

- to deliver oxygen
- to remove carbon dioxide.

Action by our lungs

Our lungs breathe faster and deeper
(increased tidal volume)

↓

Increased exchange of gases

- more oxygen taken into our blood
- more carbon dioxide removed from our blood.

As a result:

- Blood pressure rises but blood vessels then expand to reduce the pressure.
- Body temperature rises, but surface blood vessels expand to reduce heat quickly through the skin, and sweating increases, producing water on the skin which evaporates and cools us.
- Blood flow is redirected away from parts of the body not involved in exercise such as the digestive system, towards our working muscles.

AQA B only

How do these changes affect performers with different levels of fitness?

The unfit performer

The unfit performer must take care when exercising. Rises in blood pressure and heart rate can lead to stress on the heart and even a heart attack. Muscles that are unused to exertion can be strained very easily. If the exercise is too intensive it will be distressing and may lead to injury. The after-effects will be sore muscles and aching joints. This is unlikely to encourage regular training.

Unfit people should have a medical check-up before beginning an exercise programme and must begin with gentle exercise that gradually increases in intensity over a number of sessions.

The average performer
The average performer may be used to regular exercise at a fairly high level of intensity so may have to work hard to improve fitness levels. They should be able to cope with high heart rates and demands on muscles, but they must warm up well, warm down to aid recovery and allow plenty of time to rest between sessions.

The trained athlete
Trained athletes are very fit and must work at high intensity levels in order to make progress. They will have lower resting heart rates than average performers, but will work so hard that their heart rates will exceed those of most people when exercising. Muscles and joints will be strong, but trained athletes will warm up for a long time as part of the preparation for each training session. They will also warm down carefully to reduce recovery time so that they can train again after a short while.

The long-term effects of exercise on our body systems

If we follow a well planned long-term training programme, changes will occur in our bones, muscles, circulatory and respiratory systems.

We must remember, however, that training is specific. This means that the actual changes that take place will depend on the type of training we have carried out. Performers must understand that the long-term effects of aerobic, anaerobic and weight training will be different. The specific effects of different types of training are described in Chapters 11–13.

QUESTIONS

2 Health

1 It is important for everyone to stay healthy.

a Describe what is meant by healthy.
(3 marks)

b Give three general rules for a healthy lifestyle.
(3 marks)

c Explain what is meant by exercise. Give two examples of health benefits from exercise.
(3 marks)

2 Health and fitness are not the same thing.

a What is the difference between health and fitness?
(2 marks)

b Give two examples of the mental benefits of exercise.
(2 marks)

3 Fitness

Being fit is central to our health and helps us to feel good about ourselves. Fitness is vital for success in sport.

Physical fitness circuit

Working in groups of three, complete a circuit of tests designed to help you experience the different factors involved in fitness.

Circuit	Fitness circuit
Tennis ball pick-up	Place three tennis balls on the floor two metres away. Run, pick up the first ball and return both feet behind the starting line. Repeat with the second and third ball. Finish as quickly as you can. Record the time taken to complete the test.
Balancing ball	Extend your arm at right angles to the ground, fist clenched, back of the hand facing upwards. Place a volleyball on the back of your hand and time how long it can be balanced up to a maximum of 60 seconds. Your arm may be moved but not your feet.
The pinch	Have a partner pinch a fold of fat on the back of your upper arm, halfway between the elbow and the tip of the shoulder. Measure the thickness of the fold in centimetres.
Two-ball juggle	Hold two tennis balls in your preferred hand. Juggle them up to 10 times without dropping either ball. Score one point for each catch up to maximum of 10.
Shoulder raise	Lie face down on the floor with your arms stretched out in front. Hold a metre rule with your hands shoulder-width apart. Raise your arms as high as possible, keeping your chin on the ground at all times and the rule parallel to the floor. Hold the highest position for three seconds. A partner measures the height reached from the floor.
Grip test	Squeeze a hand grip dynamometer as hard as possible with one hand. Record the reading.
Standing broad jump	Start with your feet comfortably apart and your toes immediately behind the start line. Then bend your knees and jump forward as far as possible. Measure the distance from your rear heel or any other part of the body which is nearest to the start line. You are allowed two attempts.
Press-ups	Complete as many press-ups as possible in 60 seconds. Girls can perform press-ups from the kneeling position.
Metre rule drop	Ask a partner to hold a metre rule so that the side edge is between your thumb and index finger at a point 30 cm from the end. When your partner releases the rule, catch it before it slips through your thumb and finger. Do not move your hand lower to catch the rule. Record how far the rule has fallen.
Double heel click	With feet apart, jump up and tap your heels together twice before you hit the ground. You must land with your feet at least 10 cm apart. Make three attempts. Record the number of successful attempts.
Shuttle run	Complete a 10-metre shuttle run as many times as possible over a one-minute period.

KEYWORDS

Agility: the ability to change the position of the body quickly and to control its movement

Balance: the ability to maintain a given posture in static and dynamic situations

Body composition: the amount (percentage) of body weight which is fat, muscle and bone

Co-ordination: the ability to use the senses together to control the body during physical activity

Fitness: 'sufficient bodily function to carry out a specific task safely' (AQA)

Flexibility: the range of movement possible at a joint

General fitness: 'ability of the body (heart, lungs and muscles) to carry out everyday activities without excessive fatigue and with enough energy left for emergencies' (AQA)

Health: 'a state of mental, physical and social well-being' (AQA)

Muscular endurance: the ability to use voluntary muscles many times without getting tired

Muscular strength: the amount of force a muscle can exert against a resistance

Performance: the quality of physical activity

Power: 'ability to contract muscles with speed and strength in one explosive act; the combination of speed and strength' (AQA)

Reaction time: 'the time taken for the body (or part of the body) to respond to a stimulus' (AQA)

Specific fitness: 'ability of the body to carry out specific tasks effectively and efficiently' (AQA)

Speed: ability of the body, or part of the body, to move quickly

Stamina: 'ability to sustain activity; the extent to which the body can withstand the onset of fatigue and carry on working' (AQA)

Strength: 'ability to bear weight' (AQA)

Suppleness: 'the range of movement in a joint' (AQA)

Timing: ability to coincide movements in relation to external factors.

“ KEY THOUGHTS ”

'General fitness is good for health. Specific fitness is good for performance.'

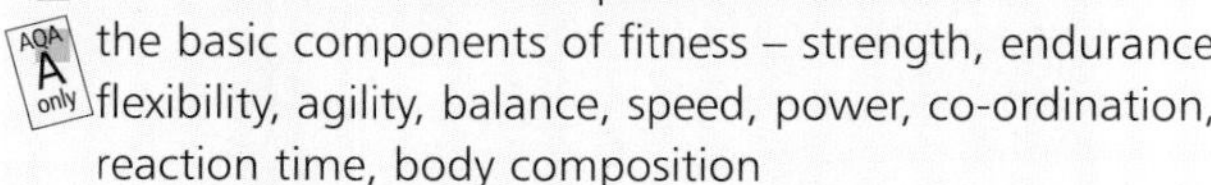

Key to Exam Success

For your GCSE you will need to know:

- how to define fitness
- the difference between health and fitness
- that fitness is related to particular activities
- (AQA A only) the basic components of fitness – strength, endurance, flexibility, agility, balance, speed, power, co-ordination, reaction time, body composition
- (AQA A only) how the different components of general fitness relate to a range of activities
- (AQA B only) the components of general fitness – speed, stamina, suppleness, strength
- (AQA B only) the components of specific fitness which contribute to skill – agility, balance, co-ordination, reaction time, timing
- (AQA B only) how to describe a test for each component and to understand/interpret the results.

What is fitness?

Fitness means different things to different people. A man who is fit for his work as a taxi driver may be dangerously unfit for a game of squash. A marathon runner may be quite unfit for lifting weights. Physical fitness is made up of a number of physical qualities which work together. These are:

- **strength**: the ability to bear weight. Strength enables us to carry out our daily tasks easily.
- **endurance**: the ability to work for relatively long periods of time without becoming tired
- **flexibility**: the range of limb movement about a joint (suppleness, mobility)

- **body composition**: the amount of body weight which is fat, muscle and bone
- **agility**: the ability to change the position of the body quickly and to control its movement
- **balance**: the ability to maintain a given posture in static and dynamic situations
- **speed**: the ability to move all or parts of our body as quickly as possible
- **power**: the ability to contract our muscles with speed and force in one explosive act
- **co-ordination**: the ability to use the senses together to control the body during physical activity
- **reaction time**: the time taken for the body (or part of the body) to respond to a stimulus
- **timing**: the ability to coincide movements in relation to external factors.

AQA B only

Types of fitness

We all need a minimum amount of physical fitness to be healthy and to cope with everyday life. This fitness protects us from stress, accidents, injury, disease and other health problems. We call this **general fitness**.

General fitness is 'the ability of the body (heart, lungs and muscles) to carry out everyday activities without excessive fatigue and with enough energy left for emergencies' (AQA).

We all take part in a variety of physical activities, from gardening to golf, and from decorating to hang gliding. To

succeed in these activities and to avoid injury, we need to develop a fitness which is specific to the activity being undertaken. We call this **specific fitness**. It is a component of skill.

Specific fitness is 'the ability of the body to carry out specific tasks effectively and efficiently' (AQA).

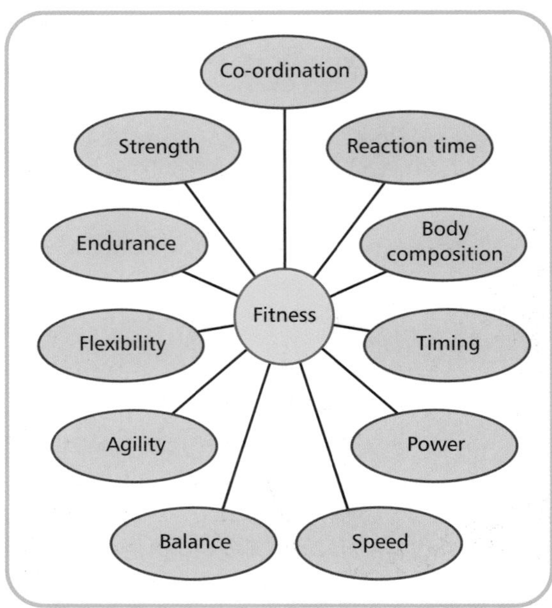

activity

Fitness factor presentation

Working in pairs or small groups, your task is to prepare and deliver a brief presentation explaining one of the factors of fitness above. Include the following in your presentation:

- a definition of the fitness factor
- an explanation of the factor
- the importance of the factor in sport
- how the factor can be measured
- how the factor can be improved.

You may wish to use Microsoft Powerpoint for your presentation.

It is important to link your presentation to your Personal Training Plan (PTP). Use the appropriate sections of this chapter to gather your information. You will also be able to obtain more information from the internet. Be sure to include the analysis of the results obtained by your group in the fitness testing. You will be expected to explain your results.

Factors of fitness

Endurance

There are two types of endurance – cardiovascular endurance and muscular endurance. We will deal with muscular endurance in the section on strength on page 47. Cardiovascular endurance is more commonly known as **stamina**.

Stamina

Stamina is 'the extent to which the body can withstand the onset of fatigue and carry on working' (AQA). It is also known as aerobic fitness or cardiorespiratory endurance.

Stamina is the ability of our heart and lung systems to cope with activity over a relatively long period of time. It is essential for work and play in our everyday lives. In order for our body to work hard for a long period we must supply our working muscles with energy and get rid of waste products. To do this, our heart, lungs and circulatory system must work well.

VO_2 Max

Our maximum cardiovascular fitness or aerobic capacity is also called our **VO_2 Max**. This is the maximum amount of oxygen that can be carried to, and used by, the working muscles during exercise, and it is often used to measure fitness (see below). A person with a high VO_2 Max can use more oxygen, work harder for longer, and will have less fatigue, than someone with a lower VO_2 Max.

How do we improve our stamina?

We can improve our cardiovascular endurance by taking part regularly in any continuous whole-body exercise, for example, running, swimming or cycling.

We must keep our heart rate between 60% and 80% of our maximum heart rate for our cardiovascular endurance to improve.

We should exercise at first for a minimum of 12 minutes, increasing this to 40 minutes as we become fitter.

We can use continuous training, interval training and circuit training to improve our cardiovascular endurance.

How do we measure our stamina?

We can measure our stamina by finding out our VO_2 Max. This is the amount of oxygen we can use in one minute of maximum exercise.

We can estimate our VO_2 Max by using tests such as the Multistage (Beep) Fitness Test, the Harvard Step Test and the Cooper 12-minute Run.

Multistage (Bleep) Fitness Test

A pre-recorded tape plays 'bleeps' at regular set intervals while you make 20-metre shuttle runs in time to the bleeps. After each minute, the time intervals between the bleeps get shorter so you have to run faster. You keep going until you can no longer keep up with the speed set by the bleeps. At this point you stop and record the level. You can then work out your VO_2 Max using published tables.

Harvard Step Test

Before starting the test, you record your resting heart rate (pulse). You then step on and off a 45cm-high bench at the rate of 30 times a minute for five minutes. You must start with the same foot each time and fully extend your leg at the top of the step. At the end of the test your pulse is taken three times, each time for 30 seconds. The first time is at 1 minute,

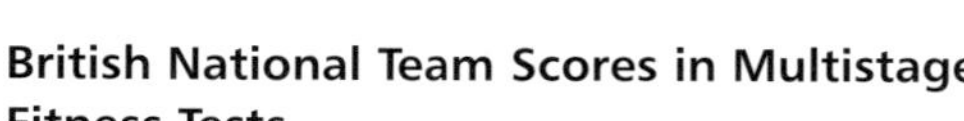

British National Team Scores in Multistage Fitness Tests

Sport	Male	Female
Basketball	11–5	9–6
Hockey	13–9	12–7
Rugby league	13–1	
Netball		9–7
Squash	13–3	

You can get an instant VO_2 Max score by using the VO_2 Max calculator at:

http://www.brianmac.demon.co.uk

Look for the links to **'Multistage Fitness test'**.

then at 2 minutes and finally at 3 minutes after the end of the exercise. Your fitness score is calculated using the following formula:

$$\text{Fitness score} = \frac{\text{Duration of exercise in seconds } (5 \times 60 = 300) \times 100}{\text{Pulse after 1 minute} + \text{Pulse after 2 minutes} + \text{Pulse after 3 minutes}}$$

For example, if Tom's three pulse rates were 160, 120 and 90 after 1, 2 and 3 minutes, his score would be as follows:

$$\frac{300 \times 100}{160 + 120 + 90} = 81$$

– which would be above average.

Harvard Step Test: comparative scores

	Males 15–16 years	Females 15–16 years
High score	Above 90	Above 86
Above average	89–80	86–76
Average	79–65	75–61
Below average	64–55	60–50
Low score	Less than 55	Less than 50

Cooper 12-Minute Run

The aim is to run as far as you can in 12 minutes around a marked area. The total distance you run is recorded. You can work out your aerobic capacity using this table:

Cooper 12-Minute Run: comparative scores

	Males 15–16 years	Females 15–16 years
High score	Above 2,800 m	Above 2,300 m
Above average	2,799–2,500 m	2,299–2,000 m
Average	2,499–2,300 m	1,999–1,900 m
Below average	2,299–2,200 m	1,899–1,800 m
Low score	Below 2,200 m	Below 1,800 m

The importance of stamina

Stamina is essential for an active lifestyle. It also enables us to cope with unexpected physical demands like running away from a dangerous situation. It is essential in all sporting activities lasting more than a few seconds. The better our stamina, the longer we can continue our activity, whether it is swimming, running, cycling or rowing. Our skill level declines as we get tired. This can be seen in team games when more goals and points are scored towards the end of matches as a greater number of mistakes are made. A player with a high level of stamina will be able to maintain his skill level for longer. It is often said that 'When fatigue sets in, skill goes out of the window.'

Strength

In everyday terms, we think of **strength** as being the ability of our muscles to carry out our daily tasks easily. This type of muscular strength is one of the factors of general fitness. However, our muscles work to produce three different types of strength:

- **muscular strength**: this is also called static strength or maximum strength
- **muscular endurance**: this is also called endurance strength
- **muscular power**: this is also called explosive strength or power.

For specific fitness it is more helpful to describe strength as the ability of a muscle or a muscle group to apply force and overcome resistance. Many sports and many everyday activities demand a combination of muscular strength, muscular power and muscular endurance.

What is muscular strength?

Muscular strength is the amount of force a muscle can exert against a resistance. It can be improved by training with heavy weights (80–100% of our maximum), using a low number of repetitions. In order to build up muscular strength it is necessary to exercise through the full range of joint movements and to work slowly when lifting.

How do we measure our muscular strength?

To measure our muscular strength, we need to find out the maximum force that a muscle group can apply. Special dynamometers can be used to measure muscular strength at different speeds and angles, and according to whether the muscles are lengthening or shortening. They can also be set up to make our limbs move in the same way as in our chosen sport.

The Repetition Max Test

We can carry out a Repetition Max Test using free weights or multigym equipment. The aim is to find out the maximum weight we can lift just once, by gradually adding weights. This is called our one repetition max. We must allow at least 2–3 minutes between each lift for recovery.

Hand Grip Strength Test

To test the strength of your hand grip, you can use a hand grip dynamometer. You simply squeeze the handle as hard as possible with your hand and record the reading on the dynamometer.

The importance of muscular strength

We use our muscles to move ourselves and everyday objects. Without strong muscles normal life would become very difficult. We need muscular strength to lift shopping and to move furniture. Attempting these kinds of activities without sufficient strength could lead to injury.

Muscular strength is extremely important in most sports. For example, a judo player needs strength when attempting to throw an opponent; a rugby player needs strength when pushing in the scrum, and an archer when drawing back the bow.

Hand Grip Strength Test: comparative scores

	Male 15–16 years	Females 15–16 years
High score	Above 56 kg	Above 36 kg
Above average	56–51 kg	36–31 kg
Average	50–45 kg	30–25 kg
Below average	44–39 kg	24–19 kg
Low score	Less than 39 kg	Less than 19 kg

Muscular endurance

Muscular endurance or endurance strength is also called anaerobic endurance. It is the ability to use voluntary muscles many times without getting tired. It refers to the efficiency of the anaerobic system within the working muscles when engaged in high-intensity, repetitive or even static exercise.

A person who has a high percentage of slow-twitch fibres will have an advantage in events involving muscular endurance. Muscular endurance is also closely linked with muscular strength.

You can improve your muscular endurance by training with light weights (40–60% of your maximum). The exercises need to be done at speed and with a high number of repetitions (20–30).

How do we measure our muscular endurance?

To measure muscular endurance you can perform repeated exercises such as press-ups or sit-ups for a given time or to exhaustion. Then you can compare your score either with those of others or with your own previous best.

The NCF Abdominal Curl Test

This test measures the muscular endurance of our abdominal muscles.

1 Lie on the mat with your knees bent, feet flat on the floor, hands resting on your thighs and the back of the head on your partner's hands. Your feet should not be held down to the floor.

2 Curl up slowly using the abdominal muscles and slide your hands up the thighs until your fingertips touch your kneecaps.

3 Return slowly to the starting position.

A complete curl should take 3 seconds, allowing 20 repetitions per minute. Repeat as many curls as you can at this rate and record the result.

NCF Abdominal Curl Test: comparative scores

	Males 15–16 years	Females 15–16 years
High score	60 and above	50 and above
Above average	45–59	40–49
Average	30–44	25–39
Below average	20–29	10–24
Low score	Below 20	Below 10

The importance of muscular endurance

Muscular endurance is important in a wide range of everyday activities, whenever the same muscle groups are used over and over again. Examples include ironing, cleaning the car and washing windows. It is particularly important in sports such as rowing, canoeing and other sporting activities where the same muscle groups work continuously with near-maximum effort.

Power

Power is the ability to contract muscles with speed and force in one explosive act:

Power = Strength × Speed

Power, or explosive strength, is the combination of strength and speed of movement. The energy for our power comes from the anaerobic system.

How can we improve our power?

We can improve our power by improving our strength, our speed of movement or both. We can train with medium weights (60–80% of our maximum), but the repetitions need to be performed at speed. Plyometrics training (see page 204) is also an excellent way of improving power. As power is a combination of strength and speed, it is important to develop both these areas of fitness.

How do we measure our power?

There are two simple ways to measure the power of your legs: the Standing Broad Jump and the Standing Vertical Jump.

Standing Broad Jump

Stand with your feet comfortably apart and your toes immediately behind the start line. Then bend your knees and jump forward as far

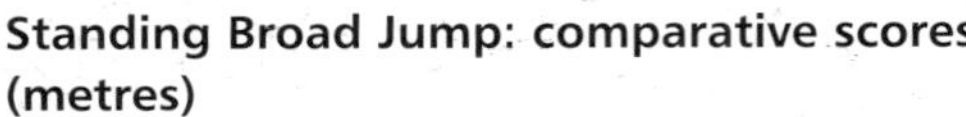

Standing Broad Jump: comparative scores (metres)

	Males 15–16 years	Females 15–16 years
High score	Above 2	Above 1.65
Above average	2.00–1.86	1.65–1.56
Average	1.85–1.76	1.55–1.46
Below average	1.75–1.65	1.45–1.35
Low score	Less than 1.65	Less than 1.35

as possible. Measure the distance from your rear heel back to the start line. You are allowed two attempts.

Standing Vertical Jump

Stand next to a wall and reach up with whichever arm is nearest to the wall. Mark the highest point you can reach with your fingers. Both feet must remain flat on the floor at this stage. Now chalk your fingers and perform a vertical jump, marking the wall at the highest point you can reach. The distance between the two marks gives a measure of how high you can leap from the ground from a stationary start. It takes into account your height and so is a fairer test than the standing broad jump.

Standing Vertical Jump: comparative scores (centimetres)

	Males 15–16 years	Females 15–16 years
High score	Above 65	Above 60
Above average	65–56	60–51
Average	55–50	50–41
Below average	49–40	40–35
Low score	Less than 40	Less than 35

The importance of power

Although power is not used a great deal in our everyday activities, we need it for certain physical tasks such as digging a hole or swinging a sledgehammer. Children often use power in their play, when they run, throw and jump.

Power is used a great deal in activities such as sprinting, throwing and jumping or when we try to move an object or ourselves as far and as fast as possible. Athletes need a lot of power, as do games players, racket players and gymnasts.

Flexibility

Flexibility is the range of movement possible at a joint. Flexibility is also known as mobility and **suppleness**. These terms all mean the range of limb movement around a joint.

Flexibility is necessary to stay healthy and avoid injury, and does not depend on our shape.

How can we improve flexibility?

We can improve our flexibility by stretching our muscles and tendons and by extending our ligaments and supporting tissues beyond their normal range of movement – for example, by holding an extended position for 20 seconds and repeating the stretch after a short rest period.

When exercising in this way it is important not to overload your muscles unless you feel comfortable. You should also stretch the prime movers and then the antagonist muscles – for example, stretching the quadriceps followed by the hamstrings. This helps your muscles recover and adapt in a balanced way.

The effects of flexibility exercises are very specific. We can, for example, be very flexible in our shoulders and yet show little flexibility in our lower limbs.

Flexibility exercise, or stretching, should be part of all training programmes.

What are the different types of stretching?

There are four main types of stretching which can be used to improve flexibility. In each case you extend your limbs beyond their normal range and hold the position. How you get to the stretch position varies:

- **Static stretching**: you use our own strength
- **Passive stretching**: a partner or coach applies external force
- **Active stretching**: you move rhythmically and under control to extend the stretch
- **PNF stretching**: you contract the muscle before stretching it.

How do we measure flexibility?

The tests used depend upon the joints that are being measured.

Sit and Reach Test

This test measures the flexibility of the hamstrings. Sit on the floor, legs straight, feet flat against the table with shoes removed, fingertips on the edge of the top plate. Bend your trunk and reach forward slowly and as far as possible, keeping the knees straight. Hold this position for two seconds.

Measure the distance from the edge of the table to the position reached by the fingertips. Be sure you make a number of warm-up attempts before the actual measurement is taken. As the 'sit and reach' table has an overhang of 15 cm, a person who reaches 5 cm past their toes scores 20 cm.

Sit and Reach Test: comparative scores

	Males 15–16 years	Females 15–16 years
High score	Above 28 cm	Above 35 cm
Above average	24–28 cm	32–35 cm
Average	20–23 cm	30–31 cm
Below average	17–19 cm	25–29 cm
Low score	Less than 17 cm	Less than 25 cm

Shoulder Hyperextension Test

This test measures your ability to stretch the muscles of your chest and shoulders.

Lie face down on the floor with your arms stretched out in front. Hold a metre rule with your hands shoulder-width apart. Raise your arms as high as possible, keeping your chin on the ground at all times and the stick parallel to the floor. Hold the highest position for three seconds while your partner measures the height reached.

Shoulder Hyperextension Test: comparative scores

	Males 15–16 years	Females 15–16 years
High score	41 cm and above	46 cm and above
Above average	31–40 cm	36–45 cm
Average	21–30 cm	26–35 cm
Below average	11–20 cm	16–25 cm
Low score	0–10 cm	0–15 cm

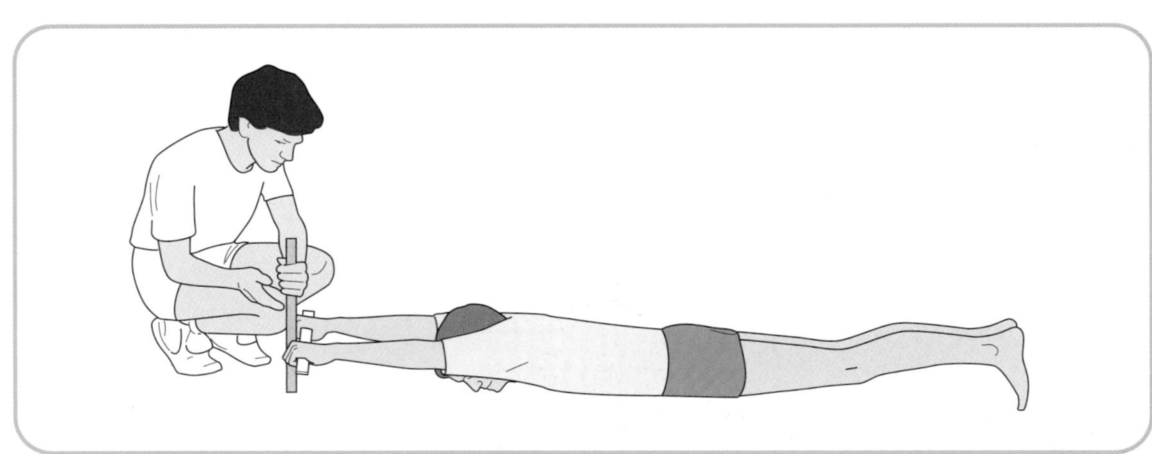

The importance of flexibility

We need a full range of movement in our joints for such everyday activities as putting on our shoes, reaching up to cupboards and twisting round as we work in the kitchen or garden. Without flexibility our movements will be limited and we are more likely to injure our joints and muscles.

All sports need a flexible body. Sports such as gymnastics and hurdling need a great deal of overall body flexibility. Other sports – for example, javelin and volleyball – need flexibility in particular parts of the body. Flexibility exercises should form a part of all training programmes, as flexible joints are less likely to be injured when put under stress.

Sportspeople often need a combination of flexibility and strength. Flexibility allows us to use our strength through a full range of movement. Strength is needed to stabilise joints and avoid injury.

Body composition

Body composition is the percentage of body weight which is fat, muscle and bone.

In everyday life the composition of our body significantly affects the way we complete our tasks. Going upstairs, for example, is more difficult if we are overweight. Shifting a large pile of sand requires a great deal more effort if we are not very strong. In the same way, sporting success comes from a combination of ability, fitness and the right body composition. Successful high-jumpers are usually tall and thin and gymnasts usually short and muscular. However, deciding what is the right body composition for each sport is complicated. We need to carry the right amount of fat and muscle for our particular sport.

How do we improve body composition?

Scientists are able to work out how much of the body is fat. The rest of the body weight is called fat-free weight (or lean body mass), and includes bone, muscle, organs and connective tissue. A healthy adult male should be approximately 12–18% fat, while a healthy adult female should be between 14 and 20% fat.

Body composition can be changed a great deal. We can reduce the amount of fat and improve the proportion of lean muscle in our bodies through careful diet and exercise.

How do we measure body composition?
Working out accurately how much of a person's weight is fat and how much of a person's weight is fat-free was once a very complicated procedure. However, modern testing equipment accurately measures the amount of fat in the body by measuring the resistance to a very small electric current flowing from the right wrist to the right ankle. Alternatively, it is possible to take skin fold measurements using a skin fold caliper and then use published tables to estimate the body fat level.

Why is body composition important?
Too little or too much fat on our body can cause problems in daily life. A certain amount of fat is necessary for our body to work properly. It provides the essential fatty acids that our body needs and is also a part of all cell membranes and nerves. Fat is a rich source of energy, particularly when we are resting or asleep, and it also cushions the internal organs. But too much fat means that we are carrying unnecessary weight, which puts extra strain on our muscles, joints and cardiovascular system.

In most sports, the higher the percentage of a performer's body is fat, the poorer the performance. Moving extra kilos of fat around the football field, the badminton court or the swimming pool is not helpful. Therefore most sportspeople try to keep their body fat low and their fat-free weight – that is, their muscle weight – high. However, long-distance runners must keep both their fat and non-fat weights as low as possible because they have to carry all the extra weight during the race.

Standard height–weight tables give an ideal weight for a particular height. But these tables are not helpful because they do not take into account body composition. If we are overweight due to extra muscle this is not a problem, but if we are over-fat, our sporting performance will suffer.

Body composition is only one of three components of body build which are important for health and sport. The other two are:

- **body size**: height compared to weight
- **body type**: a way of describing a person's physique based on muscularity, linearity and fatness.

Body size

Height and weight are important factors in determining body size, and both can be accurately measured. We can compare our height with our weight. Body size will be affected by changing weight, but a person's height will not change once he or she has reached physical maturity.

Body size is generally not important in everyday life. However, extremes of height and weight can cause practical problems and pose a risk to health.

The ideal body size for sport depends on the type of sport or the position we play in the game. For example, a height of 1.9 metres would be short for a top basketball player but very tall for a gymnast. Long-distance runners keep their weight down in order to reduce the load they have to carry. Rugby players vary considerably in height and weight. Some sports such as wrestling, boxing and weightlifting have fixed weight categories. It is essential that athletes control their diet and avoid rapid weight loss and consequent weakness through crash dieting.

Body type

Using a method known as somatotyping, it is possible to identify three main body types: endomorphs, mesomorphs and ectomorphs (see page 220). These extremes occur rarely, and most people are a combination of all three types.

Most successful sportspeople are high in mesomorphy. They are suited to sports requiring explosive strength and power. Their muscular bulk also helps them in contact sports.

Those who are high in endomorphy are likely to do well in sports needing power but only limited movement, such as weight lifting and wrestling.

People who are high in ectomorphy may be successful at long-distance events such as running or cycling. By developing muscular strength they may also do well in many non-contact sports. Tall ectomorphs may find that they are suited to basketball and high jump.

Body type depends very much on heredity, but we can make some changes. Our body type will be affected by any long-term change in the amount of fat and muscle in our body. However, we cannot change our basic bone structure.

In general body type is not important in everyday life, although extremes of endomorphy and ectomorphy can cause health problems.

Agility

Agility is the ability to change the position of the body quickly and to control its movement (AQA). It is a combination of speed, balance, power and co-ordination.

Agility can be developed by training, and by rehearsing the movements made in our chosen sport. This needs to be done at full speed and under conditions similar to those in a competitive situation. We must also improve our speed, balance, power and co-ordination, as all these fitness aspects affect our agility.

How do we measure our agility?

An expert watching us play our particular sport can make a very good assessment of our agility. We can also assess our general agility using a test such as the Illinois Agility Run.

Illinois Agility Run

Begin by setting up a course as shown in the diagram. Lie face down on the floor at the starting line. When told to start, leap to your feet and complete the course in the shortest time possible.

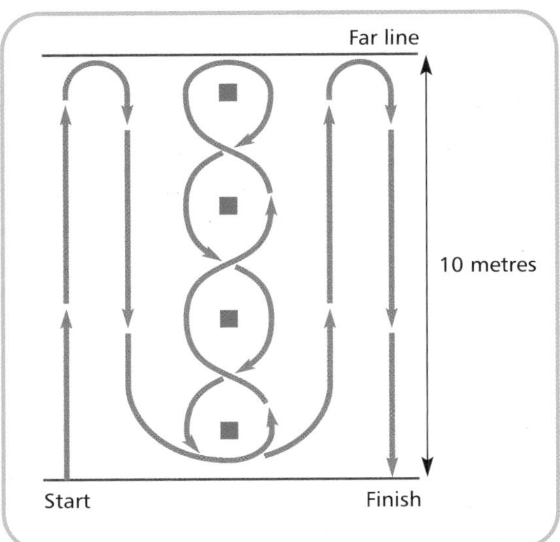

Illinois Agility Run: comparative scores (seconds)

	Males 15–16 years	Females 15–16 years
High score	Faster than 15.9	Faster than 17.5
Above average	15.9–16.7	17.5–18.6
Average	16.8–18.6	18.7–22.3
Below average	18.7–18.8	22.4–23.4
Low score	Slower than 18.8	Slower than 23.4

The importance of agility

We need a basic amount of agility to carry out our everyday tasks – for example, moving through a crowd of shoppers, getting on a train or bus or getting into a car. We need to maintain our agility as we get older, or it will deteriorate. Agility is closely linked to flexibility as it requires us to have a good range of movement of our joints.

Agility is important for most games and sports. Gymnasts, basketball players and skiers all need specific agility if they are to be successful. Only in static activities such as archery and shooting is agility of no importance.

Balance

Balance is 'the ability to maintain a given posture in static and dynamic situations' (AQA).

To maintain our posture we must keep our equilibrium.

- **static balance** is the ability to maintain our equilibrium when stationary
- **dynamic balance** is the ability to maintain our equilibrium when moving.

Maintaining equilibrium means keeping the centre of gravity over the area of support. Our base of support is the area formed by those parts of the body which are in touch with the ground. For

example, in a handstand we have a very small base of support, whereas in press-ups we have a very large base of support. If we do not keep our equilibrium we fall over. We maintain our balance through the co-ordinated actions of our eyes, our ears and the proprioceptive organs in our joints.

We can improve the balance needed in particular sports through practice and training. We can then put these skills to the test under the stress of competitive situations.

How do we measure our balance?
Dynamic balance is best measured by an expert watching us play our particular sport. Static balance can be measured in a number of ways. The Stork Stand described below is a test of static balance.

The Stork Stand
Stand comfortably on both feet and place your hands on your hips. Then lift one leg and place the toes against the knee of the other leg. On command, raise the heel and stand on your toes, balancing for as long as possible without letting either heel touch the floor or the other foot move away from the knee. Time your balance in seconds.

The Stork Stand: comparative scores (seconds)

	Males/females 15–16 years
High score	Above 49
Above average	40–49
Average	26–39
Below average	11–25
Low score	Below 10

The importance of balance

Without the ability to keep our balance, life would be impossible. Fortunately loss of the ability to balance is rare and few of us ever have to worry about it. It is only when taking up a new activity such as skiing that we realise that we have to learn how to balance.

Static balance is only seen in a few sports such as gymnastics – for example, when holding a handstand. But dynamic balance is very important in most sports; for example, snowboarders and surfers who have to move very fast over uneven surfaces and who have to constantly adjust their positions need very good dynamic balance.

Co-ordination

Co-ordination is 'the ability to use the senses together to control the body during physical activity' (AQA). Co-ordination involves carrying out a series of movements smoothly and efficiently. This will happen if the nervous and muscular systems work well together. We talk about hand–eye co-ordination being necessary to catch a ball, and foot–eye co-ordination being necessary in football. Most of us are better co-ordinated on one side of our body and favour it in sport, for example, using a racket or throwing a ball with a particular hand.

Co-ordination improves with good coaching and regular practice. Many of the toys we play with when young help to develop our hand–eye, foot–eye and whole-body co-ordination. Early PE lessons further develop our co-ordination through gymnastics and playing with balls, hoops and skipping ropes.

How do we measure co-ordination?

An expert watching us play our particular sport can make a very good assessment of our co-ordination. Observers can also assess our hand–eye co-ordination using a test such as the Alternate Hand Wall Toss Test.

The Alternate Hand Wall Toss Test

Stand two metres away from a smooth wall. With your right hand throw a tennis ball against the wall and catch it in your left hand. Then throw it with your left hand and catch it with your right. Do this as quickly as possible for 30 seconds.

Juggling test

A fun way to test co-ordination is to try juggling with first two and then three balls. Some people are able to achieve the three balls juggling much more quickly than others.

Alternate Hand Wall Toss Test: comparative scores

	Males/females 15–16 years
High score	Above 35
Above average	35–30
Average	29–25
Below average	24–20
Low score	Below 20

The importance of co-ordination

We need to be well co-ordinated to cope with everyday life. Co-ordination is involved in every movement we make, from picking up a cup to cutting down a tree.

Good co-ordination is also essential for skilful performance in sport, from movements in gymnastics such as triple somersaults to saving penalties in football. We become only too aware of poor co-ordination when we try to learn a new sporting skill.

Reaction time

Reaction time is 'the time taken for the body (or part of the body) to respond to a stimulus' (AQA).

A reaction can be simple, or it can involve choice.

- **Simple reaction time** is the time taken between the stimulus and our movement – for example, between the gun going off in a sprint race and a runner's first movement off the starting block.
- **Choice reaction time** is the time taken between the stimulus and an action which involves making a choice – for example, when we receive a ball from an opponent in a tennis match.

In both cases we have to react quickly; but in the first case, no choice has to be made. In the second case, we have to decide where and how to hit the ball. These decisions depend on where the ball is about to land, in which direction our opponent is moving and many other factors. We are therefore involved in making choices. The more skilled and experienced the player, the more likely he or she is to make the right choice and to hit the most appropriate type of return.

It is not possible to improve our simple reaction time through training. Speed of reaction to a single stimulus is due mainly to the efficiency of the nervous system. If we are lucky, our sensory and motor nerves will be capable of transmitting messages efficiently, and our muscles will get the message from our brain very quickly.

However, we can improve our choice reaction time a great deal through practice and experience. In a game like hockey, players will be receiving stimuli from their:

- **eyes**: about the position of the ball, other players and goal
- **ears**: from players, spectators and referee

- **kinaesthetic sense**: about their own body position and their options to pass, kick, etc.

Skilled players can reduce their choice reaction time by focusing on important information. They can anticipate the action of other players and the movement of the ball. This skill is developed mainly through training and experience.

Movement time

Movement time is the time that we take to move once the decision to move has been made. If we have a high percentage of fast-twitch fibres, we will be able to respond faster than people with a high percentage of slow-twitch fibres. We can improve movement time by improving our power.

How do we measure our reaction time?

A number of computer programmes are available to measure reaction time. They ask for a response as quickly as possible to a stimulus such as a sound or a visual cue. Some measure simple reaction times by only asking for one response to a single stimulus. Others measure choice reaction time by giving a variety of responses, only one of which is correct.

The importance of reaction time

All of us have to respond quickly to situations in everyday life. Examples include driving a car, riding a bike and crossing the road. Quick reactions can often prevent accidents – sometimes even save lives.

Simple reaction time is very important in sporting activities such as the 100-metre sprint on the track or in the pool. Choice reaction time is important in all games where we have to respond rapidly and effectively to the movements of other players, a ball, or both. However, movement time is critical in all sports and is most easily improved through training.

Speed

Speed is 'the time taken to move a specified distance'(AQA). More simply, speed is the ability to move all or part of the body as quickly as possible.

In order for our bodies to achieve speed, we have to supply energy to our muscles very quickly. The muscles then have to contract in the shortest possible time. We use our anaerobic energy supply system for speed work. If we have a high percentage of fast-twitch fibres in our active muscles, we will have a natural advantage.

How do we improve our speed?

We cannot increase the percentage of fast-twitch fibres in our bodies, but we can improve our speed in sport in other ways, such as:

- increasing our strength through a programme of weight training and plyometrics. Stronger muscles will give more power and therefore more speed.
- improving our reaction time
- improving our choice reaction time (see page 57)
- improving our ability to cope with lactic acid (see page 175)
- improving our skill in sport; for example, a more efficient swimming stroke will create less resistance and increase speed in the water.

How do we measure our speed?

Speed can be measured simply by recording the time it takes us to run a certain distance – for example, 50 metres – using a stopwatch. Reaction time, speed off the mark, time to reach top speed and deceleration times can all be measured as part of a training programme.

Why is speed important?

Children develop the ability to move quickly through play. Although adults do not need speed for everyday tasks, the ability to move quickly can be important in emergencies. Examples include moving out of the way of falling objects or moving to help another person at a time of need.

50-metre speed test: comparative scores (seconds)

	Males 15–16 years	Females 15–16 years
High score	Faster than 7.2	Faster than 7.8
Above average	7.2–7.8	7.8–8.4
Average	7.9–8.4	8.5–9.0
Below average	8.5–9.0	9.1–9.6
Low score	Slower than 9.1	Slower than 9.7

Speed is important in sports that require a great deal of effort over a very short period of time. Sprinters, speed skaters and sprint cyclists all need to develop speed. It is also important in many team games, when a sudden change of pace and direction is needed. Some sports require speed for the whole body, for example, long jumping; while for the javelin, shoulder and arm speed are of major importance.

Timing

Timing is 'the ability to coincide movements in relation to external factors' (AQA). It combines decision-making, co-ordination and reaction time to allow us to be in the right place at the right time.

Once there, we are able to control our body and the ball or implement that we are using. Sportspeople with good timing always seem to be unhurried when playing. As a result they are able to play consistently well. The mistimed movements of beginners are less likely to be as consistently accurate as those of experienced players.

How do we improve our timing?
Timing can only be improved by practice in drills and in competitive situations. Regular practice develops our ability to anticipate where we need to be. Anticipation helps us to improve our timing as we begin to move into position earlier. As our timing improves, the speed with which we perform will increase. In net games, players can practise beating the ball/shuttlecock to where it is going. As their timing improves they will find themselves in position waiting to play their shot.

How do we measure our timing?
There is no objective measure of good timing in sport. However, success rates in drills which include movement are a good indicator. For example, in a hockey drill such as running to meet a cross and shooting first time. 8 shots on target out of every 10 attempts would indicate good timing. If the player misses the ball, or slices it wide on a number of attempts, their timing needs to be improved. In many sports good timing is shown when the player is in position before the ball arrives. This can be practised (see above) or observed as a measure of timing.

Why is timing important?
Good timing reduces effort, improves performance and reduces the risk of injury. After a break from performing, sportspeople often report that they are 'off the pace' when they play. This refers to the fact that they are mistiming their movements. Once they are training regularly their timing returns and they play far more effectively.

QUESTIONS

3 Fitness

1 Sports performers need a number of components of fitness.

a What is meant by agility? Give one example from a named sport. *(2 marks)*

b What is meant by balance? Give one example from a named sport. *(2 marks)*

c What is meant by stamina? Give one example from a named sport. *(2 marks)*

2 Explain why heart rate is a reliable indicator of fitness. *(3 marks)*

3 It is possible to test fitness levels for sport.

a Name a method of measuring reaction time. Give two examples where fast reactions are important in sport. *(3 marks)*

b Name a test of muscular power. Give two examples where muscular power is important in sport. *(3 marks)*

4 Using examples from everyday life, describe how lack of the fitness types listed below can make simple movements or manual tasks difficult.

a Stamina *(2 marks)*

b Strength *(2 marks)*

c Flexibility *(2 marks)*

d Balance. *(2 marks)*

5 Describe four types of fitness and explain how each might be measured. *(8 marks)*

6 Explain how the fitness requirements of a gymnast and a cross-country runner are different. *(8 marks)*

4 Diet

Our sporting performance is influenced by many factors including our ability and our training programme. We can influence our performance by the way that we live. A healthy lifestyle will help us to perform to our full potential. Our diet must be balanced and should match our sporting needs.

activity

Different sports, different people

All the sportspeople pictured here are performing well in their chosen sports. They have trained hard, but their body build and their lifestyle also help them. Working in small groups, look at the pictures and discuss the following questions:

- What is it about the body build (shape and size) of each person that helps them to excel at their sport?
- How will their training differ?
- Which person is likely to eat more food each day?
- Would you expect their diets to be different?

KEYWORDS

Carbohydrate loading: eating a large amount of carbohydrate before endurance events in order to increase the amount of glycogen available to working muscles

Cholesterol: fat-like substance found in blood which can build up on artery walls

Energy equation: term to describe the relation between diet, weight and energy needs

Glycogen: chemical substance used to store glucose in the body

Nutrients: basic elements of food that provide nourishment for the body.

Key to Exam Success

For your GCSE you will need to know:

- the components of a balanced diet
- how our diet provides energy for sport
- why diet is important for sport
- how and what we should eat for specific sports.

Why do we need a balanced diet?

To be healthy and successful in sport, we need to know about different food types, what makes a healthy diet and how food can provide us with the right energy for sport.

Why do we need food?

We need food for:

- energy
- repair
- growth
- good health.

We get energy from food for our muscles to work. Food contains the basic materials needed for growth and repair. We need many different **nutrients** for good health, and a balanced and varied diet will provide them. If we are following a regular training programme for our sport we must plan our diet accordingly. We will need extra amounts of energy-producing foods as well as sufficient foods to allow repair of tissues.

What is a balanced diet?

A balanced diet contains seven essential components:

- carbohydrates
- fats
- proteins
- vitamins
- minerals
- fibre
- water.

We should limit the amounts of the three main food types: carbohydrates, fats and proteins. The Department of Health recommends that a healthy diet should contain:

- 50–60% carbohydrates (mainly from starch and natural sugars)
- 25–30% fat (mainly from unsaturated fat)
- 10–15% protein (mainly from lean meat, fish, poultry and plants).

We should also:

- decrease the amount of salt that we eat
- increase the amounts of fibre, calcium and vitamin C that we eat.

Nutrients that provide energy

Carbohydrates

Carbohydrates are broken down in the body into different sugars. There are two types of carbohydrate:

- **Sugars** (simple carbohydrates): these are found in:
  - fruits
  - cakes
  - honey
  - biscuits
  - jam
  - beer
  - sweets
  - table sugar.

Highly processed food such as sweets will give us a quick supply of energy but

no other nutrients. Biscuits and cakes often contain a lot of fat.

- **Starches** (complex carbohydrates): these are found in:
  - vegetables
  - rice and cereals
  - bread
  - pasta.

It is better to take most of our carbohydrates in the form of starches rather than sugars.

Why are carbohydrates important for exercise and energy production?

Carbohydrates give us the energy needed for our working muscles. We can also get energy from fats and proteins, but not as quickly or as efficiently as we can from carbohydrates. Large amounts of carbohydrates are stored as **glycogen** in the liver and muscles. Small amounts are stored as glucose in the blood. Intense exercise quickly uses up these stores, so active sportspeople need plenty of carbohydrates in their diet. Extra carbohydrates can be stored as fat around the body.

Fats

Fats are broken down in the body into saturated and unsaturated fatty acids. There are two types of fats:

- **Saturated fats**: these are found in animal products, and in foods made from them. These include:
  - milk
  - meat
  - cheese
  - cream
  - butter
  - cakes
  - biscuits
  - chocolate.

  Saturated fats can raise our cholesterol levels.

- **Unsaturated fats**: these are found in:
  - fish
  - nuts
  - corn
  - soya beans.

Why are fats important for exercise and energy production?

Fats provide energy, although much more slowly than carbohydrates. Fats need extra oxygen supplies to provide energy. Fats are the main source of energy when we are resting or asleep. They keep the skin in good condition, help to keep us warm and protect our vital organs. Extra fat is stored just under the skin. However, this extra weight will not help sportspeople. Too much fat can also lead to obesity and high cholesterol levels.

Cholesterol is a fat-like substance found in the blood. It is present in some foods, especially fatty animal products. Cholesterol which is not needed by the body builds up on our artery walls and may cause circulatory and heart problems.

Proteins

Proteins are broken down in the body into amino acids. There are two types of amino acids:

- **Non-essential amino acids**: for our bodies to function properly, we need 21 different amino acids. We can make 13 of these, which are called non-essential.
- **Essential amino acids**: these are the eight amino acids that we have to take from our food because we cannot make them for ourselves. They are found in both animal and plant foods.

Proteins are found in:

- fish
- meat
- milk
- cereals
- poultry
- beans
- eggs
- cheese
- peas
- nuts.

Proteins from animal products contain all the essential amino acids. However, plant proteins (with the exception of soya beans) lack some essential amino acids.

Why are proteins important for exercise and energy production?

Much of our body tissue is made up of protein, including our skin, bones and muscles. Proteins are needed for the repair, growth and efficient working of our tissues. Protein is only rarely used as an energy source, when no carbohydrate or fat is available. Excess proteins cannot be stored in the body as protein. They are either used as an energy source, stored as fat or excreted.

Other nutrients that do not provide energy

Vitamins

Vitamins enable our bodies to work normally and efficiently. We cannot make vitamins. They must be supplied in our food. Some vitamins are water-soluble (vitamin C and the B vitamins). We need these vitamins in small regular amounts. Unfortunately, because they

Sources of vitamins

Vitamin	Contained in:
A	Deep orange or yellow fruits and vegetables, dark-green vegetables, liver, codliver oil, dairy products
B1	Cereals, whole-grain bread, yeast, milk, potatoes, fish, sunflower seed
C	Most fruits and vegetables; high concentration in citrus fruits
D	Oily fish (mackerel, salmon, tuna), liver, codliver oil, butter, eggs
E	Beans, nuts, seeds, green, leafy vegetables, egg yolk, codliver oil

The function of vitamins

Vitamin	Function
A	Good vision and healthy skin
B	Energy production, stress reduction
C	Fights viruses, keeps skin and gums healthy, heals wounds
D	Helps to build bones and teeth
E	Protects cells, helps immune system, aids growth

are water-soluble, they are washed out of foods during cooking. Fat-soluble vitamins (such as vitamins A, D and E) can be stored by our body. We need to eat some foods containing fat in order to get these vitamins.

Why are vitamins important for exercise?

Vitamins do not provide energy. They regulate the activities of the body. They help in the working of muscles and in the release of energy from food. They also play a role in the growth and repair of body tissues.

Minerals

Minerals are substances found in a variety of foods which enable the body to work normally and efficiently. They do not provide energy, and the body cannot make its own minerals.

We need small but regular amounts of minerals, and a balanced diet can provide them all. Too much of some minerals can be harmful: for example, sodium in the form of salt can cause increased blood pressure.

Why are minerals important for exercise?

All minerals have their own function in helping the body to work well.

Fibre

Fibre is also called roughage or dietary fibre. Fibre is the part of a plant that

Sources of minerals

Mineral	Contained in:
Calcium	Milk, sardines and salmon with bones, vegetables, beans
Iron	Spinach, dark-green vegetables, liver, red meat, beans, peas, nuts
Magnesium	Dark-green vegetables, nuts, soya products
Potassium	Bananas, dried fruit, meat, vegetables, sunflower seeds
Sodium	Table salt, soy sauce, preserved meat, crisps, canned foods

The function of minerals

Mineral	Function
Calcium	Strengthens bones and muscles
Iron	Aids production of red blood cells, helps get oxygen to the muscles, prevents fatigue
Magnesium	Helps muscles to contract and relax
Potassium	Aids muscle contraction, maintains normal blood pressure
Sodium	Maintains body fluid levels, aids muscle contraction

cannot be digested. It does not contain any nutrients. Fibre is found on the outside of seeds, in vegetables, fruits and nuts.

Why is fibre important for exercise?

Fibre does not provide energy but adds bulk to our food. This helps the food to move through our digestive system and prevents constipation. Fibre is also involved in food absorption. It slows down the release of sugars from our food so that we get a more even release of energy. Dietary fibre adds bulk without adding extra kilojoules. A high level of fibre helps us to lose weight and to maintain good health.

Water

Although water does not provide energy it is essential for living. It comes from the fluids we drink and the food we eat. We lose water in our sweat, urine, faeces and in the air we breathe out. About two-thirds of our body weight is made up of water. It is the main component of blood and cells. As part of the blood, water carries nutrients, electrolytes, blood cells and waste products around the body.

Water in our blood also helps to control our body temperature by absorbing heat produced during exercise. This heat is then carried to the skin where it is lost to the air. Water helps to cool the body when it evaporates on the surface of the skin in the form of sweat. Heat is also lost in the water vapour in the air that we breathe out. Loss of water can lead to dehydration and heatstroke. An adequate supply of water is vital during training, especially for strenuous exercise in the heat.

Diet and energy

Eating a balanced diet is vital for health. Eating the right food to provide energy and to maintain the correct body weight is a major factor in sports performance.

Why do we need energy?

The energy our bodies use has two main purposes:

1 **To keep our body systems going**. The amount of energy we need to keep alive and healthy is called our Basic Metabolic Rate (BMR). We can think of it as the energy needed to keep us 'ticking over'. BMR is affected by our age, sex, body size and body composition.

2 **For physical activities**. This is known as our Physical Activity Level (PAL). We use energy for all our everyday activities such as walking, housework and gardening. If we take part in sport we will use a lot more energy (depending on the type of sport, and how much activity is involved). Our age, sex, work, health and lifestyle will all affect our PAL.

Remember that our total energy needs = BMR + PAL.

How is energy measured?

Energy is measured in kilocalories (kCal) or kilojoules (kJ). One kilocalorie is the equivalent of 4.2kJ. All food contains an energy value, which is usually calculated as the number of kilojoules per gram of food. Exercise is measured as the number of kilojoules used per hour.

How much energy is contained in food?

The amount of energy in our food depends on how many carbohydrates,

fats and proteins it contains. It is also greatly affected by the way the food is cooked. We can see from the table overleaf that potatoes contain 3kJ per gram when boiled, but 15kJ per gram when served as chips. A baked potato may contain fewer calories than the butter that we spread on it!

How much energy do we need?

We need to match the amount of energy in the food that we eat with the amount of energy our body needs. We will lose weight if our body needs more energy than our diet is providing. We will put on weight if our body needs less energy than our diet is providing.

The energy equation

The link between diet, energy and weight is quite straightforward. The diagrams on the next page show the effects of an imbalance between the amount of kilojoules taken in and the amount of kilojoules burned up each day.

Experts have calculated the energy needs, for growth and body maintenance, of teenagers as follows:

The energy content of food

Food	kJ per gram
Butter	31
Crisps	23
Milk chocolate	22
Sausage roll	21
White sugar	16.5
Chips	15
White bread	10
Boiled eggs	6.2
Boiled rice	5.8
Low-fat yoghurt (fruit)	3.8
Boiled potatoes	3
Milk (semi-skimmed)	1.9
Fizzy soft drink	1.5
Apple	1.4

- An average 15-year-old male needs to eat about 11,500 kJ per day.
- An average 15-year-old female needs to eat about 8,800 kJ per day.

Weight stays constant
Kilojoules taken in each day equals kilojoules burned up each day

Weight gained
Kilojoules taken in each day is greater than kilojoules burned up each day

Weight lost
Kilojoules taken in each day is less than kilojoules burned up each day

How much energy is used when taking part in activity?

The amount of energy people use depends upon the intensity of the activity.

There are many books and websites that will give you detailed information about a range of activities.

How do overeating and undereating affect sporting performance?

Imagine that you have been asked to compete in a sports tournament, but that you have to carry your rucksack when playing! You would be very quick to complain that your chances of success were being harmed by the extra weight you had to carry. It is easy to see that being overfat or obese will slow you down when sprinting, make you less able to twist and turn in a games situation and will prevent you from doing well in a long-distance race. Long-distance runners keep their weight down to reduce the load they have to carry. The lighter the load the further and faster they can run.

Energy used per activity

Activity	kJ per hour	Activity	kJ per hour
Marathon running	4158	Cycling (moderate)	1260
Basketball	3360	Gardening	1260
Brisk jogging	2520	Cleaning	798
Disco dancing	2100	Studying	420
Badminton	1848	Watching TV	378

activity

Dietary advice

Interview a friend or family member about their diet and exercise levels. List the amount of food and drink that they consume in a typical day. Write down the amount of activity they have had during the day. Then write a summary about the effect that their diet and activity pattern will have on their weight. Finally, write down the advice you would offer them about this.

Some sports such as wrestling, boxing and weight lifting have fixed weight categories. Despite being able to compete when very heavy, top performers will have much more muscle than fat, because whilst eating a lot of food they will also be training very hard.

Other sports such as gymnastics, long-distance running and horse racing require athletes to be very light. Controlled diets are essential for these athletes to avoid problems caused by rapid weight loss through crash diets. Although they need to be light, they

must make sure that they have enough energy reserves to compete and enough vitamins and minerals to stay healthy.

What is an ideal body size?

The ideal body size for sport depends on the needs of the individual sport or the position the person plays in the game. For example a height of 1.90 metres would be short for a top basketball player but very tall for a gymnast. In rugby, we see players of a variety of heights and weights.

Scientists are able to work out how much of our body is fat. The rest of our body weight is called fat-free and includes bone, muscle, organs and connective tissue.

In most sports, the higher the percentage of a participant's body is fat, the poorer the performance. Therefore most sportspeople try to keep their body fat low and their fat-free weight (i.e. muscle weight) high. However this is not the case for long-distance runners. They must keep both their fat and non-fat weight as low as possible as they have to carry the extra weight for the length of the race

Standard height–weight tables suggest a range of weights for a particular height. They do not help sportspeople to estimate their optimum weight because they do not allow for body composition. Being 'overweight' is not a problem if it is composed of extra muscle. Some people are 'heavily built'. Their bone structure is large and they have bigger muscle girth. This is often an advantage in sport. However, being overfat can certainly reduce sporting performance.

Food for sport

How do we get enough energy for sport?

When we work hard, the energy we use comes from stores of glycogen in the body. Glycogen is made from carbohydrates and also from fats. Our stores of glycogen are limited. To have enough energy for endurance activities we need to eat extra carbohydrates, which build supplies of glycogen. This is called **carbohydrate loading**. When carbohydrate-loading, we reduce our level of exercise for at least three days before competition. At the same time we increase the amount of carbohydrate (pasta, rice, etc.) in our diet.

Carbohydrates or fats?

Our bodies use carbohydrates, in the form of glycogen, and fats to produce energy. The mixture used depends on the length and intensity of the activity.

For example:

- When resting we use mainly fats.
- On a long walk we will also 'burn' mainly fat.
- If we start jogging we will begin to use glycogen.
- If we jog for a couple of hours, our glycogen stores will be used up and we will begin to utilise fats.
- Sprinting will lead to our muscles using glycogen.

Endurance training teaches our body to use more fat during exercise. This helps our limited supplies of carbohydrates to last longer.

Proteins are only rarely used as an energy supply. This happens when all other energy supplies have been used.

Eating for sport

We need to plan how we eat before, during and after exercise.

Before exercise we should:

- eat our main meal at least three to four hours and our snack meal at least one to two hours before exercise, to allow time for digestion
- include starches such as bread, cereal and fruit, to give a slow, steady release of energy
- avoid simple sugars (sweets) because they increase our insulin level, which in turn reduces our blood glucose and makes us feel tired
- avoid foods which are high in fat and protein as they take longer to digest
- include plenty of fluids to avoid dehydration.

During exercise we should:

- continue to drink water, not waiting until we feel thirsty, but taking small sips regularly
- drink a glucose-based sports drink if the activity lasts for more than one hour.

After exercise we should:

- eat foods rich in carbohydrate within an hour of exercising, even if we do not feel hungry, to restore glycogen stores quickly
- drink plenty of water to replace lost fluids.

Which sports foods will improve performance?

Food supplements for athletes are widely available and sports drinks are heavily advertised. Creatine monohydrate is becoming popular as it can help in the production of energy and in the recovery process. When we are trying to perform at our peak we are easily tempted to buy these products. However, we need to look at the scientific evidence and decide for ourselves if the product will really help us.

Drinks

We only need to drink plain water before and during activities lasting 60 minutes or less.

Sports drinks containing carbohydrates and electrolytes (sodium, potassium, chloride and magnesium) can enable us to work hard for longer if our activity lasts more than 60 minutes.

Sports drinks can help after exercise as they help to restore lost fluids, energy and minerals. They also provide useful nutrition during whole-day tournaments. But there is no need to buy sports drinks

containing extra vitamins. We do not lose vitamins when we sweat and a balanced diet should supply all the vitamins we need.

Food and food supplements

A high-carbohydrate diet will allow us to work hard for longer, but we must also train well in order to do this. If we are training very hard, our diet should consist of 65–70% carbohydrates, but we should not increase fat consumption even if we are training very hard.

Remember also:

- Extra protein in the diet does not help to make extra muscle: it is broken down and stored as fat or used for energy. Using the correct training technique is the only way to increase muscle size.
- High-protein foods are difficult to digest and we should not eat them before training or competing.
- Creatine is found in large quantities in red meat. Our bodies can make it from amino acid.

activity

What does it say on the label?

Collect a label from a sports energy drink and a snack bar. The labels will contain details about energy levels and other nutritional information. Compare a sports energy drink with an 'ordinary' fruit-based drink, or compare an energy bar with an ordinary snack bar.

Investigate and compare the claims made for each product. Some products have their own websites, but other information is also available on the internet. Decide whether or not you think the energy drink or snack bar will improve your sporting performance.

QUESTIONS

4 Diet

1 Carbohydrates are the main source of energy for exercise.

a Give examples of two foods rich in carbohydrates. *(2 marks)*

b Why are fats important in our diet? *(2 marks)*

c Suggest two rules about eating before exercise. *(2 marks)*

2 Fats and protein are important components of a sportsperson's diet.

a List three foods that are healthy sources of fat. *(3 marks)*

b List three foods that are sources of protein. *(3 marks)*

c Describe the use of fat and protein in the body. *(3 marks)*

3 Give three reasons why a sportsperson needs to eat a balanced diet. *(3 marks)*

4 The energy equation explains the reason for balancing energy intake and energy output.

a Explain how a person might become obese. *(3 marks)*

b Explain how a person who wishes to lose weight might do so healthily and effectively. *(3 marks)*

5 Athletes can get the nutrients they need from everyday foods. Give a benefit and a food source of each of the following nutrients.

a Vitamin C *(2 marks)*

b Vitamin A *(2 marks)*

c Iron *(2 marks)*

d Calcium. *(2 marks)*

6 Athletes eat to get energy.

a Name the two measurements of energy in food. *(2 marks)*

b Name the two purposes of energy. *(2 marks)*

c Give two factors which affect our everyday energy requirements. *(2 marks)*

d Give two reasons why a jockey eats less than a rugby player. *(2 marks)*

7 Explain why water intake is important for sportspeople. Give examples from a range of environments and sports to illustrate your answer. *(8 marks)*

8 Explain the link between the amount of food we eat, the amount of exercise we take and our weight. *(8 marks)*

5 Hygiene, safety and risk assessment

Many of us take part in sport because it is exciting and unpredictable, but this unpredictability can put great strain on our bodies and brings with it the risk of injury. Good preparation is important in trying to reduce the risk of injury. We should know the rules of our sport and the ways of working safely. We should wear the correct protective clothing and use safe equipment. Competition should be fair in terms of level of skill, weight, age and sex. Warming up and warming down should be essential parts of any sporting activity.

If we are to perform to the best of our ability we must avoid injury when training and competing. To do this we must assess the risks, plan to be safe and take every precaution to stay safe. If we do get injured, we must know how to recognise and treat the injury so that we recover quickly. Knowing when to return to training is also important: returning too soon can cause problems.

activity

Safety issues

Look at the following cartoons of sporting activities and copy and complete the grid listing all the potential safety hazards.

Sport	Facility	Clothing and equipment	Safety in general
Trampolining			
Climbing			
Gymnastics			
Rugby			
Cricket			
Basketball			

KEYWORDS

CPR: cardiopulmonary resuscitation – a procedure to follow if someone has no pulse

Dehydration: loss of body fluids, usually when working extremely hard in hot conditions, leading to heat exhaustion

DRABC: Danger, Response, Airway, Breathing, Circulation – a checklist to follow when dealing with an emergency situation

Etiquette: special ways we are expected to behave in our sport

Hygiene: good personal habits which keep us clean and healthy

Hyperthermia (heatstroke): when the internal body temperature becomes dangerously high through exercise in hot, humid conditions

Hypothermia: when the internal body temperature becomes dangerously low through exposure to extremely cold conditions

Heat exhaustion: state of fatigue in hot conditions caused by dehydration

Heatstroke: when the body becomes dangerously overheated through exercise in extremely hot conditions

MMV: mouth-to-mouth ventilation – a procedure to follow if someone has stopped breathing

Overtraining: continuing to train when the body needs rest and time to recover

Overuse injuries: caused by using a part of the body incorrectly over a long period of time

RICE: Rest, Ice, Compression, Elevation – a checklist to follow in the case of soft tissue injuries

Shock: an acute state of weakness caused by physical pain or emotional upset

Sprain: when we overstretch or tear a ligament at a joint

Stitch: a sudden sharp pain in the muscles in the side of the body usually caused by exercise

Strain: when we stretch or tear a muscle or tendon.

Key to Exam Success

For your GCSE you will need to:

- be able to assess the risks involved in sporting activities both to yourself and to others
- understand the common causes of sports injuries
- recognise the signs and symptoms of a range of sporting injuries
- know the procedures for dealing with an injured person in an emergency situation
- identify how preventative measures can minimise the risk of injury to yourself and to others
-  understand how keeping to the rules of the game, wearing correct clothing and footwear and taking part in balanced competition only when fit enough and properly warmed up will help to prevent injuries.

KEY THOUGHTS

'Most sporting injury is both painful and avoidable.'

Hygiene and sport

Hygiene means the different ways we look after our body to keep it healthy and clean. We should keep our bodies healthy as part of our preparation for sport. We should also develop hygienic habits after taking part in sport and ensure we get enough sleep and rest.

Skin care

Our skin protects and maintains our body. If the skin is healthy, it can resist most forms of infection. Soap and warm water removes dirt and sweat which encourage bacteria and cause body odour. We should wash our hands after going to the toilet, before meals and whenever they are dirty.

We can also keep our whole body clean by showering daily. It is essential to wash or shower thoroughly after taking part in any physical activity. Most of us use deodorants and anti-perspirants, but they are only really effective if the body is already clean.

Acne is a skin complaint which affects many teenagers. The glands in the skin, which produce grease, become particularly active at puberty and the openings of these glands can become blocked. Greasy material builds up under the skin if the blockage is not cleared, and the skin can become infected with bacteria. To prevent acne, it helps to keep the skin very clean, to avoid make-up, to eat fresh fruit and expose the skin to plenty of sunlight.

Nails

Nails should be kept clean and cut regularly. This will help to reduce injury in sport from scratches. Ingrowing toenails can be avoided by keeping nails short and having footwear of the right size.

Hair

Hair is found on nearly every part of our skin. We must wash our hair regularly to keep it clean and healthy. In some sports long hair can be a hazard and should be tied back.

Teeth

Our teeth must be kept healthy and free from decay. We should avoid sugary food and clean our teeth at least twice a day. Sugar-free gum can help to keep teeth clean after a meal, but must not be used if gum is banned in your school. Dental floss can be used to remove plaque from between teeth. We can keep our gums healthy by eating foods that need chewing. Regular dental check-ups are essential.

Feet

Shoes and sports footwear must fit well. This will help to prevent corns and other problems. We must wash our feet regularly and dry them carefully. If we also change our socks daily this will also help to prevent foot odour.

- **Athlete's foot** is a fungal infection which affects our feet, especially between the toes, causing the skin to crack open and become itchy. It can be treated by drying the feet carefully and using antifungal creams, sprays and powder.
- **Verrucas** are warts which can be found on the feet. They are caused by a virus and can be quite painful. They can be treated by applying a prescribed liquid.

Foot conditions are easy to treat if recognised at an early stage. We should check our feet for problems regularly and treat them immediately.

Clothing

We should wash and change our clothes regularly. Our underwear, in particular, can become unhygienic very quickly. We should always have a complete change of clothes for sporting activities and remember to take a towel, soap and shampoo for the shower afterwards. Sports clothing can become sweaty and dirty and should be washed after each exercise session.

Preventing injury

We can look at prevention of injury in sport under a number of headings:

- rules of the game
- footwear, clothing and equipment
- balanced competition
- warm-up and warm-down.

Rules of the game

To avoid injury we need to know and understand the rules of our chosen activity. Rules encourage good sporting behaviour, help games to flow and also protect players from harm. Rules must be followed and players punished if they break them. Injury causes pain and stops us from playing. In high-risk collision sports such as rugby, injuries will inevitably happen, but players who break rules and harm opponents must be dealt with severely. In recent years some players have been taken to court when their deliberate foul play has led to serious injury.

Some sporting activities such as mountaineering, pot holing and sky diving have no formal rules as such. However, failure to follow the appropriate safety guidelines can have disastrous consequences.

Etiquette means the special ways we are expected to behave in our sport. Etiquette is not a set of written rules as such, but a code of behaviour that has become part of each sport over a long period. Golf has many examples of etiquette; for example, when players complete a hole, they should immediately leave the green and record their scores elsewhere. Tennis players will always shake hands at the net after a match, and rugby players will clap their opponents off the pitch. Etiquette allows us to demonstrate fair play, sportsmanship, sporting spirit and respect for our opponents. In this way it helps to reduce violence and injury.

Footwear, clothing and equipment

All sports shoes must support and protect our feet as well as be comfortable. Shoes must also grip the surface for which they are used and absorb impact when we are running or landing. Cross-trainers are useful for moderate performers who play a number of sports, but top players will always choose shoes that are specially designed for their sport. They will also make sure that their shoes can provide maximum support and response to movement by tying the laces tightly when training and playing.

Always wear the correct clothing for the activity. Check your clothing and equipment regularly to see that everything is in good order. For example, a damaged fencer's outfit could be dangerous if used in competition or practice.

In extreme weather conditions it is especially important to wear the

activity

Safety rules

All sports have rules designed to minimise the possibility of injury to those taking part. For example, in football girls are not allowed to play against boys above the age of 11, players who raise their feet too high close to an opponent are penalised and all players must wear shin guards.

Choose three sports and write down three rules designed to prevent accident or injury in each one.

appropriate clothing. Sports manufacturers now produce a wide variety of clothing suitable for very hot, very cold and very wet weather.

Some sports have rules to make sure that protective equipment is worn. For example, hockey goalkeepers and school-age batters in cricket must wear helmets and other padding. Footballers must wear shin guards. Sports often lay down few rules about clothing, but players still need to take sensible precautions.

Protective equipment must:

- properly protect the player
- allow freedom of movement
- permit air to flow around the body
- be comfortable
- be safe and reliable.

In very sunny conditions, players should wear protection against harmful ultraviolet rays, such as sunglasses, hats, long-sleeved shirts and skin creams.

Jewellery

Players should remove as much jewellery as possible before playing sport. The risk of accidents due to jewellery will vary from sport to sport. For example, rings on fingers will be a much greater problem in judo than in running. People taking part in contact or combat sports should wear no jewellery at all.

Balanced competition

Many sports try to make their competition balanced for fairness and the greater enjoyment of the competitors. For combat and contact sports, balanced competition is important for safety reasons.

- **age**: most competition in school sport is based on age. However, competition between players of the same age but with different physical development can be both unfair and unsafe.
- **size and weight**: rugby and football can be very dangerous if there are large differences between the body size and skill levels of the players. For weight lifting and rowing there are

These children are all the same age.

weight categories to make competition fairer, whilst weight categories in boxing and wrestling make contests both fairer and safer.

- **gender**: mixed-sex teams are acceptable in tennis, volleyball, hockey and badminton, but not in netball. Rugby union has non-contact forms of the game which are suitable for mixed teams, whilst mixed teams are allowed in soccer up to the age of 11.
- **skill**: in karate and judo belts are awarded for different skill levels and competition takes place within these skill levels for reasons of safety and fairness. Golf has a handicap system to allow competition between players of different abilities.

Warm-up and warm-down

These are essential parts of any training session or competitive situation. They are important in preventing injury and should be closely tailored to the individual sport.

If we start strenuous activity when our muscles and joints are cold, they are likely to suffer damage because they will be unable to cope with the sudden stresses. Gentle exercise for the whole body warms up the muscles and joints and prepares them for more vigorous activity. A combination of gentle jogging and stretching exercises will help to prevent injury.

If we simply rest immediately after strenuous activity, our recovery will take much longer and there is the possibility of dizziness. Light exercise will maintain the blood circulation, prevent pooling in the skeletal muscles, lower blood pressure and so reduce the possibility of dizziness. It will also help the speedy removal of waste products which will prevent muscle soreness and stiffness.

Risk assessment

Taking part in sport always carries some risk of injury. We know that rugby or climbing carry a greater risk of injury than table tennis or swimming. In order to take part in a sport we have to be willing to accept the risk.

However, if we are organising a sporting activity for other people we have a responsibility for their safety as well as our own. For this reason organisers of sporting activities must carry out an assessment of all potential risks and ensure that these risks are minimised before the activity takes place. All those taking part must be made aware of any specific risks and be properly prepared to deal with them.

We can carry out a risk assessment by asking a number of important questions in different areas. We must then deal with any problems.

Assessing the risk to ourselves

The first step is to check that we are well prepared for our activity.

- **Health and fitness**: are we healthy and fit enough to take part in the activity?
- **Techniques and skills**: do we have the ability to compete at this level?
- **Training**: have we completed sufficient training to cope with the demands of the activity?
- **Warm-up**: have we warmed up our body to avoid injury?
- **Clothing, equipment and footwear**: do we have what is needed for the activity and conditions?
- **Jewellery**: have we removed rings and any other item of jewellery that might cause injury to opponents?
- **Rules**: do we have a good understanding of the rules?
- **Etiquette**: do we know the expected behaviour for the activity?
- **Respect**: do we have respect for our opponents?

Assessing the risk to others

We must be sure we have the right qualifications, knowledge and experience to teach, coach, train or instruct young people in an activity. If we are responsible for young people we have a 'duty of care'. This means that we must take all reasonable precautions to see that they are safe. We must ask the following questions:

- Have we prepared the group members properly?
- Have we planned the activity carefully?
- Have we the right group size?
- Have we ensured fair competition in terms of age, size, weight, sex and skill?
- Are the facilities and equipment safe?
- Will we supervise the activity well?
- Have we taken safety precautions?
- Is First Aid equipment ready?
- Have we explained any emergency procedures?

Assessing the sporting environment

We must be satisfied that the sports facilities, both indoors and outdoors, are in a safe condition.

Indoor areas

- Is the floor surface suitable for the activity?
- Is the floor surface clean, dry and free from dirt?
- Is the area clear of unnecessary portable apparatus?
- Is all fixed apparatus, such as beams, secure?

- Are there any dangerous projections or wall fittings?

Playing fields

- Is the grass clear of litter, especially glass and cans?
- Is the playing surface suitable?
- Are the weather conditions suitable?
- Is the equipment, such as goal posts, in good condition?

Swimming pool

- Are the wet surfaces around the pool clearly indicated?
- Are rules of behaviour prominently displayed?
- Are depth signs clearly visible?
- Are lifeguards on duty?

Outdoor activities

- Are competent instructors present?
- Are the weather conditions suitable?
- Is appropriate specialist clothing and equipment available?
- Are First Aid facilities available?
- Are emergency procedures known and understood?

activity

Organising a tournament

Imagine that you are organising a tournament for your chosen sport. Describe the basic organisation of the event including the age of teams, the number of teams and the number of pitches, courts or other facilities involved.

Complete a risk assessment and describe the safety precautions you will take. Set it out in the form of a table as shown below:

Hazards	Risk factor (1–5) (1 = low risk; 5 = high risk)	Precautions (actions/instructions)

Sports injuries

Injuries

Working in groups, look at the following photos of injured sportspeople. See if you can agree on the following:

- What type of injury have they sustained?
- What was the likely cause of their injury?
- How could the injury have been avoided?

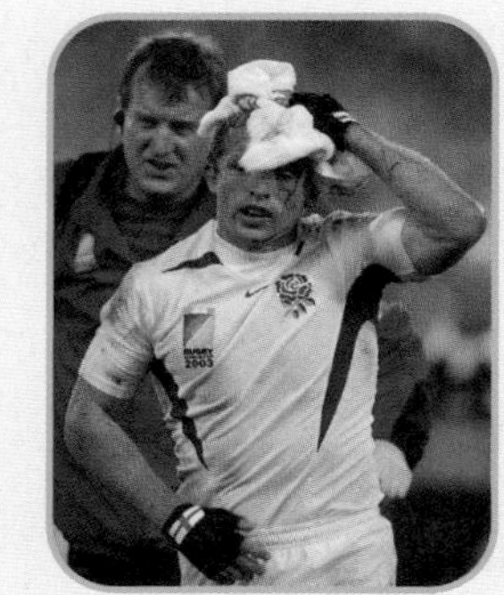

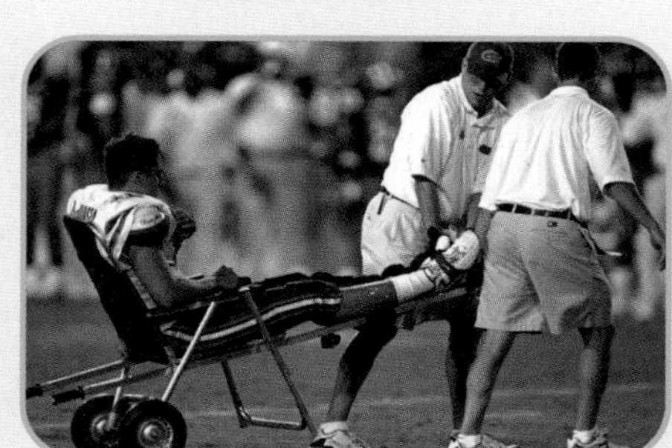

Causes of sports injuries

In order to avoid sports injuries, we need to know what they are and why they happen. A sports injury can be any damage caused to a sportsperson whilst in action. This can include hypothermia brought on by cold weather conditions as well as broken bones and pulled muscles.

Some sports have a greater risk of injury than others – for instance, we are more likely to be injured when playing rugby than when taking part in archery. Being aware of the risk can help to reduce it.

Sports injuries can be caused in many different ways. They can be classed as:

- accidental injuries (due to violence or the environment)
- overuse injuries
- chronic injuries.

The force that causes accidental and overuse injuries can be:

- **internal**: from inside our bodies
- **external**: from outside our bodies.

Accidental injuries

Accidental injuries are those that surprise us by happening when we least expect them. They can be caused by internal and external forces.

- **Internal forces** are those created when our body works during exercise. When we perform at our highest level, the extra strain on some body parts can cause damage. A sudden stretch or twist can strain or tear muscles, tendons or ligaments. These injuries may be caused by forgetting to warm up, by very sudden powerful movements or by lack of skill. For example, sprinters can tear hamstrings in a race. Footballers often suffer groin strain through stretching for the ball or knee ligament damage through twisting.
- **External forces** come from outside our bodies. Direct contact, or violence, from another player is one external force. Another external force is the environment.

Violence

Injuries caused by violence are due to direct contact between players or equipment. Many sports involve violent contact between opponents. Collisions may result in fractures, dislocations, sprains and bruises. They may also be caused by being hit by equipment such as balls, sticks or rackets. Breaking the rules can lead to violent injury.

The environment

The environment can lead to injury in two different ways:

- An injury may involve equipment or facilities – for example, you might trip and land heavily on the playing surface or collide with the goalposts.
- Alternatively, an injury may be due to weather conditions. Extreme heat can cause dehydration, heat exhaustion and then heatstroke. Extreme cold may lead to hypothermia.

Overuse injuries

Overuse injuries are caused by using a part of the body again and again over a long period of time. These injuries produce pain and inflammation.

Common overuse injuries include:

- 'tennis elbow' or 'golf elbow' – an inflamed elbow joint
- 'shin splints' – pain on the front of the shins
- 'cricketers' shoulder' – damage and inflammation to the front of the shoulder
- blisters and calluses – caused by gripping equipment very tightly during the activity, for example, in rowing.

The only cure for overuse injuries is rest. However, where injuries are caused by incorrect technique, the action must be corrected to prevent the injury recurring.

Chronic injuries

All injuries must be treated immediately and given time to heal. If we put an injury under stress before it is healed it will get worse. If this continues, we will develop a chronic injury, which is difficult to heal. Chronic injuries can lead to permanent damage such as arthritis in the joints.

Recognition and treatment of sports injuries

Whenever we have to deal with an injury the first step is to look for signs and symptoms. These help us to assess the injury and decide on any action.

- **Signs**: what we can see, feel, hear and smell – for example, swelling, bruising, bleeding, skin colour
- **Symptoms**: what the sufferer feels and describes – for example, pain, discomfort, nausea.

Fractures

A fracture is a break or crack in a bone. There are two types:

- In a simple (closed) fracture the bone stays under the skin.
- In a compound (open) fracture the bone breaks through the skin.

More complicated fractures also involve damage to nerves and muscles. Whenever the skin is broken there is a danger of infection. All fractures are serious and need urgent medical treatment.

Stress fractures

These are small cracks in a bone, often the result of an overuse injury, such as too much running on hard surfaces. The signs of a stress fracture are steadily increasing pain in a particular part of a limb, swelling and tenderness. In such cases the sufferer needs to:

- use ice to reduce inflammation
- get immediate rest
- keep fit by doing other activities
- check running action and footwear for problems
- run on softer surfaces after recovery.

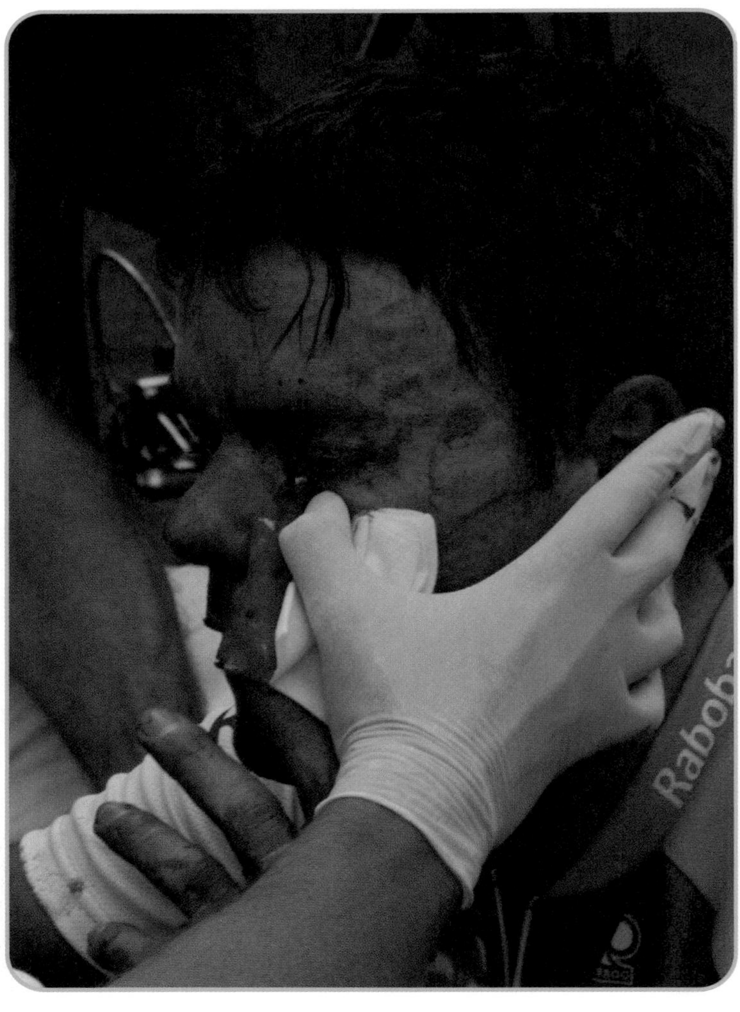

Joint injuries

The joints of our body are often extremely complex and vulnerable to injury. Simple joint injuries may be treated using the **RICE** procedure – that is, Rest, Ice, Compression, Elevation (page 95). However, if serious damage or dislocation are suspected, the injury should be treated as a break and medical help sought.

Dislocations

A dislocation means that a bone is forced out of its normal position at a joint. The ligaments around the joint may also be damaged. The cause may be a strong wrench to the bone, perhaps in a rugby tackle. Treat all dislocations as fractures (see above). Do not attempt to replace the bone into its socket.

Tennis and golf elbow

These two injuries to the tendons at the joints are both caused by overuse. The tendons become inflamed and should be treated using RICE in the first instance. If the symptoms persist after a lengthy period of rest, then further medical advice should be sought to prevent chronic injury and the development of arthritis.

Cartilage injury

We have two cartilages between the bones of our knee joint which act as shock absorbers. They can be torn when the joint is twisted or pulled in an unusual way, for example, during a tackle in football. Sometimes cartilage injury causes the knee to lock. If this happens, medical advice should be sought.

Twisted ankle

This refers to damage to the ankle when the joint is forced beyond its normal range of movement. This is a relatively common injury in games such as hockey, football and rugby. The ligaments supporting the joint are torn, causing pain, swelling and loss of movement. Immediate treatment should be RICE.

How do we treat bone and serious joint injuries?

The first step is to identify the problem. The following are all possible indicators of serious bone or joint injury:

- a recent blow or fall
- snapping sound of breaking bone or torn ligament
- difficulty in moving the limb normally
- pain made worse by movement
- tenderness at the site (fracture)
- severe 'sickening' pain (dislocation)

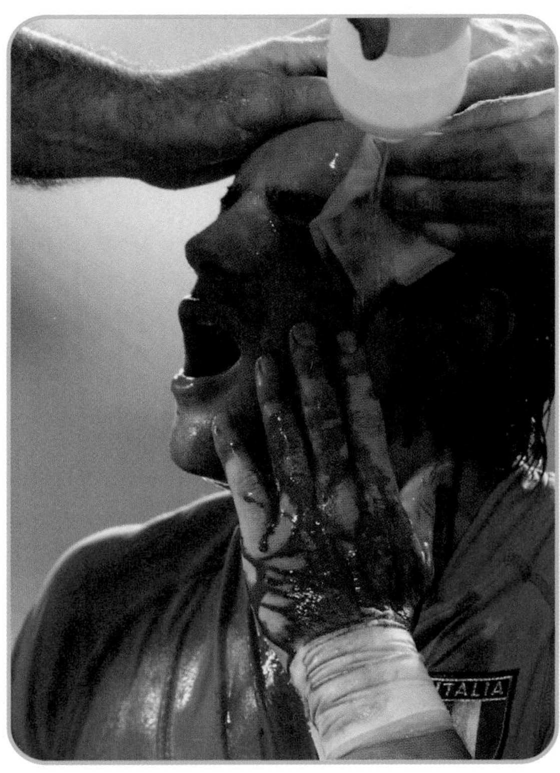

- deformity – that is, the limb has an unusual shape
- swelling, bruising
- signs of shock.

Some injuries are hard to diagnose. A sprained ankle and a broken ankle are very similar. An early sign of a break is that the casualty becomes pale and the skin is clammy. This is a sign of shock that does not often occur when the ankle is only sprained. If in doubt, treat the injury as a fracture:

- Keep the casualty still, steady and comfortable.
- Support the injured part.
- Reassure the casualty.
- Send for medical help.

Soft tissue injuries

Soft tissue injuries include damage to:

- muscles
- ligaments
- tendons
- cartilage.

When soft tissues are injured they become inflamed. Treatment aims to reduce the swelling, prevent further damage and ease the pain. Soft tissue injuries are usually dealt with by using the RICE treatment.

- A **sprain** happens when we over-stretch or tear a ligament around a joint. A sprain can be caused by a twist or sudden wrench, for example, a sprained ankle. In this case we must use the RICE treatment. If the injury is severe, we would treat it as a fracture.
- A **strain** happens when we stretch or tear a muscle or tendon. This can be caused by a sudden stretch or extra muscular effort (for example, a pulled muscle). In this case we must use the RICE treatment.

Even minor problems should be attended to quickly and carefully. If ignored, they may become more serious.

Skin damage

- **Cuts**: clean the cut with running water. Dab dry and cover with a dressing. Clean and dry the skin around the cut. Use an adhesive plaster over the dressing. Some lint-free dressings stick directly to the wound. These are designed to remain in place until they fall off naturally.
- **Grazes (abrasions)**: the top layer of skin has been scraped off through friction with a rough surface. Treat it as a cut, but use a specialist non-stick dressing. Be careful to check that the wound is clean.
- **Blisters**: damage to the skin by heat or friction can cause a bubble to form to protect the skin. Do not break the blister. Cover it with a special plaster that stays in place until it falls off naturally. This will ease pain and protect the area from further damage.
- **Bruises**: these are formed by damaged capillaries bleeding under the skin and are the result of an impact. The skin changes colour, the area is painful and can swell. Treat by raising and supporting the bruised part. Put a cold compress (ice pack) on the affected area.

- **Cramp**: this is a sudden and painful muscle contraction caused by strenuous exercise or loss of fluid and salt through sweating. Treat by drinking fluid, stretching and massaging the muscle.
- **Stitch**: a sharp pain in the abdominal area caused by a cramp in the diaphragm. Treat by sitting down and resting. Light massage can also help.

The RICE procedure

The treatment known as **RICE** (Rest, Ice, Compression, Elevation) is a checklist to follow in the case of most soft tissue injuries, including sprains, strains and impact injuries. We should treat such injuries as soon as possible after they occur to prevent them from becoming worse.

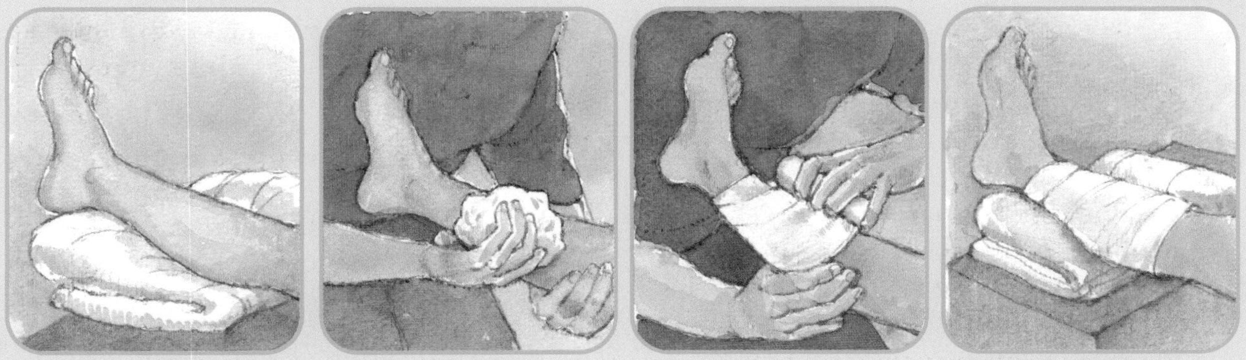

	Rest	Ice	Compression	Elevation
Reasons	■ Reduces internal bleeding ■ Prevents further injury	■ Reduces blood flow, pain and swelling	■ Reduces internal bleeding and swelling	■ Reduces internal bleeding, swelling and throbbing
Action	■ Stop activity ■ Support the injury in a comfortable position	■ Apply an ice pack to injury for 10–15 minutes every hour. Remove pack after 15 minutes or blood flow will increase to try to heat up the area	■ Wrap a bandage firmly around injured area. Do not stop blood flow	■ Raise injury above level of heart

Returning to sport

All injuries need time to heal. We can reduce the time before we return to sport by acting quickly when we are first injured. We also need to continue to treat the injury properly throughout our recovery period. If we try to return to play too soon, we can make the injury worse.

There are three stages of treatment for sprains and strains.

Stage 1: The first 48 hours

Ice should be applied for 10–15 minutes every hour during this period.

Remember **HARM** – things to be avoided in the first 48 hours after an injury:

- Do not use **Heat** because it increases internal bleeding.
- Do not drink **Alcohol** because it increases the swelling.
- Do not **Run** because the weight and impact will cause further injury.
- Do not **Massage** the injured area because it increases internal bleeding.

Stage 2: 48–72 hours

Apply ice and heat alternately for five-minute periods to increase blood flow to and from the injured area. This will encourage healing.

Stage 3: 72 hours onwards

Use heat from baths, hot water bottles, etc., to increase blood flow and encourage healing. Most injuries will now be at the stage where some movement will help to speed up recovery, but do not try to move or play at full strength until you are sure you can do so safely.

This phase is called rehabilitation. It can last for between 10 days and 6 weeks. It has four stages:

1. **Active movement**: gentle movements that do not cause any pain. If movement is painful it should not be continued.
2. **Passive stretching and active exercise**: stretching and light endurance work that does not cause any pain.
3. **Active strengthening**: the muscles will have lost some strength during the period of injury. You should first train to improve endurance and only then develop power and speed.
4. **Re-education**: if you have no pain or swelling, your muscles and joints will need to be worked through their full range of movement. You can return to full training and then return to play.

Emergency procedures

DRABC

Although you should always get medical help if possible, there are times when

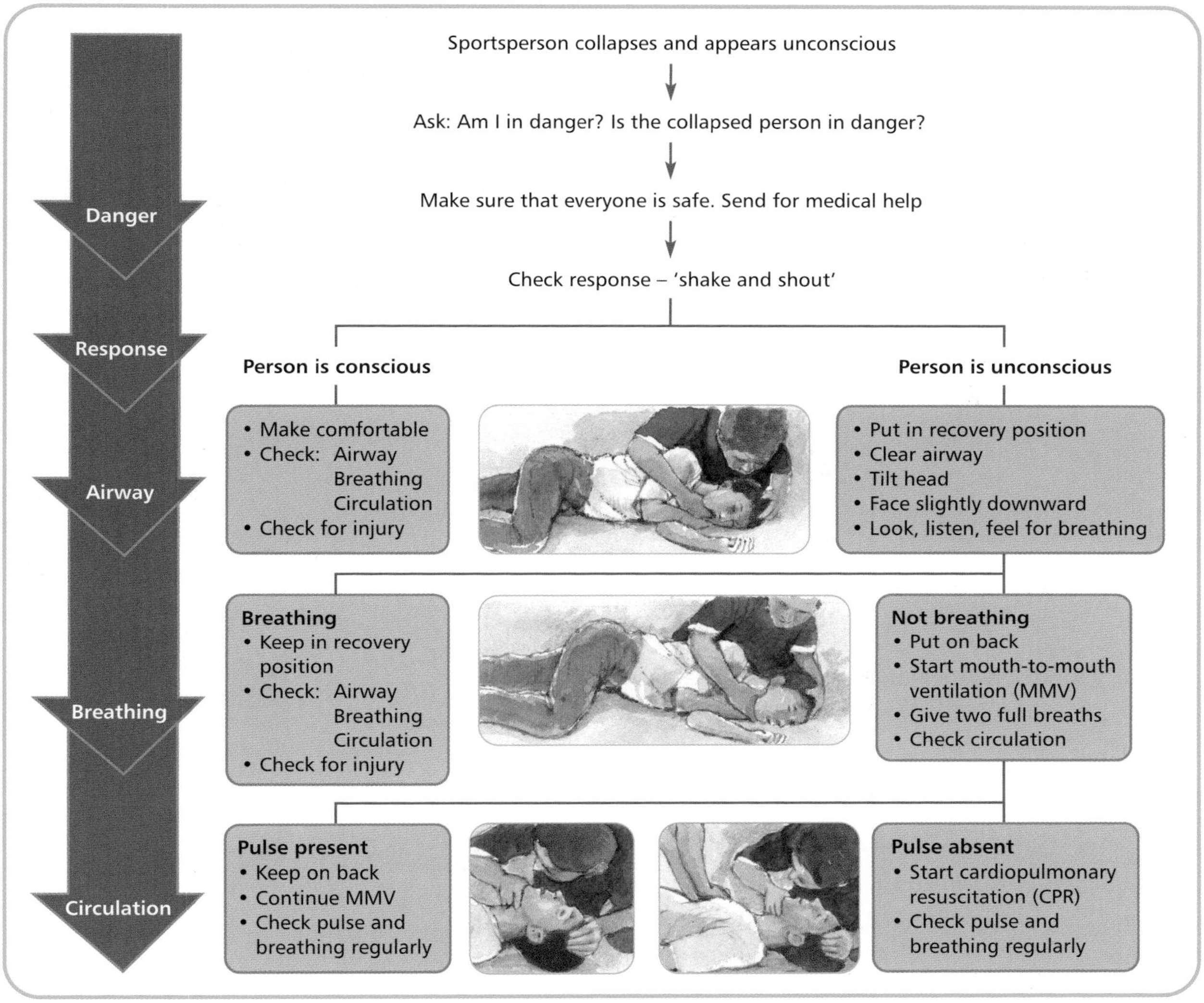

Danger

Response

Airway

Breathing

Circulation

Sportsperson collapses and appears unconscious

↓

Ask: Am I in danger? Is the collapsed person in danger?

↓

Make sure that everyone is safe. Send for medical help

↓

Check response – 'shake and shout'

Person is conscious

- Make comfortable
- Check: Airway
  Breathing
  Circulation
- Check for injury

Person is unconscious

- Put in recovery position
- Clear airway
- Tilt head
- Face slightly downward
- Look, listen, feel for breathing

Breathing

- Keep in recovery position
- Check: Airway
  Breathing
  Circulation
- Check for injury

Not breathing

- Put on back
- Start mouth-to-mouth ventilation (MMV)
  Give two full breaths
- Check circulation

Pulse present

- Keep on back
- Continue MMV
- Check pulse and breathing regularly

Pulse absent

- Start cardiopulmonary resuscitation (CPR)
- Check pulse and breathing regularly

you may have to deal with an emergency involving a serious injury on your own. It is important to keep calm and to make sure that the first treatment is correct. **DRABC (Doctor ABC)** will help you to focus on the key points. Make sure you follow the points in the right order.

When a casualty has stopped breathing we can breathe for them and help restart their breathing by increasing carbon dioxide levels in their blood. We do this by giving **mouth-to-mouth ventilation (MMV)**. If their heart has stopped beating we can try to get it going again by giving **cardiopulmonary resuscitation (CPR)**.

Mouth-to-mouth ventilation (MMV)

1. With the casualty lying on his or her back, open the airway by lifting the chin and tilting the head well back.
2. Clear the mouth and throat of any obstruction.
3. Check for breathing with your face close to the casualty's mouth. Look for chest movement. Listen for sounds of breathing and feel for breath on your cheek.

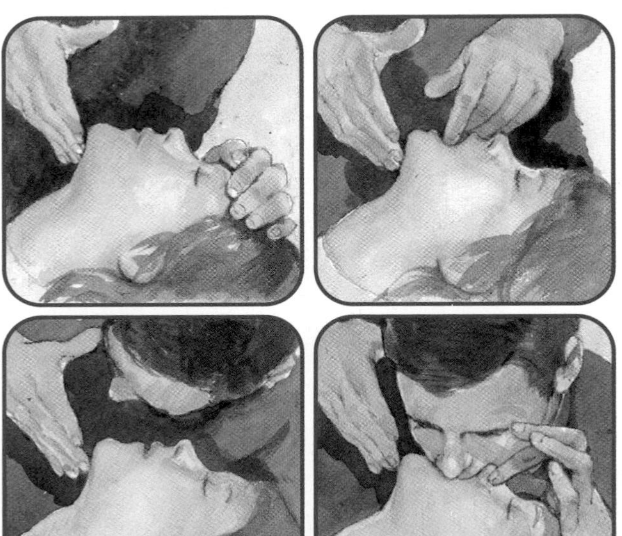

4 If the casualty is not breathing, pinch his or her nose. Take a deep breath. Seal your lips around the mouth. Blow into the mouth, and watch the chest rise. Take your mouth away and watch the chest fall back. Take another breath and repeat.
5 If the chest does not rise, check again for an obstruction in the mouth, check that the airway is open, and that you have a firm seal around the mouth.
6 Check for a pulse before continuing. If there is no pulse, start chest compressions (see CPR below).
7 If the casualty has a pulse and the chest has risen, continue blowing into the mouth. Use ten breaths a minute and continue until breathing starts. Then place the body in the recovery position.

Cardiopulmonary resuscitation (CPR)

If you are certain that a person has no pulse, use chest compressions to get the heartbeating again whilst waiting for medical help to arrive.

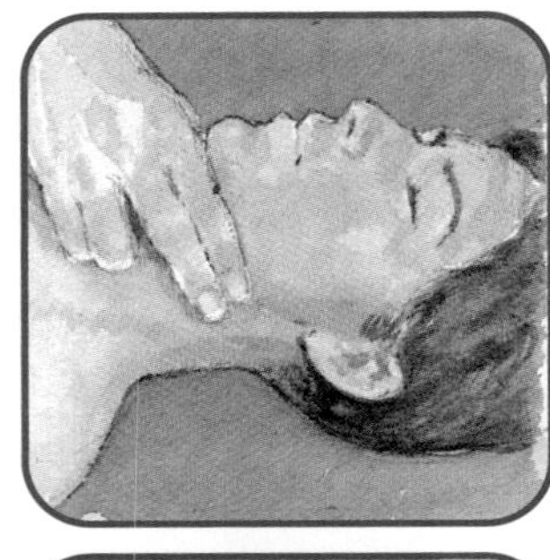

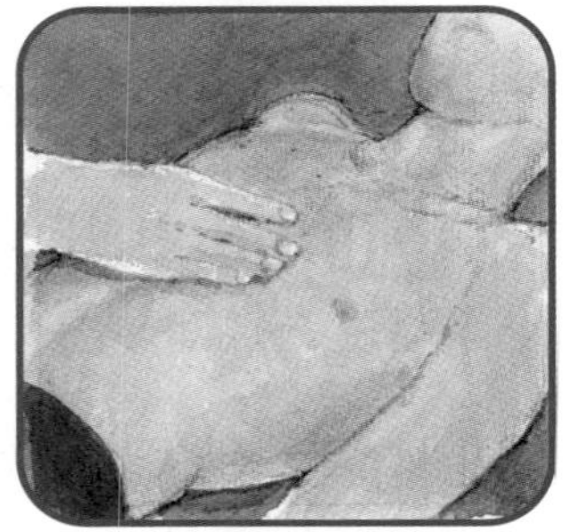

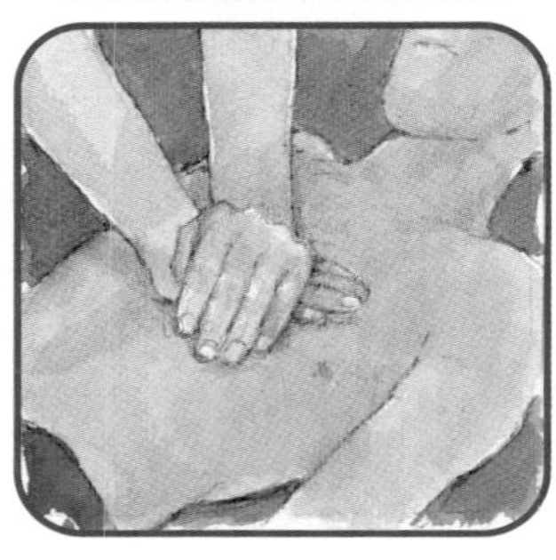

1 Check for a pulse. If the heart has stopped, you will not be able to feel a pulse. The skin will be pale, the lips blue and the arms and legs will be limp.
2 Place the person on his or her back and use your fingers to find the point where the ribs meet the breastbone. Put your middle finger over this point and your index finger higher up on the breastbone.
3 Put the heel of your other hand on the breastbone, just above your index finger. This is the spot where pressure should be applied.
4 Move the heel of your other hand over the top of this hand. Interlock your fingers.
5 Lean over the casualty with your arms straight. Press down firmly into the breastbone to a depth of 4–5 cm. Then rock backwards to release the pressure. Keep your hands in place. Repeat at a rate of about 100 compressions a minute.
6 Check the pulse rate regularly. Stop compressions as soon as the pulse returns.

MMV and CPR combined

If you are alone with a person who has no pulse and no breathing, you need to take the following five actions:

1. Open the airway. Give two breaths using MMV.
2. Give 15 chest compressions (CPR).
3. Give two breaths (MMV).
4. Give 15 chest compressions (CPR).
5. Continue until help arrives – keep checking breathing and pulse.

If you have help you can share the work.

Dealing with serious injuries

We expect help whenever we are injured whilst playing sport and we also expect organisers and helpers to have a knowledge of First Aid. Every sports club should have a qualified First Aider at every match and training session. We can all become qualified quite easily and should take the opportunity to do so. The St John Ambulance Brigade and the Red Cross organise First Aid courses. With a little training we may be able to provide life-saving help in an emergency. There are a number of serious injuries and conditions that need prompt action. We should all know what to do if we have to deal with someone who is seriously injured.

The recovery position

Always use the recovery position for an unconscious person who is breathing. You may need to alter the position slightly if the person is injured, but you can roll the body towards you and into the basic recovery position as follows:

- Tilt the head well back. This prevents the tongue blocking the throat.

- Keep the neck and back in a straight line.
- Keep the hip and knee both bent at 90°. This keeps the body safe, stable and comfortable.
- Use the casualty's hand to support their head, which should be slightly lower than the rest of the body. This allows fluids to drain from the mouth.

Remember to:

- check pulse and breathing regularly
- send for medical help.

Unconsciousness and concussion

All blows to the head are potentially dangerous. A person may lose consciousness after a violent blow to the head and may suffer from concussion on recovery. Sometimes there is a delay between the injury and losing consciousness. This is a sure sign of concussion.

If you suspect concussion, you should check for dizziness, sickness and headache. People suffering from concussion often cannot remember what has happened to them. Always put someone with concussion in the recovery position and check their breathing and pulse regularly. Never allow anyone who

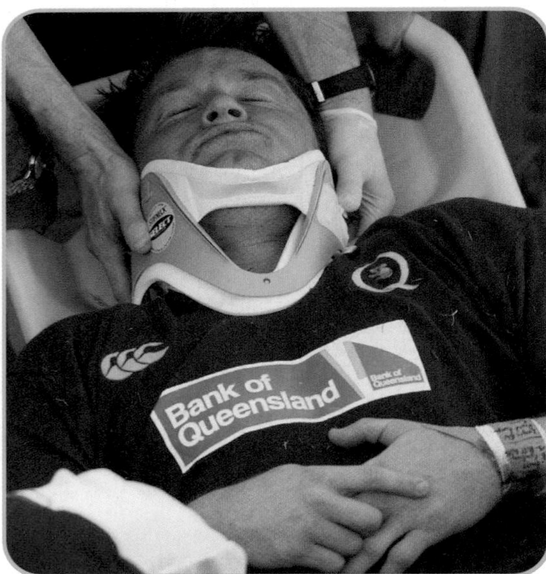

has been knocked unconscious to continue with activity until medical advice has been obtained. In many sports, players who have suffered concussion are barred from playing again for a period of time in order to prevent further injury to the brain.

Shock

Serious injuries of many types may cause shock. If you suspect that a person is suffering from shock you should check for:

- a rapid pulse
- paleness
- cold, clammy skin
- light-headedness
- nausea (feeling sick)
- thirst.

Eventually the person may become restless, anxious and aggressive, may yawn and gasp for air or even become unconscious.

Treat shock by removing or treating the cause, if possible, then:

- lie the person down, with head low and feet high to assist blood flow to the brain
- give room and air, loosen tight clothing to assist breathing and increase oxygen intake
- keep the person warm
- send for medical help
- give reassurance
- keep checking for pulse and breathing.

Extreme conditions

Extreme sports are becoming very popular. These, and many mainstream sports, take place in very cold or very hot conditions. Such conditions can create very serious problems for sportspeople. Three common but dangerous conditions that we should be able to recognise and treat are **hypothermia**, **heat exhaustion** and **heatstroke**.

Hypothermia

Hypothermia is a condition in which the internal body temperature becomes dangerously low. It can be caused by being outdoors in the cold and wind, or being in very cold water. Signs of hypothermia include:

- shivering
- cold, pale, dry skin
- slow, shallow breathing and slow, weakening pulse
- feeling confused and lacking energy.

If someone is suffering from hypothermia, send for help and then:

- insulate the person with extra clothing and cover their head to keep in heat

- move to a sheltered place and protect them from the ground and weather
- use a survival bag, if you have one
- give hot drinks if the person is conscious
- check pulse and breathing regularly.

Heat exhaustion

When the temperature around you is the same as your body temperature, your body cannot lose heat by evaporation. If the air is also humid, then sweat will not evaporate from the body and heat exhaustion or heatstroke can occur.

Heat exhaustion develops during activity in hot conditions. It is caused by dehydration – that is, loss of fluid and salt from the body due to excessive sweating.

Signs of heat exhaustion include:

- headaches and light-headedness
- feeling sick
- sweating
- pale, clammy skin
- muscle cramps
- rapid, weakening pulse and breathing.

If someone is suffering from heat exhaustion, send for help and then:

- lie them down in a cool place
- raise and support the legs
- give plenty of water and sips of weak, salty water
- if they are unconscious, place them in the recovery position.

Heatstroke is the result of the body becoming dangerously overheated after being in the heat for a long time. Signs of heatstroke include:

- headaches
- dizziness, restlessness and confusion
- hot, flushed, dry skin
- very high body temperature
- a full, bounding pulse.

If someone is suffering from heatstroke, send for help and then:

- move them to a cool place
- remove outer clothing
- cool the body with wet towels or a cold, wet sheet
- if they are unconscious, place them in the recovery position.

Careful planning and proper training, together with the right clothing and equipment, can help to prevent all the dangerous conditions described above.

QUESTIONS

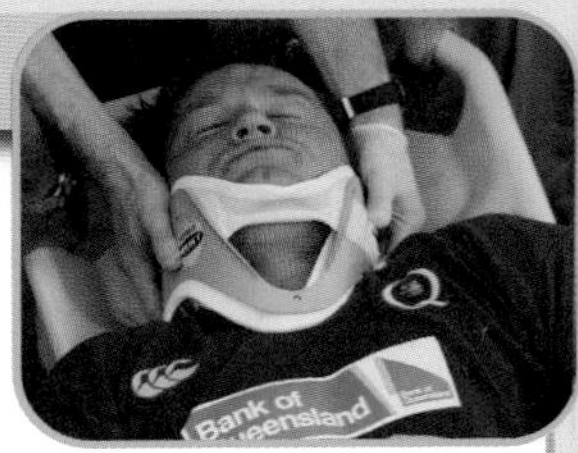

5 Hygiene, safety and risk assessment

1 All sports can be dangerous. For each named sport, list one possible risk and one way to reduce the risk.

a Basketball (2 marks)
b Rugby union (2 marks)
c Weight lifting. (2 marks)

2 The correct treatment of sports injuries is essential.

a Name two signs and symptoms of concussion. Suggest one method of treatment. (3 marks)

b Name two signs and symptoms of a sprain. Suggest one method of treatment. (3 marks)

c Name two signs and symptoms of heat exhaustion. Suggest one method of treatment. (3 marks)

3 The RICE treatment is used for soft tissue injuries. R stands for Rest. What do the other three letters stand for? (3 marks)

4 Hygiene means the way we look after our bodies to keep them healthy.

a Describe three ways in which we should look after our feet. (3 marks)

b Describe three ways in which we should look after other areas of our body. (3 marks)

AQA A only

5 There are a number of ways in which injuries can be prevented. For a named sport:

a Give one rule and explain how it reduces the risk of injury. (2 marks)

b Give one aspect of fitness and explain how it reduces the risk of injury. (2 marks)

c Name one item of clothing or footwear and explain how it reduces the risk of injury. (2 marks)

d Name one item of equipment and explain how it reduces the risk of injury. (2 marks)

6 When dealing with a sportsperson in an emergency situation we should use the DRABC procedure. If D stands for Danger:

a define and explain the letter **R**. (2 marks)

b define and explain the letter **A**. (2 marks)

c define and explain the letter **B**. (2 marks)

d define and explain the letter **C**. (2 marks)

7 Explain the procedure you would follow when dealing with an unconscious sportsperson in an emergency situation. You should include DRABC in your answer. (8 marks)

8 Sport often presents performers with risks. Using examples from sport, describe common methods of reducing risk.

Fitness for physical activities

6 The skeletal system and joints

Without our skeletal system we would look very different indeed. Our bodies would have no framework, our delicate organs would be unprotected, and we would be unable to move.

Although we all have the same number of bones and joints, our skeletal systems vary a great deal due to the wide difference in the size of our bones. This difference greatly affects our ability in sport. The longer the bone, the greater the range of movement possible and the greater the amount of force produced. This is why top-class rowers are usually very tall, with the necessary long levers to row a boat at speed.

We are all limited in the choice of sport in which we might be successful because of the size of our skeletal system. Gymnasts usually have shorter limbs. This enables them to produce a burst of power very quickly and also to move their body with great control. At the highest sporting level, height is necessary for success at, for example, basketball, high jump and volleyball. However, even if we are of medium height we can still have some success in these sports if we are skilful and determined enough.

How do we move?

Our skeleton has many joints. Our muscles are positioned around these joints. If we want to make a movement, our muscles contract and pull on the bones around the joints. In this way our whole body can move as quickly or as slowly as we want. We have over 100 different joints in our body. The different arrangements of bones and joints, together with our muscles, allow us to perform intricate and powerful movement patterns in dance and gymnastics, as well as to make a full-blooded tackle in rugby.

Our body is flexible, and this is due to the combination of many of our joints. For example, our vertebral column has 33 small vertebrae, all of which can move a little. The result is that we can bend our back in many different ways in gymnastics, from performing a forward somersault to a backward walkover. The joints of our upper body allow us to serve in tennis and those of the lower body enable us to high-jump. In contrast to these powerful movements, the joints in our hands and wrist enable us to spin a ball in cricket, throw a dart and aim an arrow. We are able to adjust our body position constantly in sport and everyday life by using our muscles and joints together.

activity

Joint observation

Roll up the sleeve of your right arm. Bend your elbow to bring your arm across your chest.

Look at the back of your hand and your forearm near the elbow as you wiggle your fingers. What's going on? Notice how your muscles create movement using some very long tendons. Now move your thumb around and note the muscles creating this movement.

KEYWORDS

Abduction: limb movement away from the middle line of the body

Adduction: limb movement towards the middle line of the body

Calcium: mineral that is vital to healthy bones, found in milk, cheese and yoghurt

Cartilage: a tough but flexible tissue which cushions and protects many bones in the skeleton

Circumduction: movement in which the end of a bone moves in a circle

Extension: limb movement straightening a joint

Flexion: limb movement bending a joint

Joint: a place where two or more bones meet

Ligament: a band of tough fibrous tissue which binds bones together at the joint

Rotation: circular movement in which part of the body turns whilst the rest remains still

Skeleton: the bony framework of the body

Synovial joint: joint containing synovial fluid, allowing a wide range of movement

Tendon: strong cords of fibrous tissue which fix muscles to bone

Vertebrae: irregular bones which make up the vertebral column.

Key to Exam Success

For your GCSE you should be able to:

- explain the functions of the skeleton and relate them to exercise and sport
- define the term joint and know its importance in exercise and sport
- understand the structure of a synovial joint
- identify different types of joint and explain their function in movement
- understand the importance of joint flexibility in sport and everyday life
- explain the different terms used to describe movement
- explain how efficient joints with increased flexibility can improve sporting performance
-  AQA A only: describe the functions of cartilage and ligaments in physical movement
- AQA A only: identify and classify all the common bones of the body
- AQA A only: relate the common bones of the body to exercise and sporting performance.

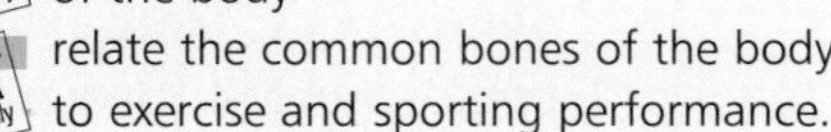

KEY THOUGHTS

'Movement is a joint exercise with muscles.'

What does our skeleton do?

Our **skeleton** gives shape to our body, protects our organs, moves our body, supports our organs and produces blood.

Gives shape

Our body needs a framework and the skeleton gives shape to our bodies, enabling us to achieve a good posture.

When playing sport we need a firm basic shape from which to develop the many different body positions required, from a smash in tennis to a tuck in gymnastics. Sports such as golf, speed skating and riding also require a variety of sporting postures.

Protects

Our delicate organs need the protection of a strong structure of bone, particularly to prevent injury in contact sports such as rugby and judo. The cranium protects the brain, the vertebral column protects the spinal cord and the ribcage protects the heart and lungs.

Moves

Different sports require an extremely wide variety of muscle movements and different amounts of force, from the delicate touch required for a badminton drop shot to the power and control of the hammer throw.

Our muscles use our bones to cause movement. The muscles are attached to the skeleton, which is jointed to allow a wide range of movement. Different joints allow different types of movement.

Supports

We change our body position in most sports and in gymnastics and trampolining we are often upside down. Our organs need to be able to function in these positions.

The skeleton holds our vital organs in place, the vertebral column playing a central part in supporting much of our body.

Produces blood

In sport, as in life in general, we need white blood cells for protection and red blood cells to provide the working muscles with oxygen. In endurance sports, the ability of the red blood cells to carry oxygen is vital for success. Red and white blood cells are produced in the bone marrow of the ribs, vertebrae and femur.

What are the different bone types?

We have four basic types of bone in our body. Their size and shape are linked to how we use them.

Long bones
These are the large bones in our legs, arms, fingers and toes. We use them in the main movements of our body.

Short bones
These are the small bones at the joints of our hands and feet. We use them in the fine movements of our body.

Flat bones (or plate)
These are the bones of our cranium, shoulder girdle, ribs and pelvic girdle. We use them to protect the organs of our body. Large muscles are attached to our flat bones.

Irregular bones
These are the bones in our face and vertebral column. We use them to give our body protection and shape.

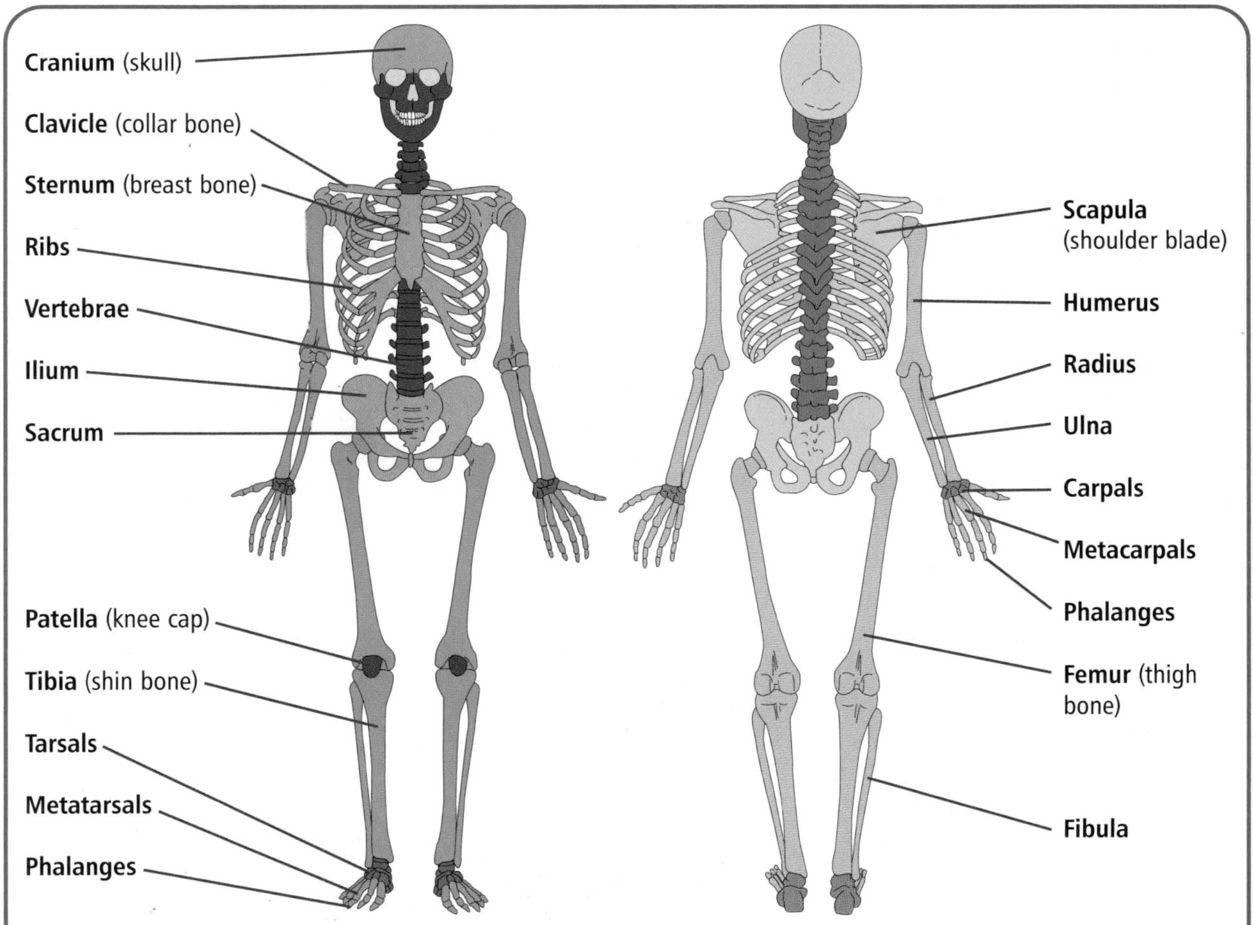

Cranium (skull)
Clavicle (collar bone)
Sternum (breast bone)
Ribs
Vertebrae
Ilium
Sacrum
Patella (knee cap)
Tibia (shin bone)
Tarsals
Metatarsals
Phalanges
Scapula (shoulder blade)
Humerus
Radius
Ulna
Carpals
Metacarpals
Phalanges
Femur (thigh bone)
Fibula

Note: The sesamoid bones are a special type of short bone within a tendon, for example, the patella (kneecap)

Bones in the upper body

The most important bones in the upper body are:

- the shoulder girdle
- the ribs and sternum
- the arms
- the wrist and hand.

The shoulder girdle

The shoulder girdle consists of two clavicles and two scapulas:

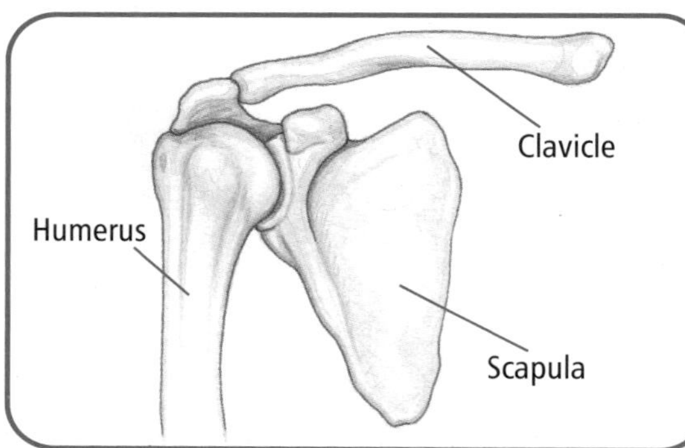

- **Clavicles** are thin, flat, slightly curved bones.
- **Scapulas** are large, flat bones with many muscles attached.

The shoulder girdle is only linked by muscles to our vertebral column. This gives us great flexibility in our arms and shoulders, which is very helpful in sports such as gymnastics and swimming. However, it limits the force we can use.

The ribs and sternum

The sternum is a large, flat bone forming the front of the ribcage and giving it added strength.

- 12 pairs of ribs are joined to the vertebral column, but only 7 to the sternum.

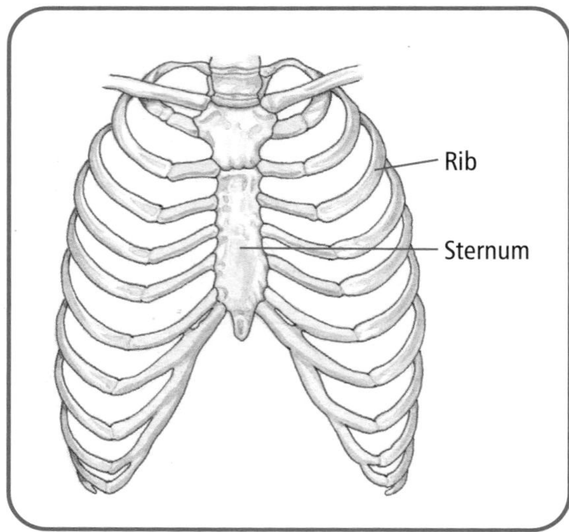

- 3 pairs are joined to the seventh rib (false ribs) and 2 ribs are unattached (floating ribs).

The ribcage protects our lungs and heart in combat and contact sports. It provides attachment for the intercostal muscles which are vital for deep breathing during strenuous exercise.

The arms

The arms consist of humerus, radius and ulna.

The long bones of the arm enable us to make major movements of the body, applying force over a large range of movement.

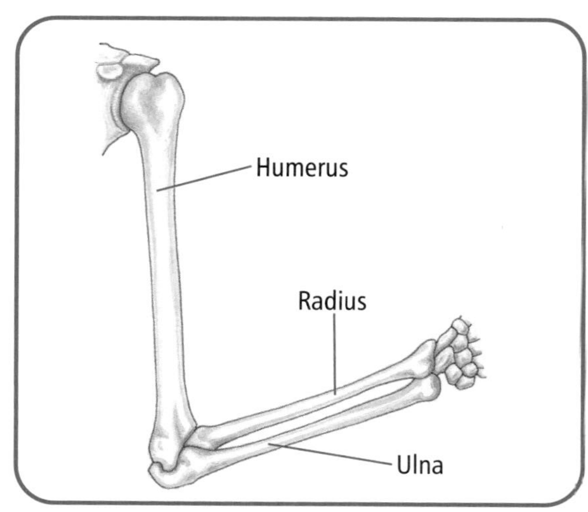

The wrist and hand

There are 8 carpal bones in the wrist, and 5 metacarpal bones and 14 phalanges in each hand.

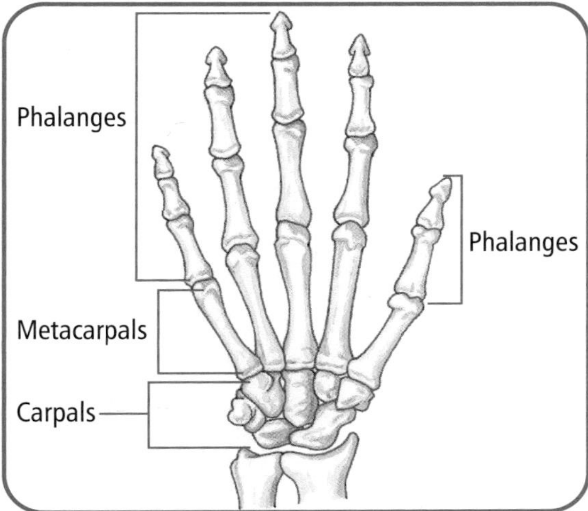

The small bones of the hand enable us to make precise and delicate movements in sport.

Bones in the lower body

The most important bones in the lower body are:

- the pelvic girdle
- the legs, ankle and foot.

The pelvic girdle

The pelvic girdle is made up of two halves, each formed by three bones (including the ilium) which are fused together on each side. This forms a very stable joint with the vertebral column and passes the weight of the body to the legs. It supports the lower abdomen and provides a strong joint for the femur.

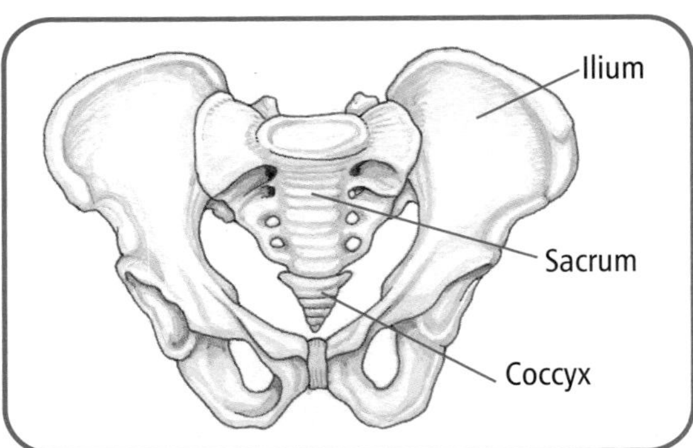

The female pelvis is wider and shallower than the male pelvis. This is to make childbearing easier, but it does make running less efficient.

Legs

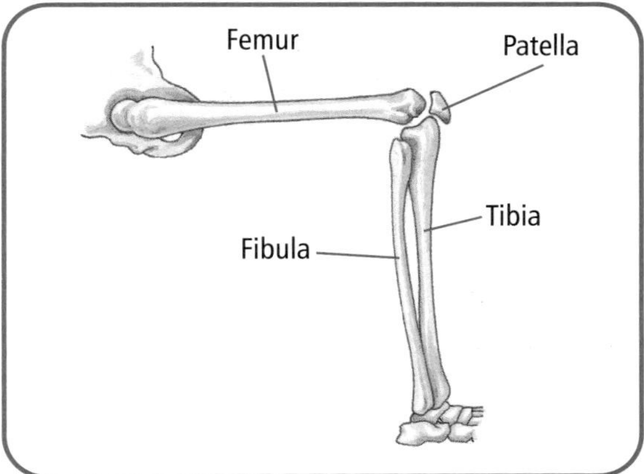

The legs consist of the femur, tibia and fibula. These long bones enable us to make major movements of the body, applying force over a large range of movement.

Ankle and foot

There are 7 tarsals in the ankle, and 5 metatarsals and 14 phalanges in each foot.

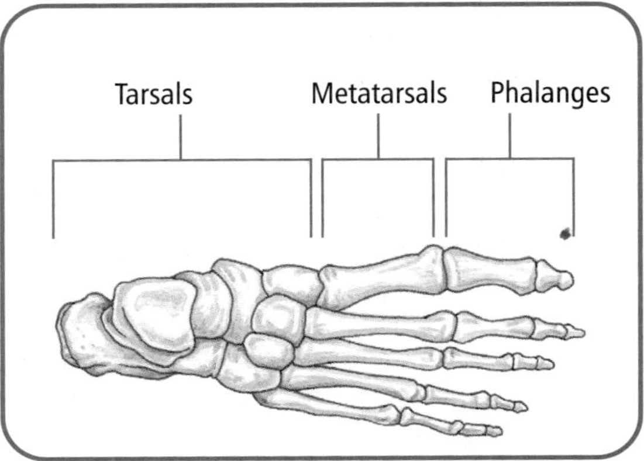

In order to perform most skilful actions, we need our feet to provide a solid base for our body. This is true of a drive in tennis, a shot in hockey or a take-off in the long jump. Even simple running requires a solid base for the thousands of steps which take place. All sportspeople should check the soles of their footwear for signs of abnormal wear.

The vertebral column

The vertebral column is also called the spine or spinal column. It is made up of 33 small, specialised bones called **vertebrae**. The vertebral column is divided into five regions. Each region has its own type of vertebrae which work in their own way.

Seven cervical vertebrae

- Our smallest vertebrae.
- The neck muscles are attached to them.
- They support our head and neck.
- The top vertebra, the atlas, fits into the cranium and lets the head nod.
- The second vertebra, the axis, lets the head rotate.

Twelve thoracic vertebrae

- Our larger vertebrae.
- Our ribs are attached to them.
- They support the ribcage.
- They allow us some slight movement, bending forward, backward and from side to side.

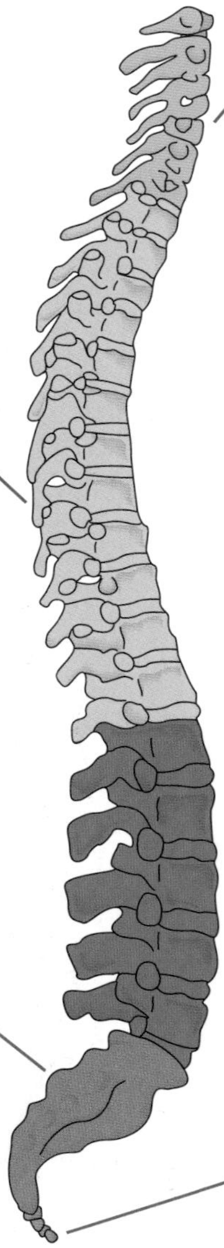

Five lumbar vertebrae

- The largest vertebrae.
- Our back muscles are attached to them.
- They allow much bending forward, backward and from side to side.
- The large range of movement means that this region can be easily injured.

Five sacral vertebrae

- These vertebrae are fused together. They are also fused to the pelvic girdle.
- They make a very strong base, which supports the weight of the body.
- They also pass force from the legs and hips to the upper body.

Four coccyx

- Our other fused vertebrae.
- They have no special use.

Vertebral discs

Between each pair of vertebrae is a disc of cartilage. Each disc is a thick circle of tough tissue which acts as a shock absorber for the vertebral column and allows movement between the vertebrae.

Functions of the vertebral column

The vertebral column:

- protects the spinal cord
- supports the upper body
- gives us a wide range of movement
- is important for posture
- passes force to the other body parts.

The vertebral column and sport

Our vertebral column is important to all sporting movements. It has many joints and is both flexible and strong. This allows us to bend and stretch our bodies into very many different positions. We must always learn the correct technique in our sport to help avoid injury to the vertebral column.

This is especially important in weight lifting, bowling in cricket and the throws in athletics. All spinal injuries should be treated very seriously. The injury can become permanent and even life-threatening.

Our bones and body shape

The size of our skeleton is largely decided by heredity. This means that if our parents are tall and heavy, we are likely to be of a similar body build. If we follow a balanced diet with all the nutrients we need for bone growth, especially calcium, then we are likely to reach our maximum height and maximum bone size.

Our actual body shape will depend not only on the height of our skeleton and the size of our bones, but on a number of other factors. These include the capacity of our bones to carry muscle, our body type (mesomorph, endomorph, ectomorph – see page 220), our diet and our regular exercise patterns.

This gymnast has bent her back into a hyperextension position. This should only be tried after much specialised training. Sportspeople can develop back injuries as a result of hyperextension.

Whatever size we are in terms of height, we need to maintain our optimum weight for our body type. This will ensure that we do not carry excess fat which will not only be a disadvantage in sport, but may also cause health problems.

Our bones and exercise

Exercise helps the development of the skeleton in young people. Exercise can increase bone width and density and therefore bone strength, but it has no effect on bone length.

In particular, regular physical activities which include weight-bearing exercises can help to keep our bones in good condition.

Children and young people should not overdo some types of exercise during the growing period in adolescence. For example, lifting heavy weights, taking part in strenuous contact sports and long-distance road running can all damage the growth plates in the bones and lead to abnormal growth.

If muscle strength develops faster than skeletal strength, bones can break up at the attachment point of the tendon on the bone. This happens in Osgood-Schlatters disease at the knee.

The vertebral column of this tennis player is able to extend to allow him to serve with strength.

This diver is able to change her body position with great precision whilst moving at speed through the air. Our vertebrae and discs are arranged to form a flexible but strong unit.

y important for this rugby player that the weight pushing against his shoulders is passed to his legs through a straight vertebral column. A bent back with his vertebrae out of line could lead to injury.

Strength training during adolescence must be planned and supervised by a qualified instructor. Injuries to bone need careful treatment to avoid damage to growth areas.

If we are unable to exercise through injury or illness we will lose both bone size and strength.

What are the different types of joint?

A **joint** is a place where two or more bones meet. The function of joints is to hold our bones together and to allow us to move our limbs and body.

Joints can be divided into three main groups, based on the amount of movement they allow:

- immovable (fibrous) joints
- slightly movable (cartilaginous) joints
- freely movable (synovial) joints.

Immovable (fibrous) joints

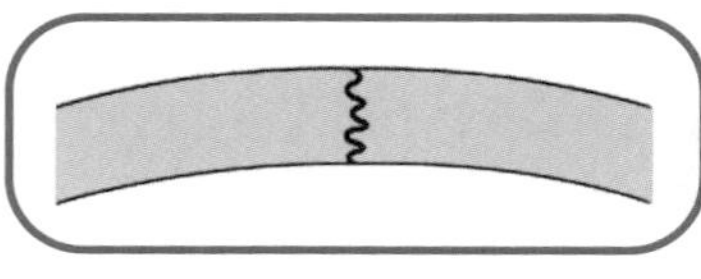

These are fixed joints with no movement possible between the bones. They have no significance in sport.

Slightly movable (cartilaginous) joints

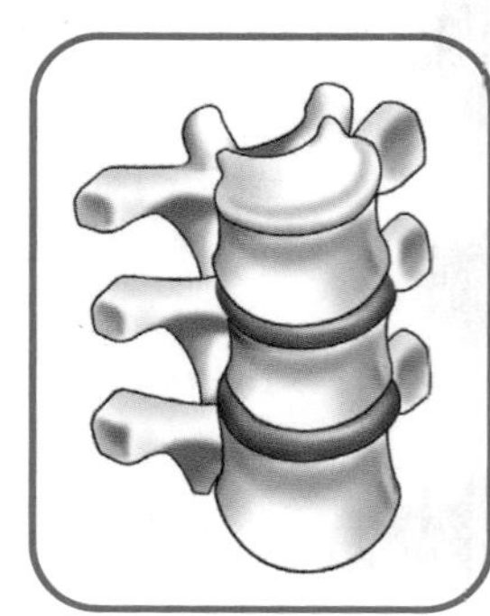

- The bones have a pad of cartilage between them.
- Movement is possible between the bones.

- Examples are found in the joints between the ribs and sternum and between the vertebrae.

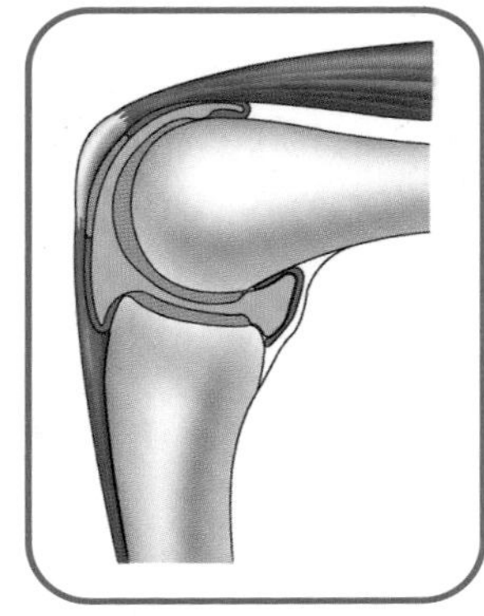

Note: the knee joint is a synovial joint although there are pads of cartilage within the joint capsule.

What is cartilage?

Cartilage is a tough but flexible tissue found on the ends of bones and as a pad between bones.

Hyaline cartilage is found on the ends of our bones and around the joint socket in all our synovial joints. It is a hard, slippery layer which protects the bones from wear and tear, greatly reducing the friction between the bones during movement. Older people may suffer from osteoarthritis. This causes damage to the layer of hyaline cartilage, resulting in severe pain whenever the bones are moved. Modern surgery has made it possible for the heads of the damaged bones to be replaced in, for example, the hip joint, and for the lining of the joint socket to be renewed. This allows the joint to work smoothly again.

In the vertebral column and knee, the pads of tough cartilage act as shock absorbers, forming a gristly cushion which can be squashed. In the vertebral column the discs of cartilage lie between each pair of vertebrae. Severe back pain is caused if these discs are damaged or slip out of place.

Many sportspeople suffer damage to the cartilage in the knee, especially in games like football. Since the cartilage does not have a blood supply, it does not repair itself easily. If the cartilage is torn it may be removed as this does not badly affect joint flexibility. However, the muscles around the knee will need strengthening to keep the joint stable.

What are ligaments?

Ligaments are bands of tough fibrous tissue which bind our bones together at joints. Some ligaments form a capsule which surrounds the joint and contains synovial fluid. Other ligaments remain outside the capsule, but also hold the joint stable. The ligaments make joints more stable by preventing excessive movement. They also limit the direction of movement. In general, the more ligaments around a joint, the stronger the joint will be.

If a lot of force is put on a ligament, it will stretch, although it can be damaged quite easily. In games like tennis, football and hockey, excessive twisting movements can cause damage to ligaments at the knee and ankle. The hip is a more stable joint because of the strength of the ligaments around it and therefore it is damaged less often. When ligaments are stretched or torn, this is known as a sprain (see page 94). The blood supply to ligaments is poor and so sprains heal slowly.

Freely movable (synovial) joints

Synovial joints are complex joints. The amount of movement they allow depends first of all on the shape of the bones within the joint. Movement will also depend on the arrangement of the muscles and their tendons around the joint, together with any ligaments which bind the bones together.

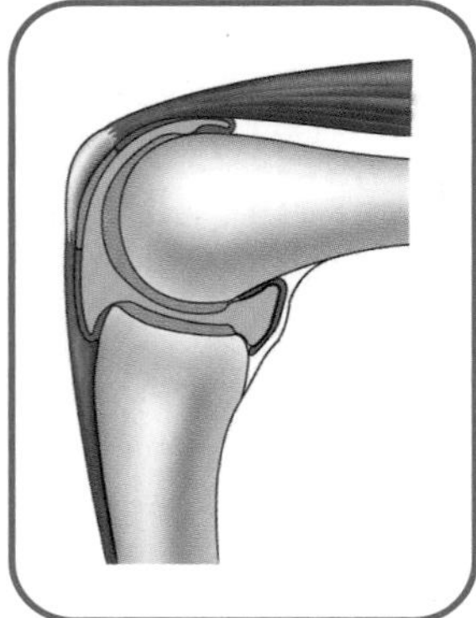

Synovial joints are found throughout the body including at the knee, hip and shoulder. They usually permit a wide variety of movement.

How are synovial joints constructed?

- **Hyaline cartilage** covers the head of the bones and the joint socket. It forms a hard, tough, slippery layer which protects bones and reduces friction in the joints.
- **Synovial membrane** forms a layer on the inside of the joint capsule and produces synovial fluid.
- **Synovial fluid** lubricates the joints and allows friction-free movement.
- A **joint capsule** made of fibrous tissue holds the bones together and protects the joint.

What are the different types of synovial joint?

Synovial joints have different structures, depending on how they work. This means the shape of the bones varies, as does the arrangement of the ligaments.

There are six basic types of synovial joint, all with different structures. The three most important for sport are:

- ball and socket
- hinge
- pivot.

The other three types are saddle, condyloid and gliding (plane) joints.

Some joints fit into more than one category. For example, the knee joint has a condyloid joint structure, but actually works as a hinge joint.

Ball and socket joint

- Moves freely in all directions.
- Ligaments are often used to keep the joint stable.
- Examples: hip and shoulder.

Hinge joint

- Movement is in one plane only.
- Will open until it is straight.
- Movement is limited because of the shape of the bones and the position of the ligaments.
- Examples: elbow and knee.

Pivot joint

- Only rotation is possible because it has a 'ring-on-peg' structure.
- Example: between the atlas and axis vertebrae in the neck.

Saddle joint

- Allows movement in two planes at right angles to each other.
- Bones are shaped like saddles and fit neatly together.
- Movement is back and forward and side to side.
- Movement is limited because of the shape of the bones.
- Example: thumb.

Condyloid joint

- Movement is possible in two planes.
- The rounded end of one bone fits into the hollow of another.
- Movement is back and forward and side-to-side.
- Ligaments prevent rotation.
- Example: wrist.

Gliding (plane) joint

- One bone slides on top of another.
- A little movement is possible in all directions.
- Ligaments limit the movement.
- Example: vertebrae, carpal bones in the hand.

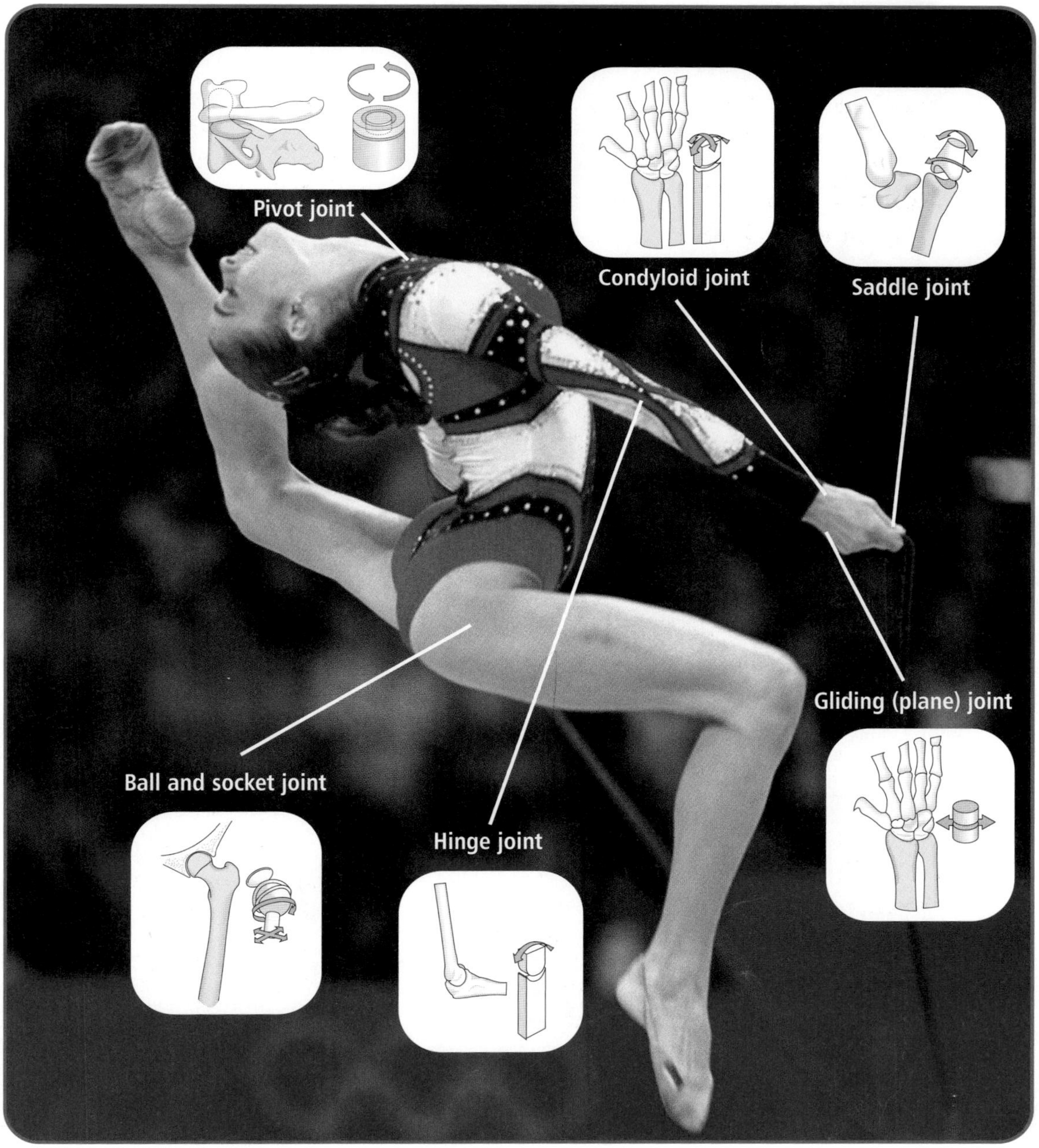

Pivot joint

Condyloid joint

Saddle joint

Gliding (plane) joint

Ball and socket joint

Hinge joint

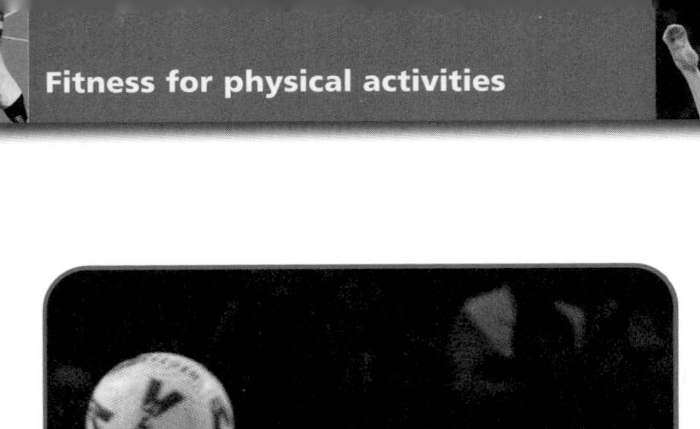

Our joints and sport

Our different joints work smoothly together when we make skilled sporting movements. They must be capable of a full range of movement in order to help us perform well. The muscles, tendons and ligaments surrounding each joint must be strong enough to give stability to the joint.

The demands of sport put severe stress on our joints. We must ensure that our joints are in good condition to reduce the chance of injury and to give us the opportunity to improve our sporting performance. We can do this by:

- eating a healthy diet to ensure strong bones, ligaments, tendons and cartilage

- strengthening the muscles around the joints to provide stability
- exercising regularly to prepare our joints for additional strain
- using flexibility exercises to increase the range of movement at the joints
- warming up thoroughly before each activity and warming down afterwards
- training to meet the needs of our particular sport.

How does our body move?

When we play sport we move our limbs in many different directions. We use special words to describe these movements: **extension**, **flexion**, **abduction**, **adduction**, **rotation** and AQA B only **circumduction**.

A. Abduction: our limbs are moved away from a line down the middle of our body.

B. Rotation: a circular movement in which part of the body turns whilst the rest remains still.

C. Flexion: our limbs bend at a joint.

D. Adduction: our limbs are moved towards a line down the middle of our body.

E. Extension: our limbs straighten at a joint.

Type of joint	Movement allowed
Ball and socket	Flexion and extension Abduction and adduction Rotation and circumduction
Hinge	Flexion and extension
Pivot	Rotation only
Condyloid	Flexion and extension Abduction and adduction
Gliding	Some gliding in all directions (no bending or circular movements)

activity

Movements at joints

Look at the pictures of movement above and on page 121. List the joints used and the type of movement shown, then try to think of examples of other sporting situations where the same, or a similar, action might be performed. Show your results in a table like the one below.

Photo	Joint(s) used	Movement	Further example(s)
A			
B			
C			
D			
E			

QUESTIONS

6 The skeletal system and joints

1 The skeleton gives shape and supports the body. Give three other functions of the skeleton and describe an example from sport for each.

(6 marks)

2 The body moves in many ways. Describe each of the types of movement below and explain how it is used in a sporting situation.

- **a** Extension *(3 marks)*
- **b** Rotation *(3 marks)*
- **c** Adduction. *(3 marks)*

3 Joints allow the skeleton to move. Give one example of:

- **a** a hinge joint
- **b** a pivot joint
- **c** a ball and socket joint.

(3 marks)

4 Name two types of synovial joint and explain the function of each in movement.

(6 marks)

5 For each type of bone listed, give one example and state where it is located in the body.

- **a** Short *(2 marks)*
- **b** Long *(2 marks)*
- **c** Flat *(2 marks)*
- **d** Irregular. *(2 marks)*

6 Joints have a number of components. Describe the role of each component in movement.

- **a** Ligaments *(2 marks)*
- **b** Hyaline cartilage *(2 marks)*
- **c** Tendons *(2 marks)*
- **d** Synovial fluid. *(2 marks)*

7 Explain how efficient joints with increased flexibility can improve sporting performance.

(8 marks)

8 List four types of freely moveable joints and discuss the function of each in sport.

(8 marks)

7 Muscles and muscle action

Nearly all the movements of our body are caused by the contraction of our muscles. The speed and power which enables us to jump out of the way of danger also enables us to do well in contact sport. The muscles which control our vision in everyday life also allow us to follow the ball in racket sport. Our heart muscle beats constantly throughout our life to pump blood around our body and enable us to work, rest and play. Silent muscles within us meet the needs of our body for both energy and nutrients. Above all, our muscles have the special ability to change chemical energy into mechanical energy. This means that if we supply our muscles with food and oxygen they will produce movement. Without movement in sport, we can achieve nothing.

activity

Muscle analysis

Working with a partner, carry out the activities below while your partner identifies which major muscle groups are being used.

Examples of muscle groups include:

- upper back
- lower back
- upper arm
- lower arm
- chest
- shoulder
- stomach.

Begin by lying flat on your back. Then complete each action when instructed to do so by your partner.

Activity	Major muscle groups being used
Move to sit-up position	
Stand up	
Raise hands above head	
Raise one knee and hold for five seconds	
Complete one press-up	
From standing position, jump as high as possible	

KEYWORDS

Antagonist: muscle that works in combination with the prime mover to control movement at a joint

Atrophy: loss of muscle mass due to physical inactivity

Circumduction: the end of a bone moves in a circle

Core stability: balanced position with the body's centre of gravity over the base of support, ready for movement

Extension: limb movement straightening a joint

Fast-twitch muscle fibres: used for anaerobic activity, providing fast, powerful contractions for a short period

Flexion: limb movement bending a joint

Hypertrophy: growth of muscles as a result of regular physical activity

Insertion: the end of the muscle which is attached to the bone which moves

Isometric contraction: muscular contraction that results in no movement at a joint

Isotonic concentric contraction: muscular contraction where the muscle shortens, resulting in movement at a joint

Isotonic eccentric contraction: muscular contraction where the muscle lengthens, resulting in movement at a joint

Muscle tone: voluntary muscles in a state of very slight tension, ready and waiting to be used

Origin: the end of the muscle which is attached to the fixed bone

Posture: the way in which body parts are positioned in relation to one another

Prime mover: muscle that is responsible for movement at a joint

Rotation: a circular movement in which part of the body turns whilst the rest remains still

Slow-twitch muscle fibres: used for aerobic activity, providing contractions over a long period of time

Synergist: muscle that reduces unnecessary movement at a joint when prime mover contracts

Tendon: strong fibrous tissue that joins muscle to bone.

Key to Exam Success

For your GCSE you should be able to:

- know the name, position and functions of the main skeletal muscles of the body
- understand why and how muscles work in pairs
- understand the importance of fast- and slow-twitch muscle fibres in sporting activity
- describe posture and muscle tone
- understand how muscles change when exercised
- know the importance of muscles and muscle action for sport, fitness and training
- AQA A only: classify and know the importance of the three different types of muscle
- AQA A only: Explain how muscles attach to bone
- AQA B only: Know how muscles work isometrically and isotonically.

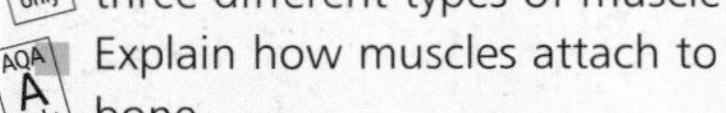

KEY THOUGHTS

'Muscles are the machines of the body.'

All the movements we make happen as a result of the shortening (contracting) and lengthening (extending) of the voluntary muscles which are found around our joints. Our muscles can only pull; they cannot push.

Our muscles:

- enable us to move our body parts
- give us our own individual shape
- protect and keep in place our abdominal organs
- stabilise our joints during movement
- enable us to maintain a good posture
- help in the circulation of our blood
- generate body heat when they contract.

There are over 600 voluntary muscles in the body – 150 in the head and neck. Skeletal muscle accounts for over 40% of our body mass.

Types of muscle

We can divide muscles into three main types, depending on the way they work.

Voluntary muscles

Our voluntary, or skeletal, muscles work as we instruct them and are under our conscious control. They make our bodies move. We use them for everyday sporting activities such as walking, running and jumping. We also use them for all the specialised movements of sport and training, ranging from somersaults to forward defensive strokes, from press-ups to golf swings. With regular training they will adapt and improve our sporting performance.

Involuntary muscles

Our involuntary, or smooth, muscles work automatically. They are not under our conscious control. They work our internal organs such as the stomach, gut, bladder and blood vessels. We rely on them to provide the nutrients we need for sport and training and to remove waste products from the body. The walls of the blood vessels contract to keep our blood flowing at all times.

Cardiac muscle

Our cardiac, or heart, muscle is a very special type of involuntary muscle which is found only in the walls of the heart. It contracts regularly, continuously and without tiring. It works automatically, but is under constant nervous and chemical control. The ability of the heart to adapt to the stresses of training enables us all to improve our cardiovascular fitness to the level required by our sport.

What are muscle fibres?

Our muscles are made up of many tiny thread-like fibres packed together in bundles. These fibres contract and make the muscle shorter. In voluntary muscle, the fibres come together at the ends of the muscles into a tough

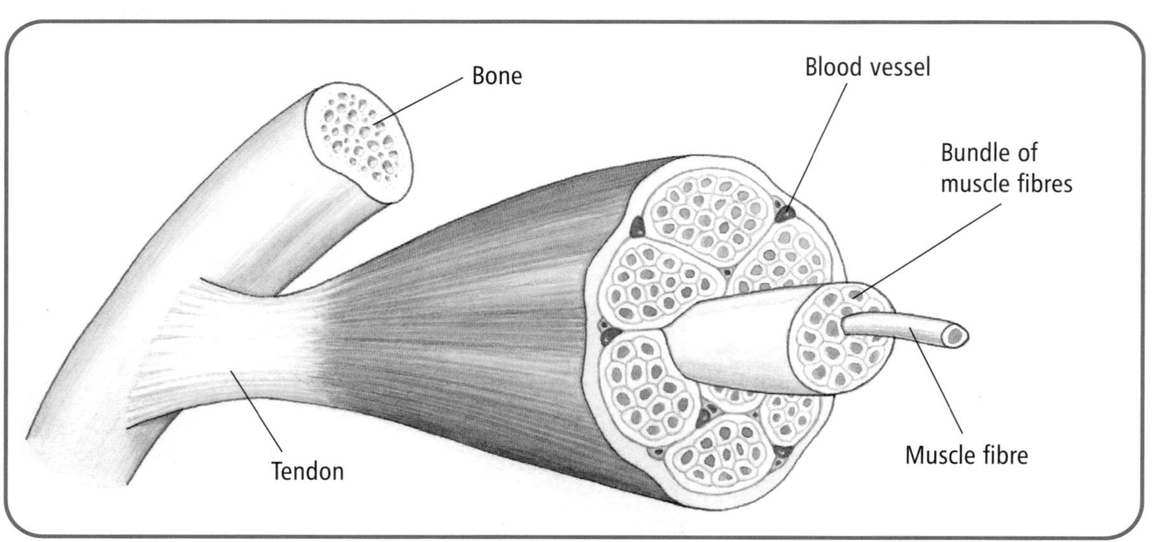

cord-like tendon. Each tendon is attached firmly to the bone. Voluntary muscles are usually long and thin. When they contract they become shorter and thicker.

We have two different types of fibres in our voluntary muscles: **fast-twitch** and **slow-twitch**.

Slow-twitch muscle fibres:

- have a very good oxygen supply
- work for a long time without tiring
- are not as strong as fast-twitch fibres
- take longer to contract
- are used in all types of exercise
- are used especially in aerobic activities which need cardiovascular fitness, such as long-distance running and cycling.

Fast-twitch muscle fibres:

- do not have a good oxygen supply
- tire very quickly
- are stronger than slow-twitch fibres
- contract very quickly
- are used when we need fast, powerful movements
- are used only in high-intensity exercise
- are used in anaerobic activities which need bursts of strength and power such as sprinting and jumping.

Our muscle fibres and sport

If we jog slowly, only a few of our slow-twitch muscle fibres contract to move our legs. When we increase our speed, we use more slow-twitch fibres. As we run faster, our fast-twitch fibres also start to contract to help out. More and more will start to work as we run even faster. At top speed, all of our fast- and slow-twitch muscle fibres will be working.

In many sports we need to use the different fibres at different times. In hockey, for example, we need to use our fast-twitch fibres for quick sprints and our slow-twitch fibres for jogging when not involved in the action.

Our muscles are usually an equal mixture of both fast- and slow-twitch fibres. The exact amount of each depends on what we inherit from our parents, and the mixture can vary widely. A person with more slow-twitch fibres is likely to be better at sports needing cardiovascular endurance such as cycling, running and swimming. Someone with more fast-twitch fibres is likely to be better at sprinting, throwing and jumping. For many team games we need both short bursts of activity and constant, less demanding activity. Our training programmes for games will therefore contain activities to develop both slow- and fast-twitch muscle fibres. We can train our muscle fibres to contract either more often (slow-twitch) or more powerfully (fast-twitch).

Our major muscles

Muscles of the upper body

Note: Movement terms are explained on pages 121–122.

Biceps

- Location: front of the upper arm
- Function: flexes the forearm at the elbow
- Examples: drawing a bow in archery, rowing
- Strengthened by: curls of various sorts.

Triceps

- Location: back of the upper arm
- Function: extends the forearm at the elbow; extends the arm at the shoulder
- Examples: smash in badminton, throwing the javelin, press-ups
- Strengthened by: press-ups, triceps curls above the head.

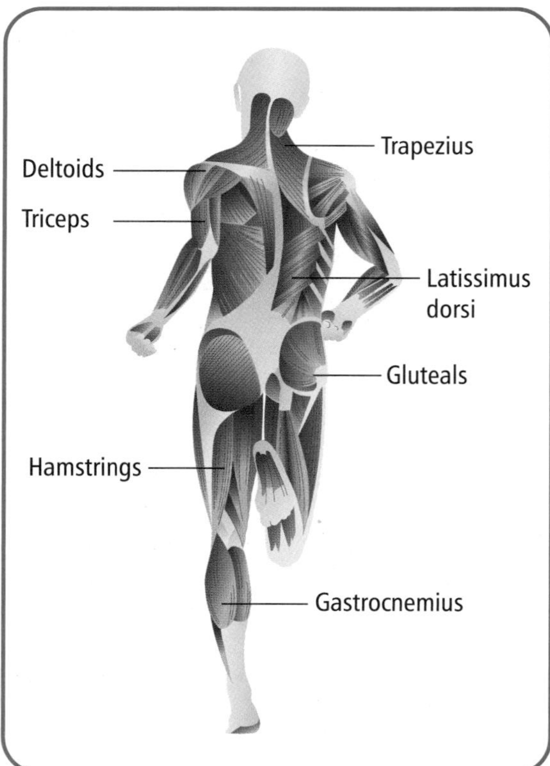

Deltoids

- Location: front and rear of the shoulder
- Function: moves the arm in all directions at the shoulder; adducts (raises) the arm
- Examples: bowling in cricket
- Strengthened by: bent-over rowing, bench presses.

Trapezius

- Location: rear of the shoulders and neck
- Function: helps to raise and control the shoulder girdle; holds back the shoulders; moves head back and sideways
- Examples: holding the head up in a rugby scrum, head back to follow high ball, head back in 'Fosbury Flop'
- Strengthened by: upright rowing.

Latissimus dorsi

- Location: lower back
- Functions: adducts (raises) and extends the arm at the shoulder
- Examples: butterfly stroke, rowing, pulling on the javelin
- Strengthened by: pull-downs.

Abdominals

Four separate muscles.

- Location: front of the abdomen
- Function: rotate, raise and allow the trunk to bend side to side; strengthen the abdominal wall; help with breathing
- Examples: performing upward circles on the bar in gymnastics, pulling the body down in hurdling
- Strengthened by: sit-ups of various sorts.

Pectorals
Consist of pectoralis major and pectoralis minor.

- Location: front of the chest
- Function: adduct (raise) the arm and shoulder; used for deep breathing
- Examples: playing a forehand drive in tennis, putting the shot, front crawl
- Strengthened by: bench presses.

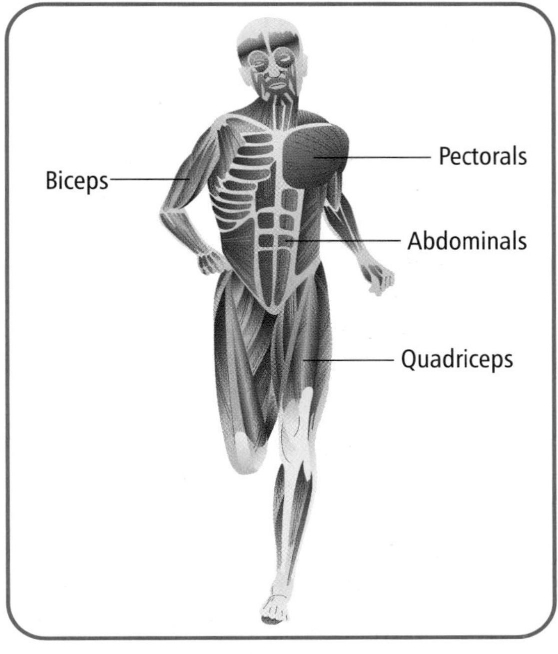

Muscles of the lower body

Hamstrings
Four separate muscles.

- Location: back of upper leg
- Function: extend the hip joint; flex the knee joint
- Examples: drawing the leg back before kicking a ball, jumping activities with knees bent before take-off
- Strengthened by: leg curls.

Quadriceps
Four separate muscles.

- Location: front of upper leg
- Function: flex the hip joint; extend the knee joint
- Examples: taking off in high jump, raising knee in running, kicking a ball
- Strengthened by: squats, leg extensions and leg presses.

Gluteals
Consist of gluteus maximus and two other muscles.

- Location: form the buttocks
- Function: abduct (move away from body) and extend the hip joint
- Examples: stepping up during rock climbing, sidestepping, pulling back leg before kicking a ball
- Strengthened by: squats and leg presses.

Gastrocnemius

- Location: back of the lower leg
- Function: flexes the knee joint and points the toes
- Examples: running, take-off in jumps
- Strengthened by: heel raises.

activity

Muscle analysis using ICT

Using a digital camcorder, record a sporting movement – for example, a sprint start – and play it back in slow motion. Use the freeze-frame facility to try to identify exactly how the muscles work. Determine which muscles are the prime movers and the antagonists in the leg action, and which muscles are acting as extensors and which as flexors.

By moving the video on frame by frame, it should be possible to see how the roles of the muscles change. If a printer is available, print out each of the still frames and label the muscles and their actions.

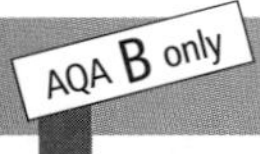
AQA B only

How do our muscles work?

Our muscles can work in different ways according to the actions we are performing. Although our muscles can only contract to cause movement, the way the muscles are positioned in our body means that this movement can vary enormously. For example, the very large muscles in our thighs not only drive us forward at a sprint start, they can also be used to help us hold a delicate balance in gymnastics.

There are two main types of muscular contraction: **isometric** and **isotonic**.

Isometric muscular contraction

In isometric contraction, the muscle tension is increased but the muscle length does not alter and there is no movement around the joint. Throughout sport we can see isometric muscle contraction at work, for example, when we hold a handstand, hold the bow bent in archery or push in the scrum in rugby. Many of our muscles help to stabilise our body as our limbs move. They do this by working isometrically.

Isotonic muscular contraction

Isotonic contraction is muscular contraction that results in limb movement. It takes place when our muscle fibres shorten or lengthen causing movement around our joints. Most sporting action involves isotonic muscular contraction.

Isotonic contraction can be either **concentric** or **eccentric**.

- **Concentric muscular action** takes place when the contracting muscle fibres shorten. This is the action we see most often in sporting movement. For example, when we do pull-ups on a bar, the muscle fibres in the biceps shorten as they contract, to bring the shoulder up, level with the wrist.
- **Eccentric muscular action** takes place when the contracting muscle fibres lengthen. For example, when lowering yourself from the pull-up position on the bar, the muscle fibres of the biceps lengthen as they contract, to move the shoulder down, away from the wrist. Plyometric exercise uses eccentric contractions (see page 204).

Isotonic contraction with muscles working concentrically

- The muscles shorten as they contract.
- The ends of the muscle move closer together.

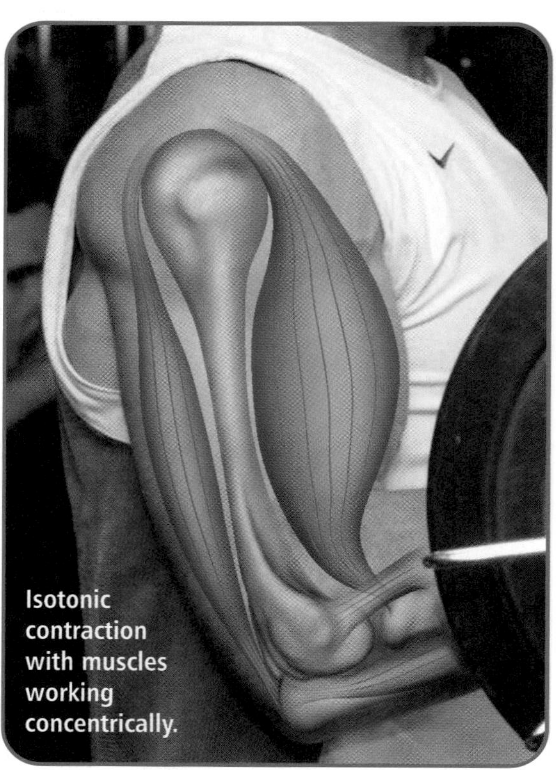
Isotonic contraction with muscles working concentrically.

Isotonic contraction with muscles working eccentrically.

Isotonic contraction with muscles working eccentrically

- The muscles lengthen as they contract under tension.
- The ends of the muscle move further apart.

Isometric contraction.

Isometric contraction

- The muscles stay at the same length as they contract.
- There is no movement, so the ends of the muscles stay the same distance apart.

activity

Feel the difference

This activity will help you to understand the three different ways in which muscles work.

1 Hold a textbook in your preferred hand with your arm extended by your side.
2 Bend your arm to raise the book to your shoulder. Place the fingers of your other hand on your biceps and feel the contraction. This is an isotonic, concentric contraction.
3 Slowly lower the book to the starting position and feel your biceps contracting as it lengthens. This is an isotonic, eccentric contraction.
4 Raise the book again but pause before your forearm is parallel to the floor. Hold the book steady and feel your biceps contracting. This is an isometric contraction as there is no movement taking place.

How do our muscles work together?

Our voluntary muscles can pull by contracting, but they cannot push. If one muscle contracts across a joint to bring two bones together, another muscle is needed to pull the bones apart again. Therefore muscles always work in pairs. Even for simple body movements we need a large number of pairs of muscles to work together in different ways. Our muscles take on different roles depending on the movement we are performing.

They can work as:

- **flexors**, contracting to bend our joints
- **extensors**, contracting to straighten our joints
- **prime movers** (or **agonists**), contracting in order to start a movement
- **antagonists**, relaxing to allow a movement to take place.

activity

What am I doing?

From the following description, try to work out what action is being performed.

The body begins in a standing position with the arms by the side. The deltoids contract to raise the arm so that it is parallel to the ground. The muscles of the fingers are flexed to grip an object. The biceps contract slowly and then the triceps contract powerfully and the fingers extend as the object is released.

Write your own movement description, then see if your partner can work out what action is being performed. Be prepared to demonstrate some or all of the action if necessary. You may need to refine your description following discussion.

How are our muscles attached to our bones?

Our voluntary muscles are usually attached to two or more different bones. When the muscles make the bones around a joint move, usually one bone stays fixed and the other moves. The end of the muscle that is attached to the fixed bone is called the **origin**. The other end of the muscle is called the **insertion**. It is attached to the bone which moves. As the muscle contracts, the insertion moves towards the origin.

The muscle fibres end in a strong flexible cord called a **tendon**. The tendon is fixed deeply into the bone and is very strongly attached. Tendons vary in shape and size. Some of our muscles are divided into more than one part. They may end in two or more different tendons, which may be fixed to different bones.

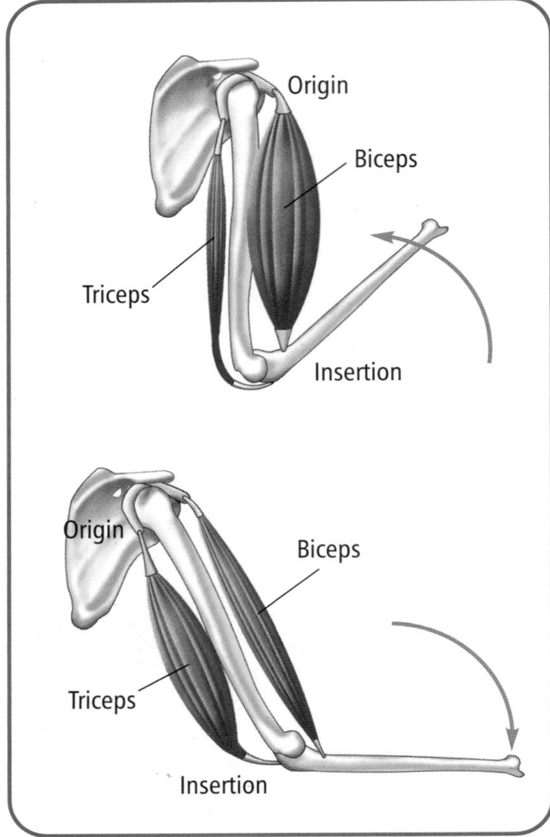

What are tendons?

Tendons are very strong cords of fibrous tissue which attach muscle to bone. They allow us to apply the power of the contracting muscles to the bones at the joint. They are made of tough fibres and are quite small so they can pass over joints and rough bone where the muscle itself would be damaged.

Tendons only stretch a little – much less than ligaments. Although they can be torn or bruised in contact sports, tendons are strong and the muscle itself is more likely to be damaged than the tendon.

Tendons can, however, be damaged by fierce muscle contraction. In squash, for example, players sometimes damage the Achilles tendon in the lower leg. Adolescents who overtrain through excessive running on hard surfaces may suffer from Osgood-Schlatter's disease, a condition caused by damage to the tendon below the kneecap.

Both tendons and ligaments respond to the stresses placed upon them. Regular exercise will improve the strength and flexibility of tendons and ligaments and make them less liable to injury during sporting action.

How do our muscles work in pairs?

Our voluntary muscles are arranged in pairs around our joints to enable us to move. When a prime mover muscle contracts, the antagonist muscle must relax to allow a movement to take place. However, the antagonist muscle will keep some fibres contracting. This is to stop our prime mover moving the joint so hard that the antagonists are damaged.

Sometimes this system fails, for example, when sprinters are running flat out. In the upper legs when the knee is raised, the quadriceps are the prime movers and the hamstrings are the antagonists. Sprinters may tear their

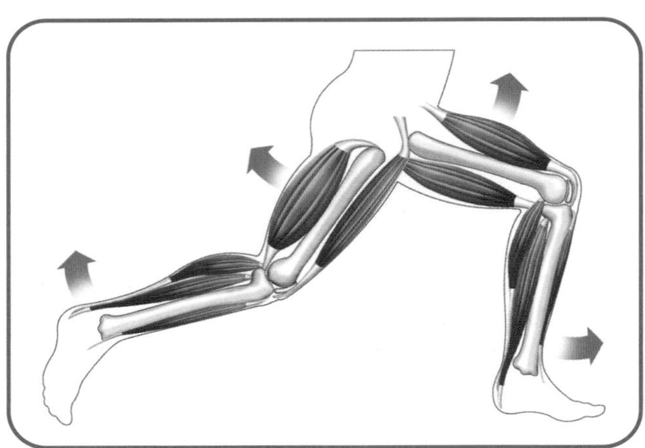

hamstrings and quickly come to a painful stop.

In isometric muscle action, both of the muscles of the pair at a joint contract at the same time and no movement is seen.

Muscle tone

Muscle tone is produced when voluntary muscles are in a state of very slight tension, ready and waiting to be used.

The way our prime movers and antagonists work against each other also gives us muscle tone. At any given time, some muscle fibres will be contracted whilst others are relaxed. This is true even when we are not moving. These contractions tighten the muscles a little, but are not strong enough to cause movement. Different fibres contract at different times in order to prevent tiredness setting in. This continuous slight contraction of our voluntary muscles is very important for good posture and keeps the body ready for instant action. Exercise improves muscle tone.

Muscle training and development

Our voluntary muscles have the ability to adapt in order to cope with the activities for which they are used. If we walk to school everyday, our leg muscles will adapt to this exercise and we will not find it difficult. If we move house and have an extra two kilometres to walk to and from school, at first we may find it tiring. However, after a few weeks our leg muscles will have learned to cope with the additional distance and we will find the walk easy again. This is exactly what happens when we train for sport. We put our muscles under an increased stress and they adapt to the new workload.

We all need a basic amount of muscular strength and cardiovascular fitness to cope with the demands of everyday life. Lifting and carrying involves strength, while walking and moving around requires stamina. As we get older it is important to maintain our fitness for life. Regular weight-bearing exercise can help prevent the weakening of bones and gentle, regular endurance exercise can help maintain cardiovascular fitness.

Muscle hypertrophy and atrophy

Our voluntary muscles become stronger the more they are exercised. If we train and exercise regularly over a long period, we will change our muscles. However, we must always remember that these changes are not permanent. The principle of **reversibility** applies (see page 188). This means that if we stop exercising, our muscles will return to their original state. 'If we don't use it, we lose it'!

Our muscles increase in size, strength and endurance when we follow a regular strength-training programme. This is called muscle **hypertrophy**. When we do not use our muscles regularly, they get smaller and weaker. We call this muscle **atrophy**. This loss of size and strength often happens when we are recovering from an injury. While waiting for a particular injury to heal, we should try to exercise the rest of the body as much as possible. Many joint injuries and weaknesses can be overcome by strengthening the muscles around the joints.

Our muscles adapt very well to an increased workload. If heavy weights are lifted, new muscle fibres develop and the muscle grows in size and also becomes stronger. This hypertrophy is known as muscle bulk. A sprinter needs large, strong muscles to provide the power required. Sprinters will also have more fast-twitch muscle fibres than the average person. With training, these fibres will become able to use the stored energy in short bursts more efficiently.

Long-distance runners do not need muscle bulk. They use distance training to adapt their muscles to use energy more efficiently, in order to delay fatigue. In fact, carrying the extra weight of large muscles over a distance will be a disadvantage. Distance runners will have more slow-twitch fibres than the average person. Through training these fibres will be able to use the stored energy in the muscle more efficiently and for longer.

Posture

Our bodies are unstable when we are upright. This is because we have a high centre of gravity and a small base of support.

If we have good **posture** we can keep our bodies upright easily by keeping our centre of gravity over our base of support. Most of the weight of the body will be supported by the bones and we will need only a little help from the voluntary muscles to keep us upright. Good muscle tone, particularly in the lower back, leg and abdominal muscles, will help posture.

Good posture reduces the strain on our muscles, tendons and ligaments. It allows our body systems to work more easily and makes us less tired. It also gives us a positive body shape which improves our self-image and helps us to feel better about ourselves.

When we slouch, the upper back muscle has to contract to move the body to the correct posture. If we continue to slouch the muscles will gradually adapt to that position. Poor posture may then become permanent, leading to deformity of the spine, strained back and abdominal muscles, and rounded shoulders which can impair breathing.

How can we have good posture when standing and walking?

- Stand with head up.
- Stretch the back upward.
- Keep shoulders straight and chest high and open.
- Balance weight evenly on both feet.
- Relax the knees.
- Wear sensible shoes.

Bad posture

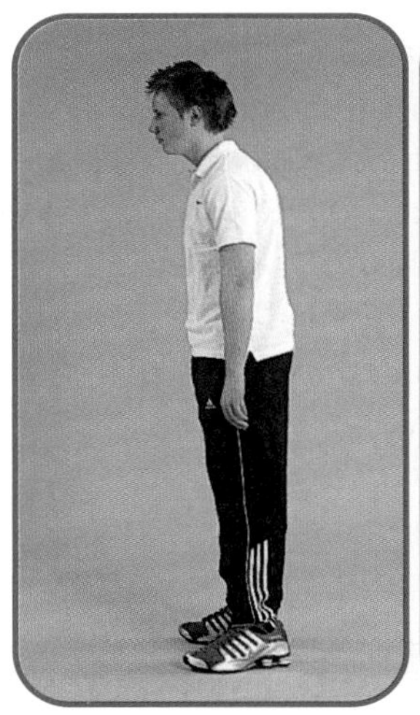

Good posture

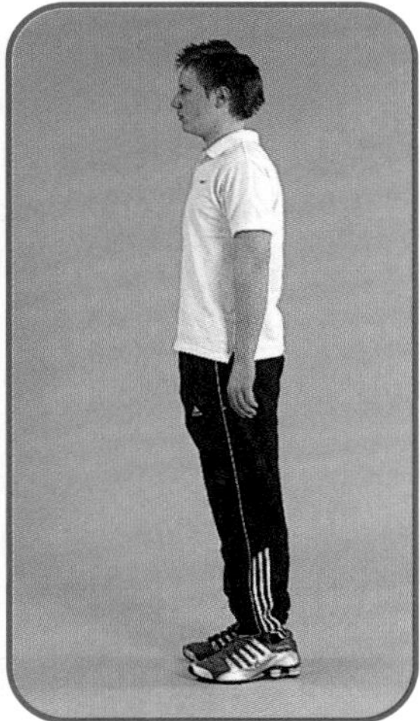

How can we have good posture when sitting?

- Choose chairs that support the small of the back.
- Sit back in the chair to support the lower back.
- Keep your feet flat on the floor in front of you.
- Try to have your knees higher than your hips.
- Check that working surfaces are at the correct height.
- Have a break every 20 minutes to gently exercise arms and shoulders.

Bad posture

Good posture

How can we have good posture when lifting?

- Never bend forward without bending the knees.
- Keep your back flat and straight.
- Try to avoid lifting anything above the level of the elbows.
- Keep objects as close to the body as possible.
- Extend legs in order to lift objects.
- Keep head up and eyes looking forward.

Posture in sport

When we play sport we use a wide variety of body positions. We must take up the right body position for the situation in which we find ourselves in our sport.

To maintain good posture, we need to consider our:

- **starting position** – for example, in movements in golf, discus and fencing (see below)
- **position during the activity**. When performing the movement or action, we must maintain our **core stability**. This means that we are in a comfortable, balanced position and are ready to perform the next sporting movement with power and control. Our centre of gravity is over our base of support. Muscle tone is essential for core stability.

We often take up a special position when preparing for a sporting movement or action. For example, in golf we need to stand in a particular way to swing through and hit the ball well. When preparing to putt, we position ourselves facing away from the direction of the

Bad posture

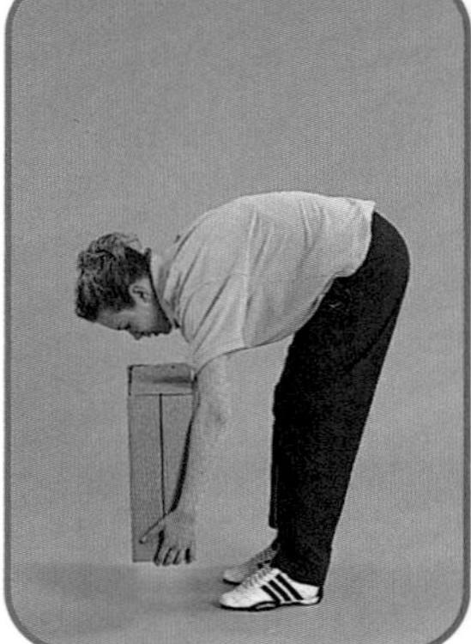

Good posture

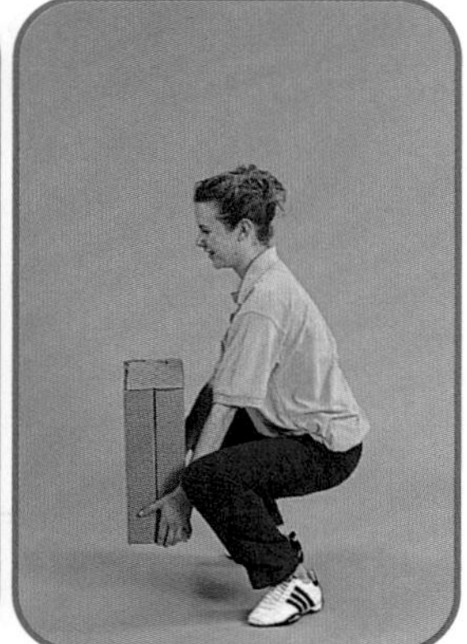

putt. In fencing, we adopt a body position which allows us to move backwards and forwards very quickly in a sideways-on position.

Core stability is essential for all sports. Some sports require a particular posture throughout the activity –for example, when we ski or ride a horse. However, this posture has to be adapted to deal with different situations – such as when we a negotiate a slalom ski course or jump fences on a horse.

In sports requiring a great deal of movement and unpredictability, core stability is essential in order to react quickly. For example, in football and netball we need to respond constantly to the position of the ball and other players.

The effects of exercise on bones, joints and muscles

What are the immediate effects of exercise on bones, joints and muscles?

- little effect on bones and joints
- increased flow of blood to working muscles
- muscles take up more oxygen from the blood
- muscles contract more often and more quickly
- more of the muscle fibres contract
- rise in temperature in the muscles.

What are the effects of regular training and exercise on bones, joints and muscles?

- bone width and bone density increases
- strengthens muscles, tendons and ligaments surrounding joints
- joint cartilage thickens, improving shock absorption at joints
- increased range of movement at joints (flexibility)
- muscles adjust to greater workload
- muscles increase in size (hypertrophy)
- depending on the type of training, the number of fast- or slow-twitch fibres will increase
- muscles can work harder and for longer.

What are the long-term benefits of exercise on bones, joints and muscles?

- increases bone strength and thickness
- increases stability of joints
- develops a full range of movement at joints
- increases muscular strength, muscular endurance and muscular power
- improves the muscles' capacity to tolerate fatigue by coping with lactic acid and oxygen debt.

QUESTIONS

7 Muscles and muscle action

1 **Muscles and bones work together to create movement. Give two examples from sport of each of the following types of movement.**

a Flexion *(2 marks)*
b Extension *(2 marks)*
c Abduction. *(2 marks)*

2 **Muscles work together to create movement.**

a Describe a muscle working as a prime mover and give an example of a specific muscle working in this way in sport. *(3 marks)*

b Describe a muscle working as an antagonist and give an example of a specific muscle working in this way in sport. *(3 marks)*

c Describe a muscle working as a synergist and give an example of a specific muscle working in this way in sport. *(3 marks)*

3 **Use examples from sport to explain the different features of fast-twitch and slow-twitch muscle fibres.** *(3 marks)*

4

a Describe muscle tone and explain its role in posture. *(3 marks)*

b Explain how muscles change when exercised. *(3 marks)*

5

a There are three types of muscle fibre. Name each type and give an example of each. *(6 marks)*

b Describe the function and give one characteristic of tendons. *(2 marks)*

6 **Name four skeletal muscles and give one movement for each.** *(8 marks)*

7 **Using examples from sport, explain the different functions of isotonic and isometric muscle contractions.** *(8 marks)*

8 **Choose four skeletal muscles and describe their role in sporting movements.** *(8 marks)*

8 The circulatory system

Our life depends upon a constant source of oxygen and nutrients in all the cells of the body. Our circulatory system works non-stop, 24 hours a day to deliver these vital supplies. The circulatory system also carries away carbon dioxide and other waste products.

activity

Recording heart rate

The simplest way to see how well our circulatory system is working is to measure our heart rate by taking our pulse. Our pulse is the surge of blood through our arteries which happens every time our heart beats. We must learn how to find and record our pulse accurately and quickly. This will enable us to assess how hard our circulatory system is working at any time.

We can easily measure our pulse rate at two specific places – in the neck at the carotid artery and in our wrist on the radial artery.

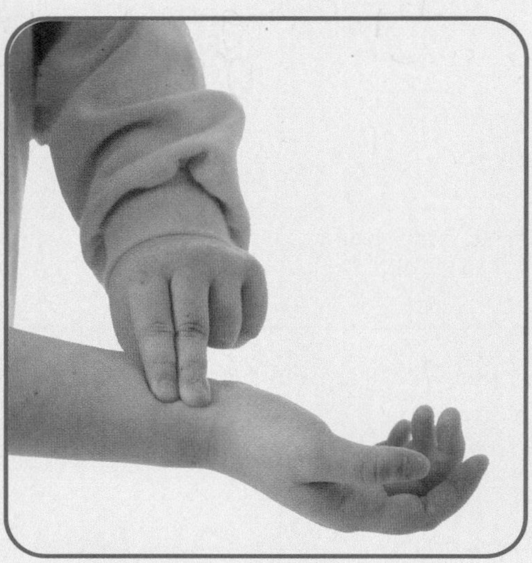

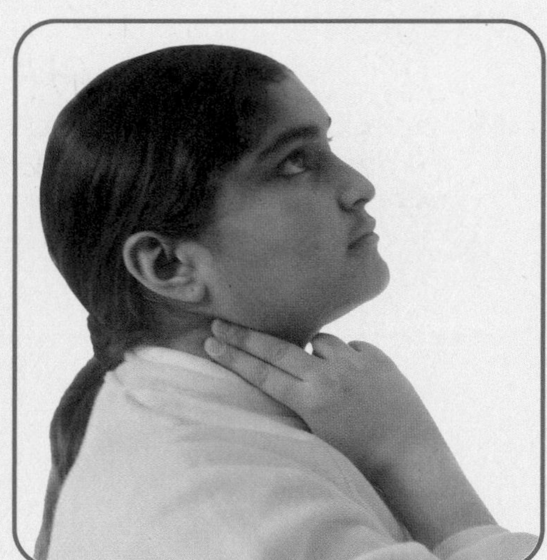

activity

1 Practise counting the number of pulses felt over a time of 15 seconds. You must use your fingers and not your thumb. Try it at both the neck and wrist. Multiply your 15-second count by 4 to get your heart rate in beats per minute. (It should of course be the same at both your neck and wrist!)

2 Practise finding your carotid and radial pulses quickly. This is important when trying to count your pulse after exercise.

3 In pairs, practise counting the pulse of your partner using both the neck and wrist locations, while sitting down at rest.

4 One of you now walks at a brisk pace for one minute. Immediately after walking, the non-active partner measures the other's pulse over the first 15 seconds and records it in beats per minute.

5 Repeat the exercise with the roles reversed.

6 The first partner now jogs for three minutes at a slow pace. Repeat the pulse-taking and swap over.

7 You both now play a game, for instance, basketball, for 10–15 minutes. Repeat the pulse-taking.

8 Your partner sprints for a total of 20 seconds. Repeat the pulse-taking and swap over.

9 You both warm down for three minutes. Repeat the pulse-taking and swap over.

10 Record your results and those of your partner on a graph. Remember, you should not join the points plotted as the data you have collected is not continuous. Explain your results and set them out as shown in the table below.

Time period	Activity	Heart rate (beats per minute)	Explanation
	Rest		
1 minute	Walk		
3 minutes	Jog		
10–15 minutes	Play game (e.g. basketball)		
20 seconds	Sprint		
3 minutes	Warm-down		

KEYWORDS

Arterioles: small blood vessels into which arteries subdivide, taking blood into the capillaries

Artery: Large blood vessel taking oxygenated blood from the heart to the body. (Exception: the pulmonary artery takes deoxygenated blood from the heart to the lungs.)

Blood pressure: force of blood against artery walls caused by heart pumping blood around the body

Capillaries: microscopic blood vessels which link arteries with veins

Cardiac output: amount of blood ejected from the heart in one minute

Cardiovascular: relating to the heart and blood vessels

Circulatory system: the heart, circulation of the blood and composition of the blood. (also known as the cardiovascular system)

Haemoglobin: oxygen-carrying substance in red blood cells

Heartbeat: one complete contraction of the heart

Heart rate: the number of times the heart beats each minute

Pulmonary circulation: carries deoxygenated blood from our heart to our lungs and oxygenated blood back to the heart

Stroke volume: the volume of blood pumped out of the heart by each ventricle during one contraction

Systemic circulation: carries oxygenated blood from the heart to the rest of our body and deoxygenated blood back to the heart

Veins: large blood vessels taking deoxygenated blood from the body to the heart. (Exception: the pulmonary vein takes oxygenated blood from the lungs to the heart.)

Venules: small blood vessels that take blood from the capillaries to the veins.

Key to Exam Success

For your GCSE you should be able to:

- identify the main parts of the heart and know how it works
- compare arteries, capillaries and veins
- understand how the heart, blood, and blood vessels work together
- explain how the circulatory system links with the respiratory system to provide energy for physical activity
- explain how the circulatory system responds to exercise and training
- 

describe the composition and functions of the blood
- AQA B only: explain how and why the body regulates temperature and water balance.

“ KEY THOUGHTS ”

‘Our circulation system is a delivery service in perpetual motion.’

The circulatory system in action

Our **circulatory system** (sometimes called our **cardiovascular system**) is made up of our heart, blood and blood vessels.

Our circulation system has two parts, our **pulmonary circulation** and our **systemic circulation**. This is called a double

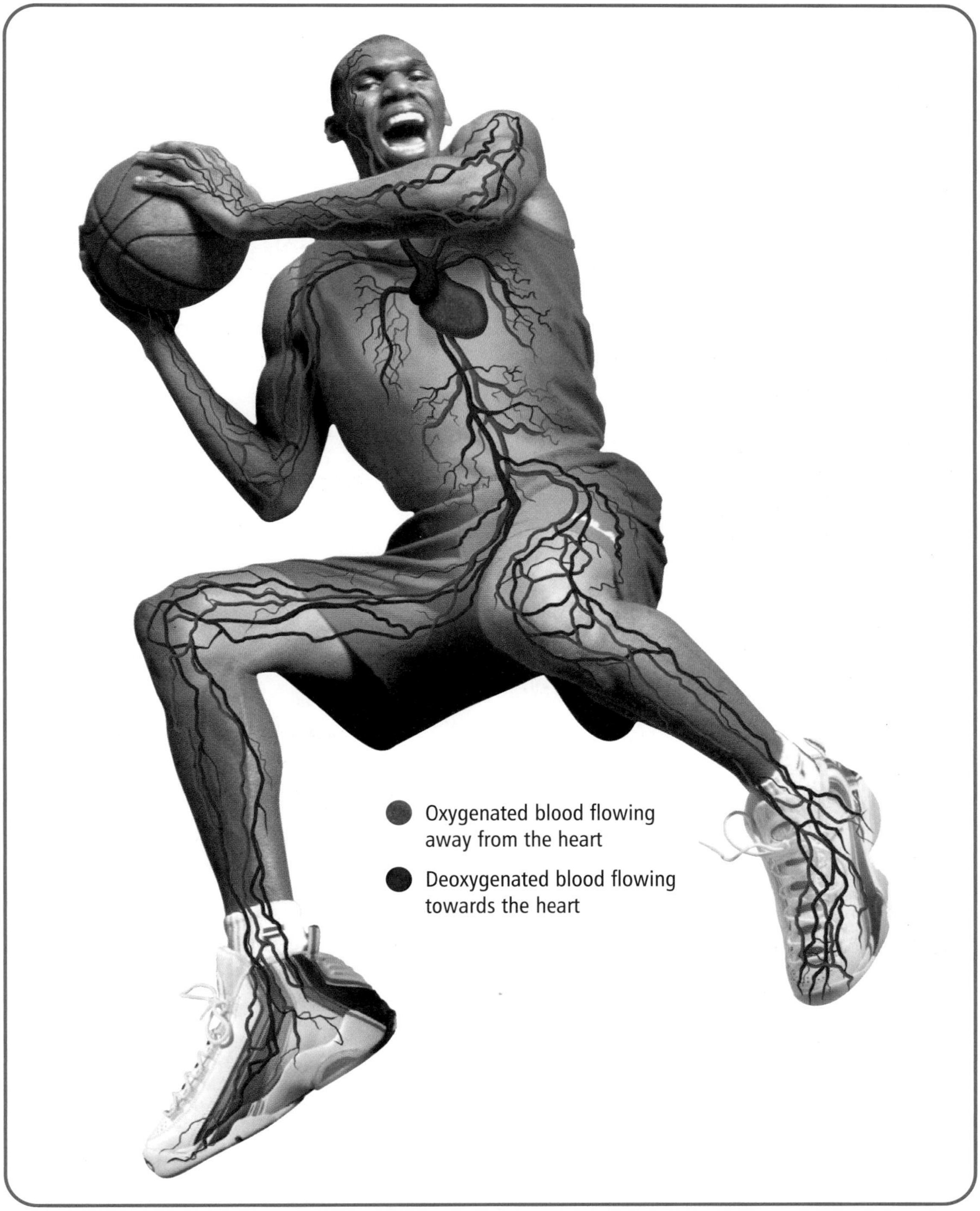

Oxygenated blood flowing away from the heart

Deoxygenated blood flowing towards the heart

circulatory system because blood is pumped simultaneously to different destinations. Our systemic circulation carries oxygenated blood from the heart to the rest of our body and the oxygen is used by the cells. Deoxygenated blood returns to the heart with waste products, which have to be removed from our body.

The function of the circulatory system is to:

- take oxygen and nutrients to every cell
- remove carbon dioxide and other waste products from every cell
- carry hormones from the hormonal (endocrine) glands to different parts of the body
- maintain temperature and fluid levels
- prevent infection from invading germs.

Our pulmonary circulation carries deoxygenated blood from our heart to our lungs. Here carbon dioxide is exchanged for oxygen. Oxygenated blood is then carried back to the heart.

How does our heart work?

The heart is a muscular pump. It is made of special cardiac muscle which contracts regularly without tiring. It pumps blood first to the lungs, to exchange carbon dioxide for oxygen. Then blood with the new oxygen is returned to the heart to be pumped out around the body.

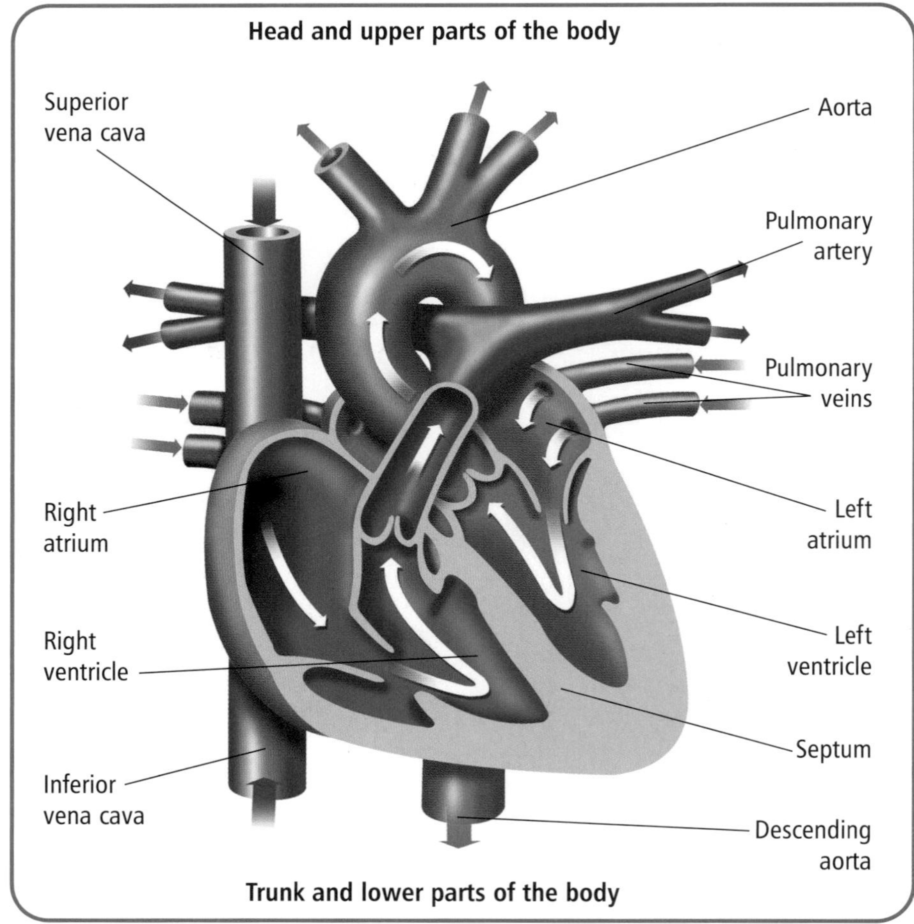

The three stages of heart action are shown below.

- Our cardiac cycle is one complete cycle of these three stages.
- Our **heartbeat** is one complete contraction of the heart.
- Our **heart rate** (pulse) is the number of heartbeats per minute.

At rest, our heart pumps between 50 and 80 times a minute. It pumps about 4.7 litres of blood around the body. At rest this journey takes about 20 seconds.

Stage 1

- Blood flows into the heart when it is between beats and relaxed.
- Deoxygenated blood from our body enters the right atrium through the two vena cava veins.
- At the same time newly oxygenated blood from our lungs enters the left atrium through the pulmonary veins.

Stage 2

- Our right atrium muscles contract to pump blood through the tricuspid valve into the right ventricle.
- At the same time, our left atrium muscles contract to pump blood through the mitral valve into the left ventricle.

Stage 3

- Our right ventricle muscles contract to pump blood through the semilunar valves into the pulmonary artery to travel to the lungs.
- Our left ventricle muscles contract to pump blood through the semilunar valves into the aorta, to travel around the body again.

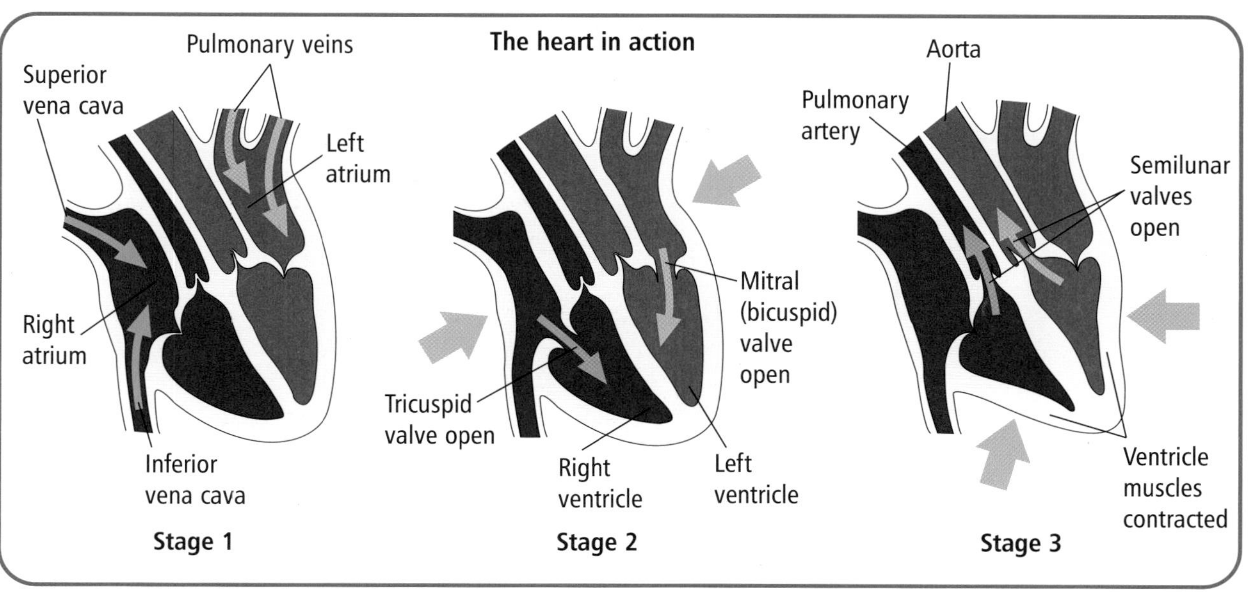

How does blood move around the body?

The heart is a double pump divided into two parts by a muscular wall called the septum.

The right-hand side of the heart deals with blood returning from our body through the vena cava. During its journey, our blood has given up much of its oxygen. It has picked up waste products, including carbon dioxide. It is now a dull red colour. The heart pumps this blood to our lungs in our **pulmonary artery**. This is the only artery which carries deoxygenated blood.

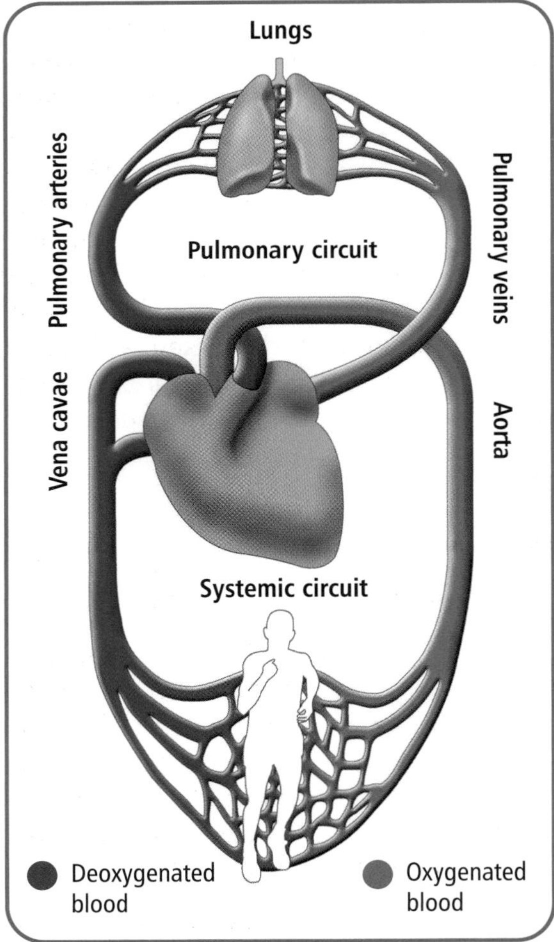

Our blood vessels include **arteries**, **veins**, **venules** and **capillaries**. These carry blood to all parts of the body and back again to the heart.

The left-hand side of the heart deals with the blood returning from our lungs in our **pulmonary veins**. These are the only veins that carry oxygenated blood. In our lungs the blood releases carbon dioxide and other waste products, and is supplied with fresh oxygen. When blood returns to the heart it is bright red. The heart pumps this blood into our largest artery, the aorta, to travel around the body.

The thickness of the walls of the heart vary according to the task that they carry out. The atria are both thin-walled, because they only pump the blood to the ventricles below. Both ventricles have much thicker walls.

The left ventricle has very thick, muscular walls. This is because the blood leaving the heart must be pumped out very powerfully at high pressure to travel the long distance around the body. In contrast, the right ventricle only pumps blood a short distance to the lungs and is therefore not so thick-walled.

The arteries carry freshly oxygenated blood from the heart. They become smaller and smaller. The smaller arteries are called **arterioles**. They take blood into the tissue where they join up with our smallest vessels – the capillaries. In turn the capillaries join up with venules, which increase in size to become veins. Our veins return deoxygenated blood to our heart.

Our heart and exercise

As we work harder, our muscles need more oxygen and we breathe in and out more deeply and quickly in order to get the oxygen to the lungs. These increased supplies of oxygen are picked up by the blood in our lungs and transported more quickly back to the heart. The double circulatory system ensures that the increased supplies of oxygen collected from the lungs are transported at an increased rate to the working muscles. At the same time, carbon dioxide and other waste products are removed at an increased rate.

The right type of training can increase the size and pumping ability of the heart – that is, the **stroke volume** and **cardiac output** of the heart. Like all muscle, heart muscle responds to training by becoming stronger as its walls thicken. In this way we can increase the amount of blood going to the lungs to pick up oxygen and therefore increase the amount of oxygen going to our working muscles. This helps us to work harder and for longer periods in our sport. During hard physical activity, our heart rate can increase to over 200 beats per minute. The heart of a trained athlete can pump up to 45 litres of blood a minute. Training will reduce the resting heart rate of an athlete considerably.

How well does our heart pump?

Our heart is made up of cardiac muscle and we cannot control its action voluntarily. Fortunately cardiac muscle never tires. The speed and force of each heartbeat are controlled by our brain. Our brain is affected by what we are doing. If we start running, our brain tells our heart to pump more blood to supply our working leg muscles with more oxygen. Like any other muscle, heart muscle can get stronger when exercised. The amount of blood pumped by the heart depends on heart rate and stroke volume.

Heart rate

Heart rate is the number of time the heart beats each minute.

At each heartbeat, blood is pumped out of our heart into the arteries. Our arteries are forced to expand and then contract, which is called our pulse. The number of pulses in one minute is our heart rate. For a normal adult when resting this will be about 70 beats per minute.

A pulse can be felt at pressure points in the body where arteries are near to the skin.

Resting heart rate

Resting heart rates can vary between people, due to factors such as sex, age and health. For a healthy resting adult it is about 70 beats per minute. Endurance sportspeople will have a much lower heart rate – perhaps as low as 30 beats per minute. This is because their hearts are stronger and are able to pump more blood in fewer beats than an unfit person. Their stroke volume is therefore greater.

Resting heart rate can be one way to measure fitness. The speed at which heart rate returns to normal after exercise is called the recovery rate. This can also be used to measure fitness.

Stroke volume

Stroke volume is the volume of blood pumped out of the heart by each ventricle during one contraction.

When we exercise, stroke volume increases for a number of reasons. Working muscles squeeze blood in our veins, forcing more blood back to the heart. The heart stretches as it fills up with the extra blood and in turn it contracts more strongly. This results in more blood being pumped out of the heart for each beat.

Cardiac output

Cardiac output is the amount of blood ejected from the heart in one minute. It is controlled by both heart rate and stroke volume.

Heart rate x Stroke volume = Cardiac output

In sport we usually want to increase the amount of blood going to the working muscles – that is, our cardiac output. We can do this by increasing stroke volume, heart rate or both.

What is blood pressure?

Blood pressure is the force of the blood against the walls of the blood vessels. It is different in different blood vessels and depends on how much blood is flowing into the blood vessels and how easily it can flow out.

In our arteries the blood pressure is high because the arteries are narrow and a lot of blood is being forced into them from the heart. Blood flows more slowly in the wider veins, which are a long way from the heart. Here blood pressure is low and so valves are needed to prevent blood from flowing backwards.

How do we measure blood pressure?

We use a special instrument to measure the pressure needed to stop the blood flowing through an artery. It is usually measured in our upper arm and two

readings are taken. One reading is our systolic blood pressure which is the maximum pressure of the blood. The second reading is of our diastolic blood pressure which is the lowest pressure of our blood, measured between heartbeats. Blood pressure should be taken when we are relaxed and resting. It will therefore be at its lowest.

What will affect our blood pressure?

- **Age**: blood pressure increases as we grow older because our arteries are less elastic.
- **Exercise**: blood pressure increases when we exercise but returns to normal afterwards. Regular exercise helps to lower resting blood pressure and prevent cardiovascular disease.
- **Stress**: stress causes hormones to be released into the blood, which increases blood pressure.
- **Smoking**: smoking increases blood pressure because nicotine reduces the efficiency of our capillaries.
- **Diet**: a diet high in fat or salt may lead to increased blood pressure. This is because fatty deposits may block up or harden arteries. Excess salt intake may lead to an imbalance in the body's chemistry.
- **Weight**: being overweight puts an extra strain on the circulatory system and so raises blood pressure.

What does high blood pressure mean?

A person has high blood pressure (called hypertension) if their blood pressure stays high over a long period of time. A high reading would be above 140 (systolic) or 90 (diastolic).

Hypertension may be caused by blockages in the smaller blood vessels, which means that the heart has to work harder to force blood around the body. Arteries taking blood to the heart muscle can also become blocked. Sudden activity can cause a sharp pain (called angina) or even a heart attack.

Blood pressure and exercise

During exercise our heart beats faster and pumps out more blood. Our blood pressure rises. This is quite normal. Regular sensible exercise linked with a healthy diet and lifestyle will actually lower our resting blood pressure. Some drugs such as erythropoietin (EPO), which has been taken by cyclists, can reduce blood pressure to dangerously low levels.

What happens to our circulatory system when we exercise?

- The hormone adrenaline is released even before we start to exercise. It prepares the body for action.
- Adrenaline in the bloodstream causes the heart to beat more quickly, so heart rate increases.
- The heart contracts more powerfully. It sends out a greater amount of blood with each contraction. Stroke volume increases.
- Blood circulation speeds up, and greater amounts of oxygen-carrying blood reach the working muscles. Cardiac output increases.
- The pumping action of muscles forces more deoxygenated blood back to the heart more quickly.
- Blood flow is reduced to the areas of the body not in urgent need of oxygen, for example the digestive system.
- Blood flow is increased to the areas in greatest need of oxygen, for example, the skeletal muscles.
- Blood vessels to skin areas become enlarged. This allows excess heat from muscles and organs to be lost more easily from the skin.

activity

Recording blood pressure

1 Depending on what equipment is available, practise taking your partner's resting blood pressure when he or she is sitting down. Record both the systolic and diastolic measures. (Remember that the systolic measure records blood pressure as the heart is contracting, whilst the diastolic measure records blood pressure as the heart is relaxing.)

2 One of you now walks at a brisk pace for one minute. The non-active partner measures the other's blood pressure immediately after walking and records it.

3 Repeat the exercise with the roles reversed.

4 The first partner now jogs for three minutes at a slow pace. Repeat the blood-pressure recording and swap over.

5 You both now play a game, for instance, basketball, for 10–15 minutes. Repeat the blood-pressure recording.

6 Your partner sprints for a total of 20 seconds. Repeat the blood-pressure recording and swap over.

7 You both warm down for three minutes. Repeat the blood-pressure recording and swap over.

Using the chart provided, plot your results and those of your partner and display them as a dual bar chart. Remember, you should not join the points plotted as the data you have collected is not continuous. Give reasons to explain your results.

Time period	Activity	Systolic blood pressure	Diastolic blood pressure
	Rest		
1 minute	Walk		
3 minutes	Jog		
10–15 minutes	Play game (e.g. basketball)		
20 seconds	Sprint		
3 minutes	Warm down		

- During very hard exercise even these blood vessels will be reduced in size. Body temperature will then rise very quickly and can cause overheating and fatigue.
- The oxygen going to the muscles can be up to three times the resting amount.
- Blood flow can be increased up to 30 times. Therefore, the working muscles can receive up to 90 times the amount of oxygen they receive at rest.

Why are our blood vessels different?

1 Arteries:

- thick-walled
- elastic, expand to carry blood
- small passageway for blood (internal lumen)
- blood under high pressure
- no valves needed, artery walls contract to move blood
- carry blood away from the heart
- carry oxygenated blood (except pulmonary artery).

2 Capillaries:

- microscopic blood vessels linking arterioles and venules
- extremely thin walls, one cell thick
- allow food and oxygen to pass out to our body tissues
- allow carbon dioxide and other waste to pass into blood from our body tissues.

3 Veins:

- thin-walled
- non-elastic
- large passageway for blood (internal lumen)
- blood under low pressure
- have valves to stop blood flowing backwards
- carry blood to the heart
- carry deoxygenated blood (except pulmonary veins).

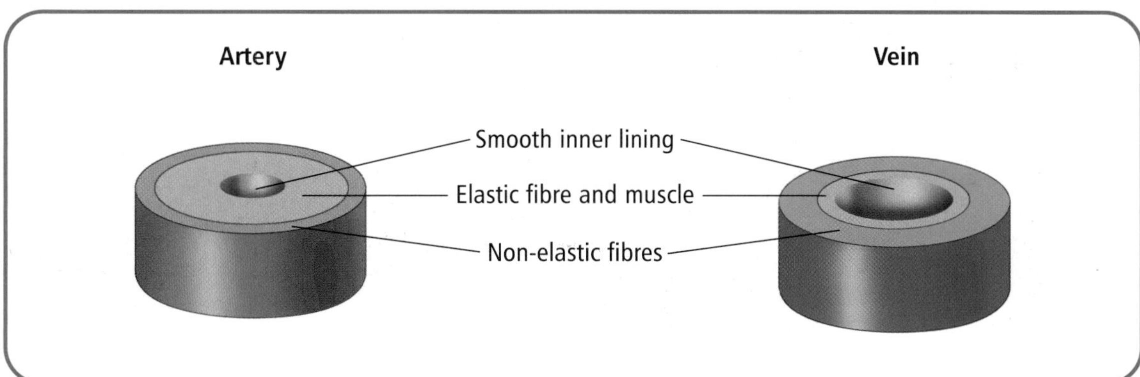

What happens in our capillaries?

Our capillary network is extremely large. It is also very dense in active tissues such as muscles. Arterioles bring oxygen and nutrients to the capillaries. In muscle tissue the oxygen and nutrients squeeze out through the thin capillary walls. This enables the muscles to work.

As a muscle contracts it produces waste products, including carbon dioxide, which squeeze back into the capillaries. The capillaries then join up with venules, which lead to veins and back to the heart. Carbon dioxide is then removed by our lungs. Other waste is removed by our kidneys.

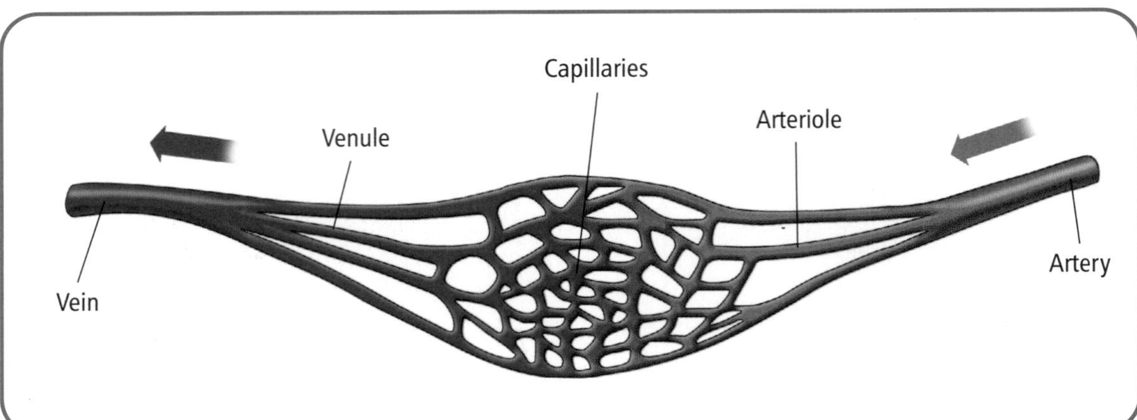

Valves

- Blood returning to our heart is under low pressure.
- Valves are needed to stop the blood flowing backwards.

Open valve

Closed valve

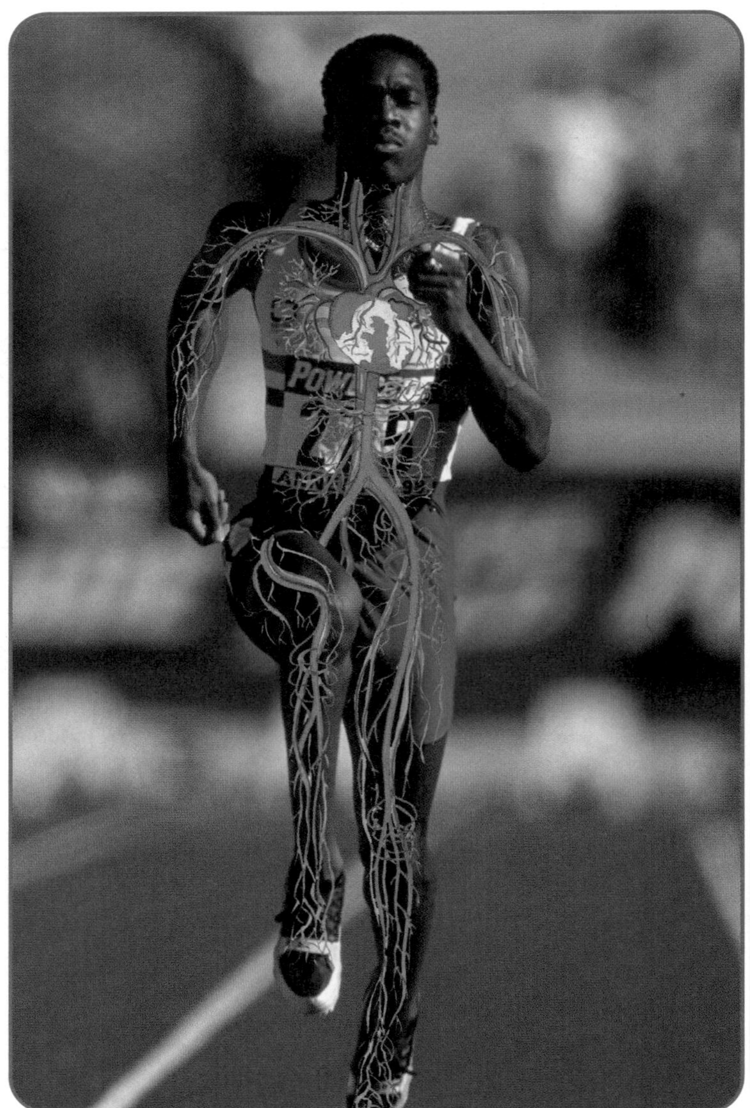

Blood circulation and exercise

The body can alter the flow of blood to different areas. At rest, our skeletal muscles need little oxygen, so only 15–20% of our heart's output goes to them. During exercise, more blood is directed to these working muscles and away from such areas as the digestive system. As much as 80% of the heart's output may go to our working muscles during strenuous exercise. Training actually increases our body's ability to redistribute blood more efficiently.

Within the working muscles the oxygen reaches actual muscle fibres through the capillary network. As a result of training, this capillary network increases, allowing more oxygen to be delivered to the working muscles. Blood pressure increases during exercise when massive amounts of blood are forced through the arteries. However, regular exercise leads to lower resting blood pressure.

Blood supply to the skin increases during exercise as the blood vessels beneath the skin expand to allow heat to escape from the skin surface.

activity

Blood circulation

The following activities are designed to reinforce your understanding of how the double circulatory system works.

Begin by selecting members of your group to represent the following:

Vena cava	Left atrium
Right atrium	Mitral valve
Tricuspid valve	Left ventricle
Right ventricle	Aorta
Semilunar valve	Arteries
Pulmonary artery	Arterioles
Lungs	Venules
Pulmonary veins	Veins.

Each member of the group has a card indicating which part of the circulatory system they represent.

1. You have five minutes to get yourself into the right order in a circle, starting with the vena cava. Now decide whether red, blue or red and blue blood flows through you.
2. A student is chosen to represent a drop of blood, and attempts to circulate through the system. In order to go past each of the various parts of the system they have to correctly answer one or more of the following questions:
   - Are you red or blue blood?
   - Which part of the system have you just come from?
   - Are you carrying oxygen or carbon dioxide?
   - Where are you going next?
3. Repeat Task 2, but with the names of the various parts of the circulatory system hidden. The blood drops have to first name the part of the system which they are visiting before they can proceed.

What makes up our blood?

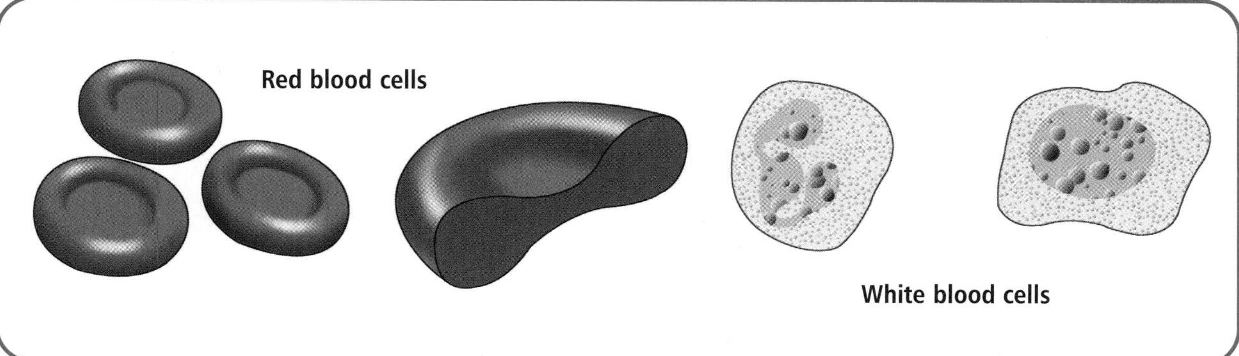

The total volume of blood in the body varies from person to person and depends mainly on body size. Men on average have 5–6 litres and women 4–5 litres.

Blood is made up of 55% plasma and 45% formed elements. The formed elements are red blood cells (erythrocytes), white blood cells (leukocytes) and platelets (thrombocytes).

- **Plasma** is a pale yellow, watery liquid which contains dissolved substances: salts and calcium, nutrients including glucose, hormones, carbon dioxide and other waste from our body cells.

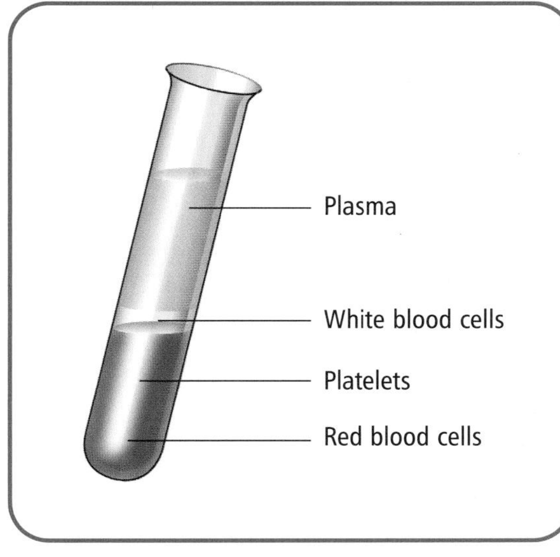

- **Red blood cells** give blood its colour. They contain haemoglobin (see below), which carries oxygen from the lungs to all our body cells, and are made in the marrow of our long bones, sternum, ribs and vertebrae. They are extremely numerous, have no nucleus, last for about 120 days and are replaced in very large numbers.
- **Platelets** are made in our bone marrow. They stick to each other easily and work with fibrinogen to produce clots when a blood vessel is damaged.
- **White blood cells** are three times the size of red blood cells but far fewer in number. They are made in our bone marrow, lymph nodes and spleen and act as a mobile guard system to deal with infection and disease. Some eat up germs, some produce antibodies to destroy germs.

How do our red cells carry oxygen?

Our red blood cells contain an iron-based substance called haemoglobin. When the blood travels to our lungs, the oxygen in the air joins up with the haemoglobin in the blood to form oxyhaemoglobin.

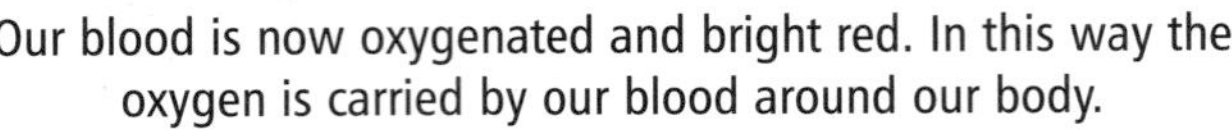

What does blood do?

Our blood links all the tissues and organs of the body together. It has four main functions:

Transportation

- carries nutrients from our digestive system to all our body cells
- takes oxygen from our lungs to our working muscles
- removes carbon dioxide from our body in our lungs
- removes waste produces and excess water in our kidneys
- takes hormones to where they are needed.

Protection

- carries white cells to sites of infection
- carries antibodies to destroy germs
- carries platelets to damaged areas to form clots.

Temperature regulation

- carries heat away from working muscles to skin
- carries heat away from centre of body to skin
- maintains temperature within the body.

Maintaining the body's equilibrium

- reduces the effect of lactic acid produced in the working muscles
- regulates fluid balance
- enables hormones and enzymes to work.

Our blood and exercise

Our muscles need a continuous supply of oxygen in order to move our body.

This oxygen is carried to the working muscles by the haemoglobin in the red cells in our blood. Regular exercise increases the red cells we produce in our bones. This enables a fit person to work harder and for longer periods of time than an unfit person.

At high altitude it is more difficult for people to carry sufficient oxygen in their blood to supply their working muscles. As a result people who live at high altitude have more red blood cells and haemoglobin than those who live at lower altitude. This helps them to take in sufficient oxygen in their activities.

Endurance athletes from high-altitude areas usually have an advantage when they compete at lower altitudes since they can carry extra oxygen in their blood. For this reason, sportspeople will train at high altitude to increase the number of red blood cells and to improve their cardiovascular endurance.

The effects of exercise on the circulatory system

Immediate effects of exercise on the circulatory system

- The hormone adrenaline enters the blood system.
- Adrenaline causes the heart to beat more quickly – increased heart rate.
- The heart contracts more powerfully – increased stroke volume.
- Blood circulation speeds up with more oxygen carried to the working muscles.

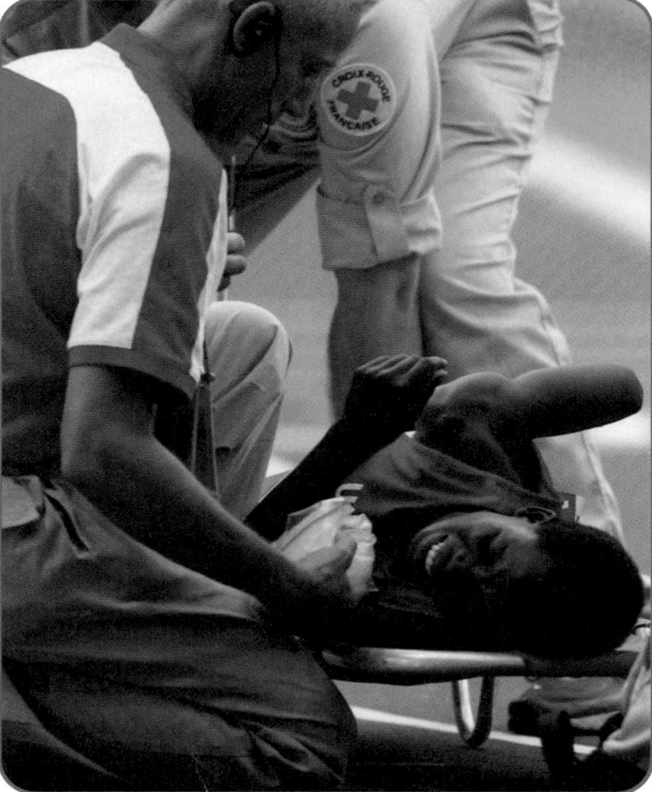

- Blood is diverted to areas of greatest need.
- Blood temperature increases, causing sweating response.
- Blood vessels to skin areas enlarge, allowing heat to be lost more easily.

The effects of regular training and exercise on the circulatory system

- Increased amount of blood pumped around the body
- Cardiovascular system copes more easily with increased demands
- Body able to carry and use more oxygen per minute
- Body able to remove waste products (especially carbon dioxide) more efficiently
- Increased recovery rate after exercise.

Long-term benefits of exercise on the circulatory system

- Healthier heart and blood vessels
- Reduced risk of heart disease
- Increased cardiovascular endurance
- Reduced blood pressure
- Lower resting heart rate and quicker recovery after exercise
- Heart muscle increases in size, thickness and strength
- Increased number of capillaries
- Volume of blood increases.

QUESTIONS

8 The circulatory system

1 **The circulatory system has a number of functions. List three functions and give an example of each from sport.**
(6 marks)

2 **The circulatory system consists of the heart, blood vessels and blood.**

a Name the upper chambers of the heart, the lower chambers of the heart and the muscular wall that divides the heart.
(3 marks)

b List three functions of blood during exercise.
(3 marks)

c Give three differences between arteries and veins.
(3 marks)

3 **Describe three ways in which the circulatory system responds to exercise.**
(3 marks)

4 **a** List three long-term effects of exercise on the circulatory system.
(3 marks)

b Explain how each effect improves performance.
(3 marks)

5 **List the four main components of blood and give one function of each.**
(8 marks)

6 **The heart has a major role in the circulatory system. Name four main parts of the heart and describe a function of each.**
(8 marks)

7 **Explain the role and function of the circulatory system in regulating body temperature during exercise.**
(8 marks)

8 **Describe the function of the heart and explain how its structure enables it to circulate blood.**
(8 marks)

9 The respiratory system

Our bodies are made up of millions of cells, all of which use oxygen to break down the nutrients contained in food. This sets free the energy which the cells need in order to work. Our respiratory system takes in oxygen from the air and transfers it to the blood in our lungs. The oxygen travels to the cells in our blood, where it is exchanged for carbon dioxide. Our respiratory system then removes the carbon dioxide.

The respiratory system and sport

The respiratory system is important for health and sporting performance, but more so for some sports than for others. For example, in archery, snooker and shot putt competitions, the efficiency of the respiratory system is not a factor. However in swimming, running, cycling, major team games and most other sports, performance will be affected by the efficiency of the respiratory system. As sportspeople we should avoid activities which reduce the efficiency of our respiratory system such as smoking cigarettes.

activity

Getting oxygen to our working muscles

Matt and Dwayne are 23-year-old middle-distance runners. When they are resting, their breathing rates are both the same: 16 breaths a minute. However, Matt has an advantage over Dwayne as he is able to get much more oxygen to his working muscles and therefore produces much faster times than Dwayne.

Read the descriptions below and try to think of three reasons to explain the difference in their times. The following questions may help your discussions:

- Body size and lung size are closely linked. Will this have any effect on cardiovascular endurance?
- Can body weight or body type have an effect on cardiovascular endurance?
- What is the importance of aerobic fitness and anaerobic fitness for running the 1,500 metres?
- Do you think the time they have given to training and the way they have trained will affect their performances at 1,500 metres?

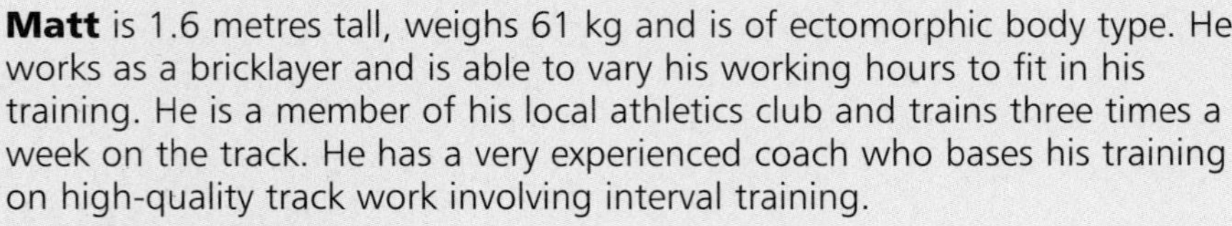

Matt is 1.6 metres tall, weighs 61 kg and is of ectomorphic body type. He works as a bricklayer and is able to vary his working hours to fit in his training. He is a member of his local athletics club and trains three times a week on the track. He has a very experienced coach who bases his training on high-quality track work involving interval training.

Dwayne is 1.9 metres tall and weighs 85 kg. He is a call-centre operator and works long, regular hours (9 am to 6 pm) five days a week. He is a member of his local athletics club but trains on his own with some advice from his father, a former athlete. His training consists mainly of long runs and a body-building session in the gym once a week.

KEYWORDS

Aerobic activity: activity when enough oxygen is available to meet the needs of the working muscles

Anaerobic activity: activity performed in the absence of sufficient oxygen from our lungs to meet the needs of working muscles

Expiration: breathing air and waste products out from the lungs

Gaseous exchange: 'the process involved in the exchange of oxygen from the air with carbon dioxide in the body' (AQA)

Inspiration: breathing air into the lungs

Lactic acid: waste product of muscular action that builds up if oxygen is not available

Oxygen debt: 'the amount of extra oxygen needed after exercise or physical activity over and above that which would have been required at rest' (AQA)

Oxygen deficit: build-up of lactic acid during activity when insufficient oxygen is available

Tidal volume: the amount of air breathed in or out of the lungs in one breath

Vital capacity: the maximum amount of air that can be forcibly exhaled after breathing in as much as possible

VO_2 Max: the maximum amount of oxygen that can be transported to the muscles and used in one minute.

Key to Exam Success

For your GCSE you should be able to:

- identify the main parts of the respiratory system and explain how it works
- describe how breathing in and breathing out takes place
- understand how respiration takes place both in the lungs and at the working muscles
- understand how the body deals with the waste products of respiration
- explain the effects of exercise and training on the respiratory system
- explain how the respiratory system links with the circulatory system
- explain how oxygen debt occurs and is repaid
- understand the terms aerobic and anaerobic in relation to exercise.

"KEY THOUGHTS"

'Cell respiration is at the centre of all human activity.'

How do we breathe?

- Air enters through the nose and mouth.
- The **nasal passages** contain mucus and hair. They moisten, filter and warm the air.
- The **palate** separates the nasal cavity from the mouth. It allows us to chew and breathe at the same time.
- The **epiglottis** is a flap at the back of the throat. It closes when we swallow to stop food from going down the trachea.
- The air passes through the **larynx**, or voice box, on its way to the **trachea**.
- The **trachea** or windpipe has rings of cartilage to hold it open. It divides into two **bronchi**. Each bronchus branches out into smaller tubes, which in turn become **bronchioles**.
- The bronchioles split up and end in **alveoli**.
- The **alveoli** are thin-walled, spongy air sacs. Most of our lung tissue is made up of large numbers of alveoli. When we breathe these tiny air sacs fill with air and then empty.
- The **lungs** are two thin-walled elastic sacs lying in our chests, in the

thoracic cavity. This is an airtight area with ribs at the back and front and the diaphragm below.

- The **pleural membranes** surround the lungs. They are slippery double skins which keep the lungs moist. They also lubricate the outside of the lungs. The membranes slide against one another as our lungs expand and contract. This reduces friction with the surrounding ribs and diaphragm.
- The **diaphragm** is a sheet of muscle which separates the thoracic cavity from the rest of the body. It is very important for breathing.
- The **intercostal muscles** are found between the ribs and control rib movement. They are very important for breathing.

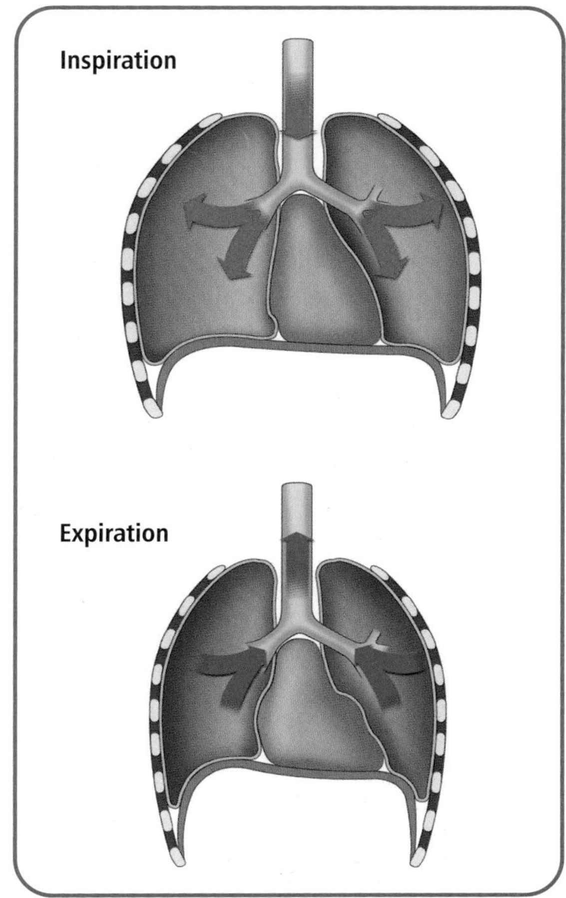

What happens when we breathe?

Breathing is the first stage in supplying oxygen to our body cells. Breathing is also called **external** or **pulmonary respiration**.

When breathing in (inspiration):

- Our intercostal muscles contract, lifting the ribs upwards and outwards. Our chest expands.
- Our diaphragm contracts. It pulls down and flattens out the floor of our ribcage. Our chest expands further.
- Our lungs increase in size as our chest expands. This is because their outside surface is stuck to the chest wall.
- The pressure inside our lungs falls as they expand. The higher pressure of air outside means air is now sucked into the lungs through the nose and mouth.

When breathing out (expiration):

- Our intercostal muscles relax. Our ribs move downwards and inwards under their own weight. The chest gets smaller.
- Our diaphragm relaxes. It is pushed back into a domed position by the organs underneath it. Our chest gets even smaller.
- Our lungs decrease in size as our chest gets smaller. They are squeezed by the ribs and diaphragm.
- The pressure inside our lungs increases as they get smaller. The air pressure outside is now lower than in our lungs. Air is forced out of the lungs through the nose and mouth.

Breathing and sport

When our body is at rest, the movements of the diaphragm alone are enough for breathing. Breathing is automatic. As soon as we start physical activity, we use our intercostal muscles to increase the depth of breathing. As a result of exercise and training, all the muscles involved in breathing (the diaphragm and intercostal muscles) become stronger, allowing us to breathe more deeply and for a longer period of time and to inhale a greater amount of air in each breath. Exercise and training will also increase the capillary network surrounding the alveoli in the lungs. This improves the process of exchanging oxygen for carbon dioxide. Regular exercise therefore makes our breathing more efficient.

When we are at rest we breathe in and out about 16 times a minute, taking in about 0.5 litres of air in each breath. If we exercise very hard, our breathing rate can increase to 50 times a minute and the amount of air taken in can exceed 2.5 litres in each breath. Therefore the amount of air breathed in can increase from 8 litres to 125 litres a minute.

Some sports performers use nasal strips which they claim help them to breathe better whilst they are playing. However, little evidence has been found to support this claim. Training can certainly improve breathing.

The effects of exercise on the respiratory system

What are the immediate effects of exercise on the respiratory system?

- Increased rate of breathing
- Increased depth of breathing
- Increased blood flow through lungs
- Increased oxygen take-up and use by the body.

What are the effects of regular training and exercise on the respiratory system?

- Increased strength of intercostal muscles and diaphragm allows deeper and faster breaths

- Greater number of alveoli
- Increased amount of oxygen delivered to the body
- Increased amount of carbon dioxide removed from the body.

What are the long-term benefits of exercise on the respiratory system?

- Healthier lungs
- Increased vital capacity and tidal volume
- Increased capacity of lungs to extract oxygen from the air
- Increased capacity of the lungs to remove carbon dioxide and other waste products from the bloodstream
- Increased tolerance of oxygen debt as lungs can work harder for longer.

How do we get oxygen to our working muscles?

The respiratory system needs two stages to supply oxygen to the working muscles and all the other body cells.

Stage 1: External or pulmonary respiration

This part of the process is what we know as breathing. It includes:

- getting air into and out of the lungs
- exchanging oxygen and carbon dioxide in the lungs
- getting oxygen into the bloodstream.

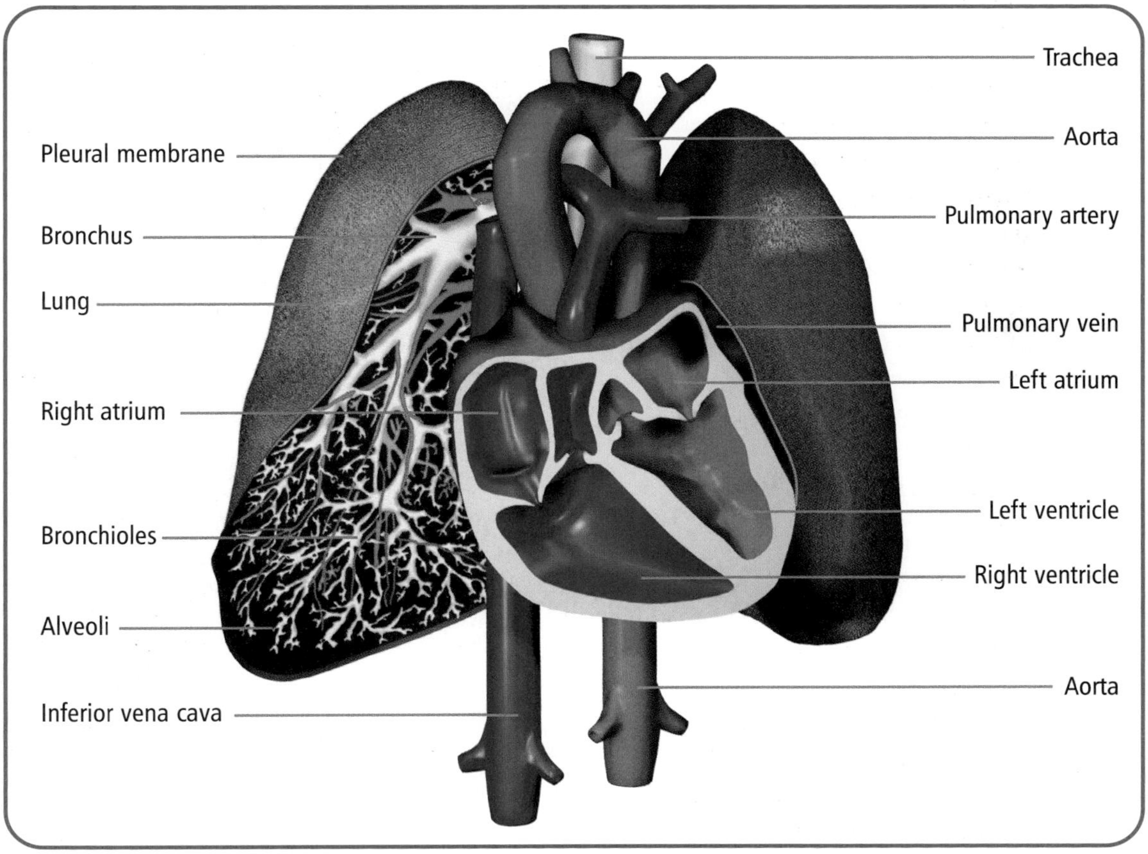

The individual steps are as follows:

- The air we breathe in passes through our trachea into our bronchi and through our bronchi into our bronchioles. The bronchioles end in tiny air sacs called alveoli. There is direct contact between the walls of the alveoli and the capillaries. The capillaries contain deoxygenated blood that has been brought to the lungs in the pulmonary artery.

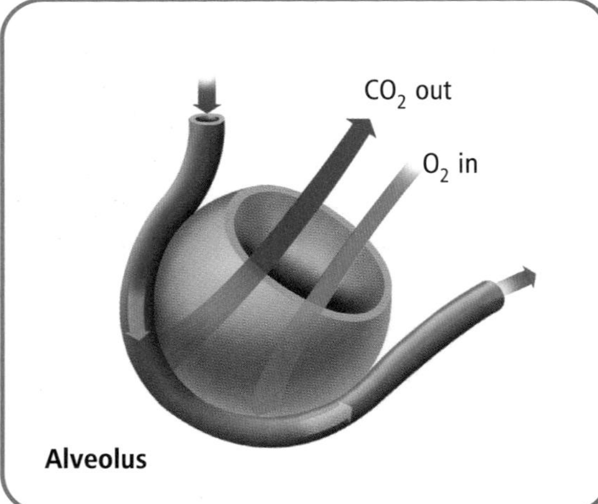

Alveolus

- The haemoglobin in the blood of the capillaries takes up oxygen from the alveoli.
- Carbon dioxide is exchanged for the oxygen and is breathed out.
- The oxygenated blood is carried in the pulmonary veins to the left side of the heart.
- The oxygenated blood is then pumped through our aorta to muscles and other body cells.
- After exchanging oxygen for carbon dioxide and other waste products in our cells, the deoxygenated blood returns to the heart in our veins.
- In the alveoli the carbon dioxide is exchanged once again for oxygen and is breathed out.

Stage 2: Internal or cell respiration

The respiratory system needs a second stage to supply oxygen to the working muscles and other body cells. This is called internal or cell respiration. It includes:

- getting oxygen into the body cells
- exchanging oxygen and carbon dioxide in the cells
- removing carbon dioxide and waste.

The individual steps are as follows:

- The heart pumps the oxygenated blood around the body in the arteries. The oxygen is carried by the haemoglobin in the red blood cells.
- The arteries get smaller and smaller, becoming arterioles. These end in a network of capillaries which cover every part of the body cells. The capillaries are tiny, with walls only one

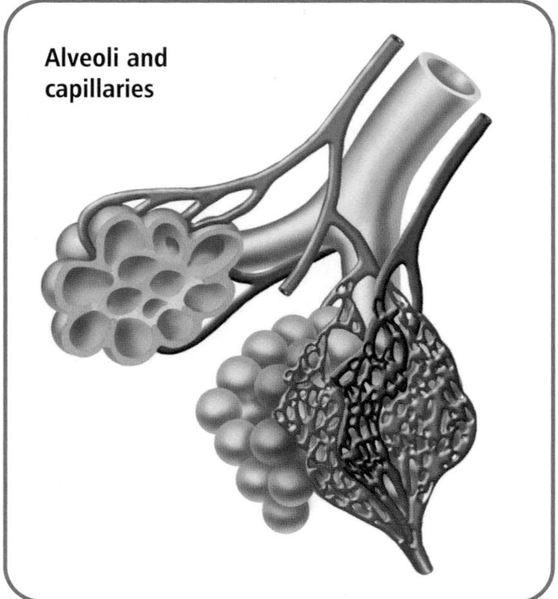
Alveoli and capillaries

cell thick. It is easy for oxygen and nutrients such as glucose to escape through these walls into the cells.

- At the same time carbon dioxide and other waste products such as water move from the cells to the capillaries. The blood has now lost its oxygen.
- The capillaries join up with small veins called venules. These carry deoxygenated blood to the veins.
- Blood returns to the heart in the veins.

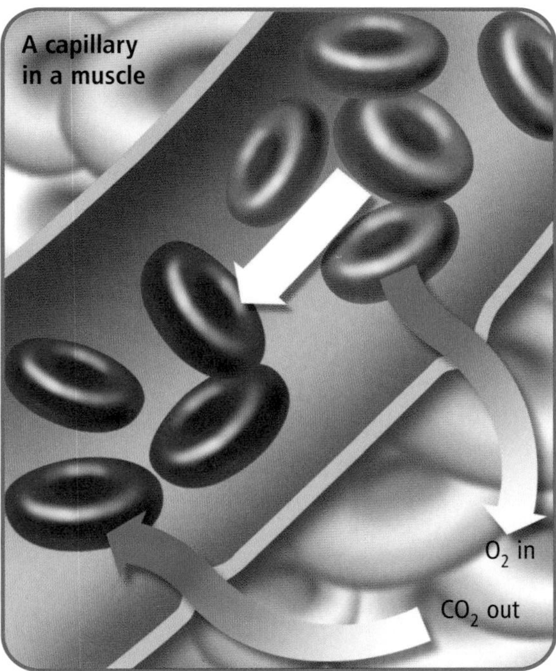

In this process we use oxygen to release the energy from glucose inside our body cells. This can be shown as:

Glucose + Oxygen	=	Energy + Carbon dioxide + Water

This glucose is obtained from glycogen stored in our muscles and liver. The glycogen comes from the carbohydrates in our diet. This is why we need to keep our intake of carbohydrates high while we are training and taking part in sport. If activity continues over a long period of time, as, for example, when running a marathon, then glycogen can also be obtained from fat reserves in our body.

As a result of training, more oxygenated blood reaches our working muscles; the exchange of oxygen and carbon dioxide is improved and waste products are removed more quickly. The overall result of training is that internal respiration becomes more efficient, improving our cardiovascular endurance and our sporting performance.

Factors affecting respiration

The air we breathe in (called inhaled air) exchanges some of its oxygen for carbon dioxide in our lungs. The air we breathe out (called exhaled air) therefore contains less oxygen and more carbon dioxide. It also has much more water vapour, which is also a waste product from our cells.

The composition of inhaled and exhaled air

Inhaled air	Exhaled air
Nitrogen 79%	Nitrogen 79%
Oxygen 21%	Oxygen 16%
Carbon dioxide 0.04%	Carbon dioxide 4%

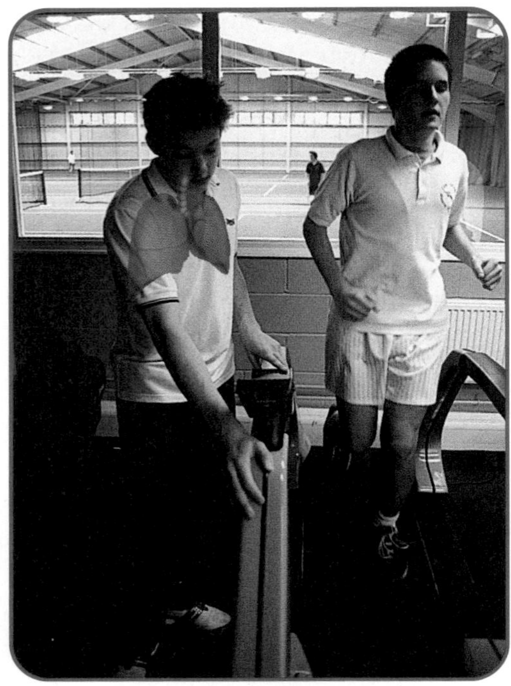

Tidal volume and vital capacity

Tidal volume is the amount of air breathed in or out of the lungs in one breath. It can vary a lot. When we are resting, only about 0.5 litres of air moves in and out of our lungs with each breath. Not all of this reaches the alveoli; some remains in our nose and throat. If we start an activity, the body will need more oxygen. We achieve this increase in our tidal volume by breathing more deeply, increasing our rate of breathing, or both.

Vital capacity is the maximum amount of air that can be forcibly exhaled after breathing in as much as possible. It is our maximum tidal volume and is usually about 4.8 litres in adults. Both tidal volume and vital capacity can be improved by a training programme, as exercise will strengthen the muscles involved in breathing. Improved vital capacity will increase the oxygen inhaled and will help improve performance.

Aerobic and anaerobic energy systems

The energy we need for sport can be found by using either of our two energy systems: the **anaerobic** or the **aerobic** system.

In the anaerobic system the body works without sufficient oxygen being supplied to the muscles, while in the aerobic system there is a constant supply of oxygen. Games players need to develop and improve both types of fitness. This can be achieved by training in both the aerobic and anaerobic target zones – i.e. keeping heart rates above a certain level during training.

Lactic acid and oxygen debt

We can continue to perform strenuous activity for some time, even when we run out of sufficient supplies of oxygen.

This is because we can draw on glycogen stores in the body as an alternative energy supply. However, in the absence of oxygen, **lactic acid** is formed in the working muscles. This makes our muscles hurt and eventually we have to stop the activity.

In the recovery period after exercise, we take in extra oxygen which is used to convert the painful lactic acid into simple waste products. The oxygen required to do this is called our oxygen debt. By following a training programme we are able to improve the ability of our muscles to use oxygen better and to cope with extra lactic acid. This means we are able to continue with our activity for longer before fatigue sets in. Through training we are also able to repay our oxygen debt more quickly.

How are waste products removed from the body?

We use three processes to remove the waste products of respiration:

- **Expiration** takes place when we breathe out carbon dioxide and other waste products from our lungs.
- **Excretion** of urine or faeces is used to remove excess water and the waste products from lactic acid.
- **Perspiration** is used to remove excess water, as sweat, from the body. It also helps us to lose heat through evaporation from the skin. Heat is a form of energy and not a waste product, but we need to regulate our body temperature or we will overheat.

QUESTIONS

9 The respiratory system

1 Describe the function of each of the following parts of the respiratory system.

a Nasal cavity and air passages *(2 marks)*
b Lungs *(2 marks)*
c Diaphragm. *(2 marks)*

2 The process of breathing is essential to life.

a Describe the process of inspiration. *(3 marks)*

b Describe the process of expiration. *(3 marks)*

c Define tidal volume and vital capacity. Explain how they differ. *(3 marks)*

3 Describe the immediate effects of exercise on the respiratory system. *(3 marks)*

4

a List three long-term effects of exercise on the respiratory system. *(3 marks)*

b Explain how each effect improves performance. *(3 marks)*

5 Exercise can be aerobic or anaerobic.

a What are the differences between anaerobic and aerobic exercise? *(2 marks)*

b Explain oxygen debt and describe how it is repaid. *(2 marks)*

c Name the waste product from anaerobic exercise and describe its effect. *(2 marks)*

d Name one waste product from aerobic exercise and describe how the body deals with it. *(2 marks)*

6

a Which two gases are exchanged in the alveoli? *(2 marks)*

b Why are our intercoastal muscles important for breathing? *(2 marks)*

c Expired air contains about 79% nitrogen. What is the percentage of:
i oxygen
ii carbon dioxide? *(2 marks)*

d Why is there more carbon dioxide in expired air than inspired air? *(2 marks)*

7 Describe aerobic respiration using an example from sport. Explain how the body deals with the waste products. *(8 marks)*

8 Describe anaerobic respiration using an example from sport. Explain how the body deals with the waste products. *(8 marks)*

The nervous, hormonal and digestive systems

All sporting activity requires our body systems to work smoothly together. This task is carried out by our **nervous system**, which controls everything that goes on in our body. Our nervous system keeps all parts of our body in touch with each other. It allows us to control our muscles for sport while other functions such as our heartbeat carry on automatically.

Our **hormonal system** (also called our **endocrine system**) works closely with our nervous system to control the way our body systems function. The nervous system acts quickly and usually has short-term effects on the body. The hormonal system can work quickly, but often works more slowly and has longer-lasting effects.

Finally, our body needs a constant supply of food as fuel to remain healthy and active. Our **digestive system** breaks our food down into elements small enough to pass into our bloodstream. It also converts our food into the basic nutrients which our body needs for building new tissue, repairing damaged tissue and for producing energy.

Key to Exam Success

For your GCSE you should be able to:

- explain how the nervous system controls movement
- describe how the hormones of the body affect exercise
- explain how food is made available by the digestive process to provide energy for physical activity.

Our nervous system

Our **central nervous system** is made up of our brain and spinal cord.

- Our brain is the control centre of our nervous system. It receives information, makes decisions and sends instructions to all parts of our body.
- Our spinal cord runs down the inside of our spinal column from our brain. It is made up of sensory and motor nerves which send messages between our brain and our body.

Our **peripheral nervous** system is made up of millions of sensory and motor nerves.

- Our sensory nerves collect information from all our body parts, including our eyes and ears, lungs, heart, muscles and joints. They tell our brain what is happening to our body as well as what is happening around us.
- Our motor nerves take instructions from our brain to our muscles and organs.

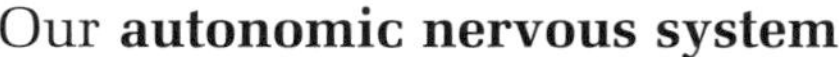

Our **autonomic nervous system** controls the automatic working of some of our body parts, especially our organs. For example, our breathing, our heartbeat and our digestive system all work quite automatically.

Our nervous system in action

- The hormone adrenaline is pumped around our body. This prepares all our body organs for sporting action. Our heart rate and our breathing both increase. Blood is diverted away from parts such as the digestive system towards the muscles.
- In cricket, for example, our eyes take in information about the bowler, the speed of his run-up, the flight of the ball and the position of the fielders. Our ears hear the talking of the players and the noise of the crowd.
- The sense organs in our muscles and joints tell us about the position of our limbs and how we are holding the bat.
- Our brain receives a lot of information from our sensory nerves. Using our previous experience, it makes decisions about what to do. It then sends messages to our muscles about how to move to play the ball.
- Our sense organs continue to send messages back to our brain as we play the ball. Our brain may alter its instructions to the muscles even as we play the ball.

Conditioned reflexes

If we are a skilled batsman, we will have learned how to play many different strokes. Our brain can choose any one of these strokes and play it automatically. We will have learned also that the stroke we choose depends on the type of ball bowled. This means we can concentrate on the speed and direction of the ball and decide where to play it without having to worry about how to play the shot.

We learn many complex skills in our lifetime. The movements we make when riding a bike, swimming or throwing a ball become automatic. These patterns of movement which we learn are called **conditioned reflexes**. We use them a lot in sport. However, we must take care to learn them correctly. Changing an incorrect conditioned reflex can be very difficult – as a golfer with a poor swing will discover.

Our nervous system and sport

Our nervous system plans, controls and co-ordinates all our movements. Therefore when we take part in sport we depend on it working efficiently. A superbly muscled and conditioned person will not necessarily be skilful. Sporting skills need to be learned and are closely linked to the working of our nervous system.

Any damage to our nervous system is likely to reduce our ability to play sport. In contact sports there is always a danger of serious injury to the brain or spinal cord. Any such injury must be treated with the greatest care.

Our hormonal system

Our hormonal system is made up of a number of glands which produce **hormones**. Hormones are the chemical messengers of our body. They are sent directly into our bloodstream when they are needed.

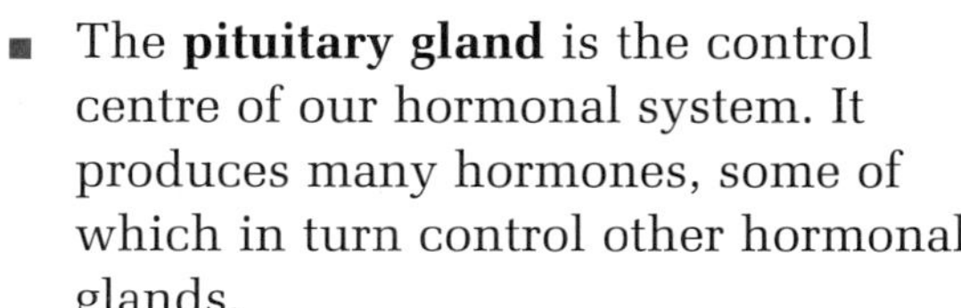

- The **pituitary gland** is the control centre of our hormonal system. It produces many hormones, some of which in turn control other hormonal glands.
- The **thyroid gland** controls the speed at which oxygen and food products are used to produce energy.
- The **pancreas** helps our digestion. It also produces insulin which controls the amount of sugar in our blood.
- The **ovaries** control the development of secondary sexual characteristics in women through the production of the hormone oestrogen.
- The **testes** control the development of secondary sexual characteristics in men through the production of testosterone. This hormone is important for the development of muscle and is sometimes used illegally to improve performance (see page 229).
- The **adrenal glands** produce adrenaline and prepare our body for instant action. Adrenaline has the effect of increasing our heart rate and of using up more oxygen in our cells to release more energy. It also moves blood away from areas such as our digestive system to our working muscles.

What happens to our hormonal system when we exercise?

We use many hormones when we take part in physical activity. They affect the body by:

- increasing our heart rate
- increasing the rate at which our body works
- increasing the use of glucose in our muscles
- increasing the amount of glucose carried in our blood
- moving blood to the skeletal muscles from other areas
- increasing blood pressure
- increasing our breathing rate
- controlling our fluid levels and preventing loss of water.

Our digestive system

- The process of digestion starts in our mouth where our food is first ground up and mixed by the action of our teeth so that it can be swallowed easily.
- Our food is moistened by our saliva which begins to turn starch into sugar.
- Our food is pushed down the gullet (oesophagus) by a wave-like muscular movement.
- In our stomach our food is churned about and mixed with gastric juices which break down protein to form simple materials. Our stomach acts as a storage tank.
- Our food moves in small amounts into the first part of our small intestine (duodenum). Enzymes break down our food into more simple substances.

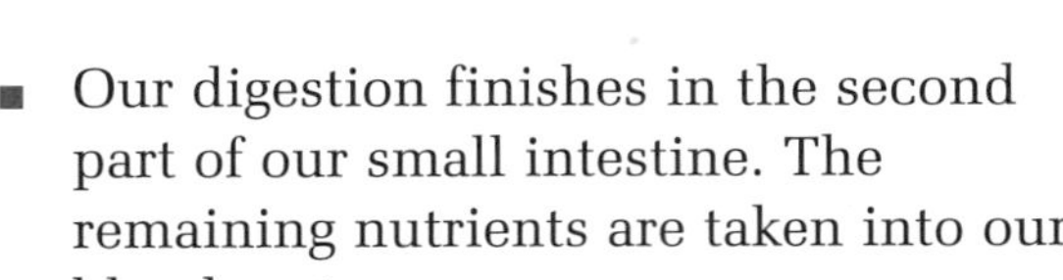

- Our digestion finishes in the second part of our small intestine. The remaining nutrients are taken into our blood system.
- The waste food passes into our large intestine (colon). Most of the water and any more nutrients are removed.
- The solidified remains leave our body through our anus. Waste fluids are taken to our kidneys. Here they are filtered and passed to our bladder as urine. The urine leaves our body through our urethra.

What happens to our digestive system when we exercise?

Our digestive system needs large amounts of blood to deal with our food. As we exercise our active muscles need more blood. The amount of blood going to our digestive system is therefore reduced. This slows down digestion. We may also feel uncomfortable exercising with a full stomach. We should avoid eating a meal for at least two hours before exercise.

Fitness training

11 Principles of training

To be successful in sport, we need our energy systems and sporting skills to be at their highest possible level. We can reach these high levels by training. Training consists of a regular programme of exercise to improve performance. Our training programmes must be based on a number of basic principles. There are many different methods of training and ways of organising a training programme. We must be sure that our Personal Training Programme (PTP) is right for our sport and our levels of fitness and skill.

activity

Training effect

This activity is an experiment to see whether or not different types of training bring about an improvement in performance. To begin with, you will need to test your ability to juggle three tennis balls using both hands. You will count the number of successful catches and record your best of three attempts.

Next, you need to join one of three groups, and to practise the following for 20 minutes:

- Group A: juggling with two tennis balls using one hand
- Group B: bouncing a tennis ball continuously on the ground
- Group C: juggling with three tissues or scarves using both hands.

After your practice session, your juggling ability with the three tennis balls will be re-tested and the results entered in a table.

Use the information from your results to answer the following questions:

1. What sort of practice is most likely to improve your juggling skills?
2. Is this true for both boys and girls?
3. Is practising bouncing a tennis ball more likely to improve your juggling skills than practising with tissues or scarves?
4. Do you think your answers would apply to other sporting skills?
5. Does slowing down the skill, e.g. using the tissues or scarves, improve learning?

KEYWORDS

Aerobic: respiration using oxygen

Anaerobic: respiration in the absence of oxygen

FITT principles: Frequency, Intensity, Time, Type – the basis for planning a fitness programme

Individual needs: specific training needs, based on your current level of fitness and the requirements of your sport

MHR: maximum heart rate

Overload: making the body work harder than normal to improve fitness

Oxygen debt: the amount of extra oxygen needed after exercise or physical activity, over and above that which would have been required at rest (AQA)

Periodisation: dividing a training programme into different parts, for example pre-season, peak season and off-season

SPORT principles of training: Specificity, Progression, Overload, Reversibility, Tedium – the basis for planning a training programme

Progression: gradually increasing the amount of training or exercise you do

Reversibility: loss of improvement when training is decreased or stopped

Specificity: training must closely resemble sporting activity for improvement to take place

Tedium: we must vary training methods to prevent boredom and overuse injuries

Training: a well-planned programme which uses scientific principles to improve performance, skills, games ability and motor and physical fitness

Training threshold: minimum rate at which heart must work to bring about certain fitness improvements

Training zone: range of heart rate within which a specific training effect will take place.

Key to Exam Success

For your GCSE you will need to:

- know how training can be planned to improve fitness
- understand and apply the SPORT and FITT principles of training to any training programme, including your own personal fitness programme
- understand the principle of periodisation
- understand the reasons for including warm up and warm down in every training session
- AQA B only: design a training session
- AQA B only: design a training programme

“ KEY THOUGHTS ”

‘Thoughtful training delivers the goods!’

Effective training

Neither health-related fitness nor sport-related fitness can be achieved by chance. We need to work at all aspects of our fitness by following a training programme.

Our training must:

- be based on sound principles
- be systematic and planned
- take account of individual needs.

Training affects our health, our fitness and our performance. For steady progress, and to avoid injury, we should follow the **SPORT principles**:

- Specificity: train for our own particular sport.
- Progression: increase training gradually.
- Overload: work harder than normal.
- Reversibility: be aware that if we stop training we lose fitness.
- Tedium: make training interesting.

Specificity

Our training must be specific to our sport and our individual needs. Every type of exercise has a particular effect on the body. The type of training we choose must be right for the type of improvement we want to see.

If we want to improve the strength of our arms, running will not help: we must use strength-training exercises that work our arms. We must always use a training programme that puts regular stress on the muscle groups or body system that we want to develop.

Our training programme must also be designed to suit the needs of our sport. For example:

- Sprinters need to include a lot of speed work in their training. This helps their fast-twitch muscle fibres to develop.
- Endurance athletes need to develop their slow-twitch muscle fibres. They train over longer distances or for a longer time.
- Games players need to include both speed and endurance training in their programmes to develop both types of muscle fibres.

Progression

The amount of work we do must begin at a level that we can cope with. Then we must gradually increase it for improvement in fitness to take place. Our body takes time to adapt to more or harder exercise. We must build up the stress on our bodies in a gradual, or progressive, way – for example, by lifting heavier weights or running further. If we build up the stress too quickly, we risk injury or find the challenge too great and give up. If we build up the stress too slowly we may become uninterested or bored and give up.

The body needs time to recover and adapt to training. Our bones, ligaments and tendons may take longer to change than our muscles or other body systems. Our training thresholds tell us if we are training at the right level.

If we are unfit we can improve our fitness level quickly. The fitter we are, the harder it is to improve.

Overload

To improve the fitness of our body systems, we need to work them harder than normal. The body will then adapt to the extra stress and we will become fitter. When we overload we can still cope with the extra level of activity, but it is hard work.

We can overload our bodies by training more often, by working harder or by spending more time on an exercise. For example, to improve aerobic fitness by running, we could run more times a week, complete the run in a shorter time or increase the distance we run. Each one of these methods will overload the aerobic system. The aerobic system will gradually adapt to cope with the overload and our fitness will improve.

Reversibility

Sometimes called reversal, the principle of reversibility means that fitness improvements are temporary and will be lost if training stops.

Just as our bodies adapt to the stress of exercise by becoming fitter, they also quickly adapt to less exercise by losing fitness. If our muscles are not used, they atrophy or waste away. We cannot store fitness for future use. It will disappear if we stop training. It takes only 3–4 weeks for our bodies to get out of condition.

We lose our aerobic fitness more easily than our anaerobic fitness. This is because our muscles quickly lose much of their ability to use oxygen. Our anaerobic fitness is less affected by not training. If we follow a strength-training programme for 4 weeks, we will lose the extra strength we have gained after about 12 weeks of inactivity.

Although it is natural to want to achieve results quickly, it is important that exercise is done in moderation, otherwise ill-effects will result. We train to improve our performance. But overtraining – that is, too much training – can be bad for our health. Our bodies need to rest and sleep between training sessions. Overtraining can cause muscle soreness, joint pain, sleeping problems, loss of appetite and extreme tiredness. After injury or illness we must start training again only gradually.

Tedium

Our training programme must be varied to avoid tedium, or boredom. By using a variety of different training methods we will keep our enthusiasm and motivation. For example:

- We can follow a long workout with a short one, a hard session with a relaxed one or a high-speed session with a long, slow one.
- We can change where we train and when we train.
- We can avoid overuse injuries by varying the way we train. For example, shin splints can be avoided by running on grass rather than on hard roads.

activity

Evaluating a training programme

Examine the following training programmes. Decide how far you think each programme has been based on the principles outlined above. Summarise your findings and be prepared to discuss them with the whole class.

Programme 1: Six-week programme for Sharon, a cross-country runner

	Monday	Tuesday	Wednesday	Thursday	Friday	Saturday	Sunday
Week 1 programme	10-mile run	Gym work, concentrating on upper body strength	Fartlek	Track work, 400-metre repetitions ×10	Rest day	Race	30-minute swim, continuous lengths
Following 5 weeks	No change	Increase weights gradually	Increase total distance run	Reduce rest time between repetitions	Rest day	Race	No change

Programme 2: Six-week programme for Errol, a badminton player

	Monday	Tuesday	Wednesday	Thursday	Friday	Saturday	Sunday
Week 1 programme	Skill practice for 1 hour	Endurance training on court – 1 hour	Light weights (high reps.) in gym	Gym work: 30-min. run, 20-min. bike, 20-min. rowing	Match practice	Stretching and plyometrics	League game
Following 5 weeks	No change	No change	Increase speed and reps.	Increase work rate	No change	No change	League game

Programme 3: Six-week programme for Mandy, a football player

	Monday	Tuesday	Wednesday	Thursday	Friday	Saturday	Sunday
Week 1 programme	5-aside matches	Power lifting in the gym	Match	Rest day	10-mile run	Match	Rest day
Following 5 weeks	No change	Heavier weights	No change	No change	No change	No change	No change

Programme 4: Six-week programme for Ahmed, a swimmer

	Monday	Tuesday	Wednesday	Thursday	Friday	Saturday	Sunday
Week 1 programme	100-metre repetitions – various strokes ×20	200-metre repetitions – various strokes ×10	1 hour technique improvement, including turns	2 miles continuous – fast	1 hour technique improvement, including turns	Competition	5 miles continuous lengths
Following 5 weeks	Reduce time for both reps. and recovery	Reduce time for both reps. and recovery	No change	No change	No change	No change	No change

Sharon

Errol

Mandy

Ahmed

Meeting individual needs

We have seen that training programmes must be designed to develop the specific fitness, strength and skills required for each sport. Training programmes must also be designed to meet the individual needs of the sportsperson. The following factors should be considered:

- **Age and experience**: a training programme designed for a 30-year-old county player will not meet the needs of a 14-year-old student who wants to get into the school team.
- **Fitness level**: training programmes must start from our current fitness level and progress from there.

- **Sporting ability**: training programmes must develop the skills which we already have and introduce new skills in a progressive manner.
- **Motivation**: our training programme must ensure a good balance of challenge and success.

Thresholds of training

We need to know exactly how hard and how long we should train in order to improve our fitness and therefore our sporting performance. If we train at too low a level we will make little improvement in our fitness. If we try to train too hard we will quickly become exhausted or suffer injury and be unable to complete the programme. We need to calculate our own individual thresholds of training so that we can work as effectively as possible.

To train effectively we must know:

- the amount of **anaerobic training** we need for our sport
- the amount of **aerobic training** we need for our sport
- our present level of fitness.

To calculate our individual threshold of training we can use our maximum heart rate (MHR). This can be estimated using the following formula:

- MHR (males) = 220 minus age
- MHR (females) = 226 minus age

Our **aerobic threshold** can then be calculated by working out 60% of our MHR. If we work above this level we will be improving our aerobic fitness.

Our **anaerobic threshold** can be calculated by working out 80% of our MHR. If we work above this level we will be improving our anaerobic fitness.

	Males		Females	
	15 years	16 years	15 years	16 years
60% MHR Aerobic threshold	123	122	127	126
80% MHR Anaerobic threshold	164	163	169	168

Different sports require different amounts of aerobic and anaerobic fitness. For example, a marathon runner will rely almost entirely on aerobic fitness, whilst a 100-metre sprinter will not use aerobic fitness at all during the race. Sprinters need instant energy which is provided in the absence of oxygen. They will therefore need to develop their anaerobic fitness. Games players need both aerobic and anaerobic fitness and their training programmes will need to develop both types. The aerobic and anaerobic energy systems are dealt with in more detail on page 207.

- **Aerobic training**: training our cardiorespiratory system to provide the working muscles with enough oxygen to work for a long period of time
- **Anaerobic training**: training our cardiorespiratory and muscular systems to work for a limited amount of time without enough oxygen
- **Aerobic threshold**: the minimum rate at which our heart must work in order to improve our aerobic fitness
- **Anaerobic threshold**: the minimum rate at which our heart must work in order to improve our anaerobic fitness.

activity

Calculating training zones

To achieve results, we must train in the appropriate ***training zone****. Consider the following training sessions for Floella, Jim, Janice and Mustafa. Calculate their individual* ***aerobic*** *and* ***anaerobic thresholds*** *and decide in which training zone they are working.*

- **Floella** is a 26-year-old racing cyclist. During a sprint training session she tries to maintain her heart rate at 155 beats per minute.

- 30-year-old **Jim** is doing a cross-country run and has maintained a heart rate of 158 for the last 15 minutes.

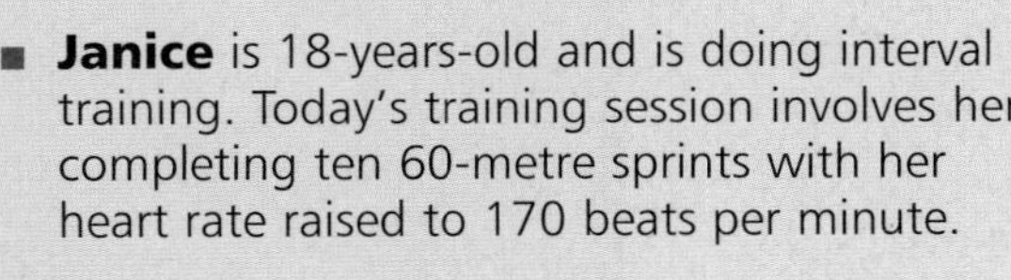

- **Janice** is 18-years-old and is doing interval training. Today's training session involves her completing ten 60-metre sprints with her heart rate raised to 170 beats per minute.

- **Mustafa**, who is 47 years old, swims regularly and keeps his heart rate above 105 throughout his swim.

Planning a training programme

We need to train to improve our fitness and therefore our performance. When planning a fitness programme we should follow the **FITT principles**:

- Frequency
- Intensity
- Time
- Type.

Frequency – how often we train

- We should train at least three times a week to improve our fitness.
- Our body needs time to recover from each training session.
- We should spread these sessions out over the week.

Intensity – how hard we train

- We will only get fitter if we work our body systems hard enough to make them adapt.
- We must start at the right intensity, depending on our current fitness.
- We must understand and use our training thresholds.

Time – how long we train

- To improve aerobic fitness, our training sessions should last longer and our working heart rate should rise.
- Each session must last at least 20 minutes to achieve real benefit.

Type – what kind of training we do

- We should analyse our particular sport to know the fitness and skills we need.
- Our training programme should include different types of activity to develop these skills and fitness.

Periodisation

If we take part in competitive sport we will naturally want to be at our best at the time of our most important competition. This is called peaking. Our training programmes will vary with the type of sport and the level of competition. We therefore need to plan well ahead. Dividing a training programme into different parts is called **periodisation**. For example, for many sports we could talk about three main periods: pre-season, peak season and off-season.

Pre-season

During the pre-season period you should:

- focus on fitness for your particular sport
- concentrate on muscular endurance, power and speed work
- develop the techniques, skills and strategies for your particular sport.

Peak season

During the peak season you should:

- emphasise speed
- practise your skills at high speed and in competitive situations
- add extra fitness sessions if you do not compete enough.

Off-season

Following the competitive season, you need a period of active rest at first. You then need to:

- maintain a high level of general fitness through moderate activity
- develop muscular strength, flexibility and aerobic fitness
- develop your sports skills.

Some sports and events require all-year round training. Athletes in these sports will only rest for a few weeks each year. Warm-weather and altitude training are often used by top performers in sports such as tennis and athletics to ensure that they can always train effectively.

activity

An annual training schedule

Draw up an annual training schedule, applying the guidelines about periodisation outlined above to your own sport. This may help you in the planning of your training programme.

Designing an individual training programme

The training programme for an elderly, recreational tennis player would be very different from one for a young, competitive pole vaulter. We must design our training programme for:

- a particular sport
- a specific level of ability
- an individual sportsperson or group of sportspeople at a similar level of ability.

Before planning the programme we must find out about:

- the sport (skill requirements)
- the type of fitness needed (body composition, muscular strength, cardiovascular endurance, flexibility, power, muscular endurance, speed, agility, co-ordination, balance, reaction time)

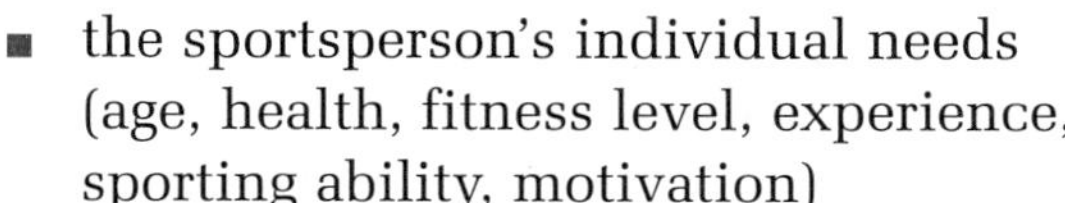

- the sportsperson's individual needs (age, health, fitness level, experience, sporting ability, motivation)
- the principles of training (SPORT: Specificity, Progression, Overload, Reversibility, Tedium and FITT: Frequency, Intensity, Time, Type)
- the types of training available (continuous, fartlek, interval, circuit, weight, flexibility, plyometric)
- the training year for the sport (pre-season, peak season, off-season).

Applying the principles of training to your training programme

- In order to ensure a successful training programme, you must apply the principles of training (SPORT). Your programme must be specific to your specific sport and to your current level of fitness. It must be progressive and involve overload in order to gradually and safely increase your cardiovascular strength, muscular strength, muscular endurance and flexibility. You must maintain your programme over time in order to avoid reversibility and vary your training to avoid tedium. You must also remember that your body needs time to recover from training and that moderation in training is important.
- Detailed planning of your programme must also involve the FITT principles, that is how often you train, how hard you train, how long you train and what type of training you do.
- You must be aware of the aerobic and anaerobic demands of your sport and plan your training to ensure that you achieve the appropriate thresholds of training.
- For each individual training session you must include a warm-up and warm-down, whilst your main activity will be dependent on the particular skill development and fitness training required for your sport. Remember that your training programme must be designed to satisfy your individual needs in your chosen sport.

Planning individual training sessions

To avoid injury and to get the most out of training, we should divide each session into three phases: warm-up, main activity and warm-down.

Warm-up

Our warm-up should include:

- gentle exercise for the whole body, such as light jogging. This gradually increases heart rate, breathing and blood supply to the muscles. It warms up our muscles and prepares us mentally for the session.
- gentle stretching, to prepare muscles, ligaments and joints and to prevent injury
- practising techniques and skills to be used in the session.

Main activity

Our main activity could be fitness training, skill development or a combination of both, depending on our needs. If our sport is a game, then one activity should be a conditioned game.

Fitness training

Our fitness activities will depend on the demands of our sport, but we can design fitness activities to develop skills as well.

If training is too intense at the start of the session we may be too tired to practise our skills well later. However, games players need to practise their games skills when they are tired.

Skill development

The techniques and skills we need to develop will depend on our particular sport. We may need to work in pairs, in small groups, or in teams as well as on our own. We may play small-sided and modified games (see below).

Conditioned games

Skill development practice must lead naturally into small-sided and modified games. In this way skills will be transferred from training to the match situation.

Warm-down

Every training session should end with a period of lighter exercise. Always avoid going from hard exercise immediately to rest. Light exercise during the warm-down decreases recovery time by helping to remove carbon dioxide, lactic acid and other waste products from the body. It also ensures that the blood continues to circulate well and prevents it pooling in the skeletal muscles, which may reduce blood pressure and cause dizziness.

While the muscles are thoroughly warm, flexibility exercises can be carried out with less chance of injury through over-stretching. Light exercise will also prevent muscle soreness and stiffness later.

Planning an individual training session

Prepare a training session specific to your chosen sport. Be sure to consider periodisation – in other words, match what you include in the training session with the training period in which it is to take place (pre-, peak or off-season). Include enough detail to allow someone else to lead the session if necessary.

QUESTIONS

11 Principles of training

1 SPORT stands for five principles of training.

a What does the letter **S** stand for? Give an example from a training programme. *(2 marks)*

b What does the letter **O** stand for? Give an example from a training programme. *(2 marks)*

c What does the letter **R** stand for? Give an example from a training programme. *(2 marks)*

2 Training programmes should be planned to meet individual needs.

a Give three aspects we should consider when assessing individual need. *(3 marks)*

b Explain target zones and training thresholds. *(3 marks)*

c Explain how to calculate the aerobic training zone. *(3 marks)*

3 Explain what is meant by periodisation when preparing a year-long training programme. *(3 marks)*

4 A warm-up and warm-down should be completed each time we train.

a Give three reasons why a warm-up is important. *(3 marks)*

b Describe the three parts of a warm-up. *(3 marks)*

5 The FITT principles should be used when planning a training programme.

a What does the letter **F** stand for? Explain how this applies to training *(2 marks)*

b What does the letter **I** stand for? Explain how this applies to training. *(2 marks)*

c What does the first letter **T** stand for? Explain how this applies to training. *(2 marks)*

d What does the second letter **T** stand for? Explain how this applies to training. *(2 marks)*

6 A training session should include three phases of activity.

a Name the first phase and give an example of an activity in this phase. *(2 marks)*

b Name the second phase and give an example of an activity in this phase. *(2 marks)*

c Name the third phase and give an example of an activity in this phase. *(2 marks)*

12 Methods of training

Success in sport only comes with dedicated training – and the key to success is to select the right methods of training. There are many different training methods available and it is important to understand their individual benefits and disadvantages. Together with the practical application of the principles of training, this will help you to achieve your potential in your chosen sport.

activity

Training for success

Look at these photographs of sportspeople in action. What methods of training do you think they used to reach this level of performance?

Discuss your ideas.

KEYWORDS

Aerobic activity: 'with oxygen'. If exercise is not too fast and is steady, the heart can supply all the oxygen the muscles need

Altitude training: aerobic exercise at higher altitudes where oxygen levels are low

Anaerobic activity: 'without oxygen'. If exercise is done in short fast bursts, the heart cannot supply oxygen to the muscles as fast as the cells can use it

Circuit training: performing a series of exercises or activities in a special order or sequence

Continuous training: working for sustained periods of time using all major muscle groups of the body

Fartlek: 'speed play' – a method of training in which the pace and training conditions are varied

Flexibility training: using a series of exercises to improve the range of movement at a joint

Interval training: using alternating periods of very hard exercise and rest to improve fitness

Oxygen debt: 'the amount of extra oxygen needed after exercise or physical activity, over and above that which would have been required at rest' (AQA)

Lactic acid: waste product produced in the working muscles

Plyometrics: training method using explosive movements to develop muscular power, for example, bounding and hopping

Pressure training: putting a technique or skill under stress

Recovery rates: length of time for cardiorespiratory system to return to normal after activity

Repetitions ('reps'): the number of times an exercise is repeated without resting (e.g. '10 reps')

Sets: the number of times we repeat a series of reps (e.g. '3 sets of 10 reps')

Training zone: the range of heart rate within which we work in order to bring about a specific training result

Weight training: using either free weights or weights in machines as a form of resistance training.

Key to Exam Success

For your GCSE you will need to:

- describe the different methods of training and apply them appropriately
- recognise the difference between aerobic and anaerobic training methods
- understand the meaning and use of recovery rates, training thresholds and training zones
- be able to monitor training in order to bring about improvements.

“ KEY THOUGHTS ”

'Train well, play well.'

Training options

There are many different training methods. They are all based on the different ways our body adapts to regular exercise. They include:

- continuous training
- interval training
- fartlek training
- circuit training
- weight training
- plyometric training
- flexibility training
- pressure training.

The aerobic training methods are sometimes used at altitude where the oxygen level in the air is lower. **Altitude training** encourages the development of extra oxygen carrying capacity in the blood which improves performance when the athletes return to competition near to sea level. **Pressure training** is a method for putting a technique or skill under stress.

Continuous (aerobic) training

Continuous training consists of working for sustained periods of time, using all major muscle groups of the body. Activity can include running, swimming, cycling, rowing, taking part in aerobics or any other whole-body activity.

Continuous training requires working at the same pace for between 30 minutes and two hours and being moderately active, that is, working in the aerobic training zone at 60–80% of MHR (Maximum Heart Rate).

Why use continuous training?

- to improve cardiovascular endurance
- to help improve health-related fitness
- to reduce amounts of body fat
- to maintain fitness in the off-season.

Who uses continuous training?

Everyone, because it forms the basis of all health-related fitness. In sport it is essential for all activities which continue over a period of time. Examples include all major team games, racket sports, swimming and running.

Interval training

Interval training consists of using alternating periods of very hard exercise and rest. Rest periods are essential for recovery and enable you to train for longer.

During interval training you can vary:

- the time or distance of each exercise
- the amount of effort (intensity) you put into each period of exercise
- the type of activity you take part in during each period of rest
- the number of exercise and recovery periods in the training session. For example, an interval training session on the track could involve six 200-metre runs in 30 seconds with 90 seconds rest between each.

Why use interval training?

The aim of interval training is to improve anaerobic and aerobic fitness. Your aerobic fitness will improve if you train for a long period at 60–80% of MHR. Your anaerobic fitness will improve if you train over a short period at 80–95% MHR.

Using this high-quality speed training you will need rests of 2–3 minutes, but it will develop your ability to work when tired.

Who uses interval training?

Interval training is a specialist training method for serious sportspeople and is not normally used for health-related fitness. It can be used to meet the needs of a variety of sports. Sprinters, for example, will allow sufficient time between sprints in order to recover fully. Games players will use programmes which alternate between hard and light working – which is what happens in a game.

Fartlek training

The name **fartlek** comes from a Swedish word meaning 'speed play'. Fartlek involves deliberately varying the speed and intensity at which you walk, run,

cycle or ski and the type of terrain over which you travel. A fartlek session normally lasts a minimum of 30 minutes.

Why use fartlek training?

- to improve aerobic and anaerobic fitness, depending on how you train
- to help games players who need both aerobic and anaerobic fitness
- to enable you to enjoy moving quickly but within your own ability
- to reduce tedium in training.

Who uses fartlek training?

Everyone can benefit from this type of training, as it can improve both aerobic and anaerobic fitness. In sport, it is regularly used in the training programmes of runners and skiers and can also be used simply to avoid tedium.

Circuit training

Circuit training involves performing a series of exercises or activities in a special order, called a circuit. A circuit usually consists of 6 to 10 exercises or activities, which take place at stations. At each station, a set number of repetitions is completed as quickly as possible, or as many repetitions as possible are completed in a fixed time, for example, one minute.

Circuits should be designed to avoid working the same muscle group at more than one station in succession. They should also include exercises that work opposing muscles around a joint.

As fitness improves, the circuit can be made more difficult by increasing:

- the number of stations
- the time spent at each station
- the number of repetitions at each station
- the number of complete circuits.

Why use circuit training?

Circuit training enables you to improve either aerobic or anaerobic fitness, or both at the same time. A great variety of exercises can be included, making it extremely adaptable for the needs of different sports.

Who uses circuit training?

Circuit training is a valuable training activity for almost all sports. For example, high jumpers can use programmes which concentrate on

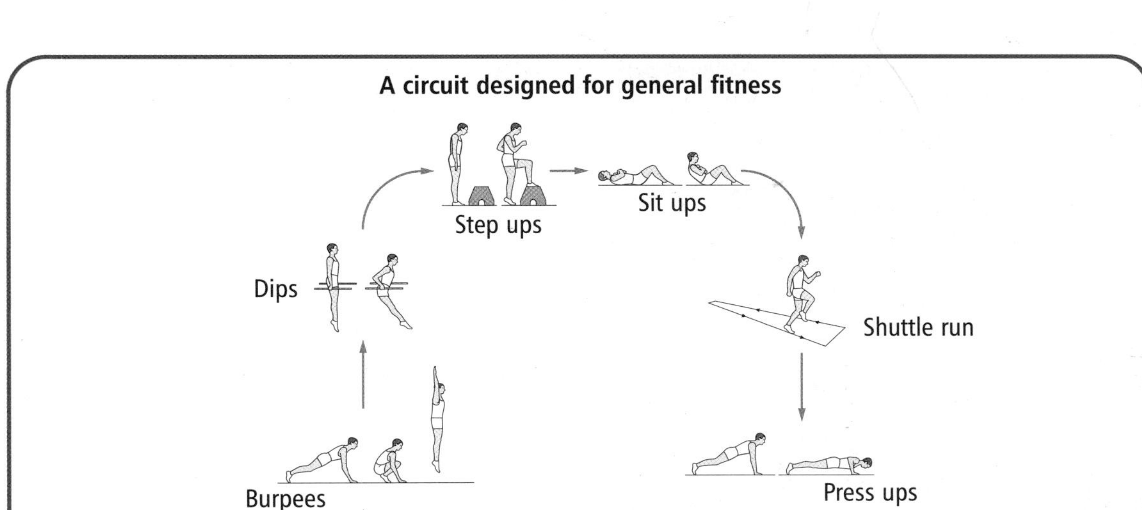

developing leg power, whilst basketball players can use programmes which develop leg power together with upper body strength and aerobic fitness. It is also possible to construct circuits for games players in which exercises are replaced by short skills practices – for example, passing a ball against a wall. At the same time, anyone who wants to achieve a basic level of health-related fitness can benefit from a suitably designed circuit.

Weight training

In **weight training**, free weights or weights in machines are used to provide resistance to muscle power. Training consists of sequences or sets of exercises, and the weights used are gradually increased, allowing you to overload your muscles safely over a sensible period of time.

Any weight training programme can take account of your current state of fitness. Below are some guidelines for weight training:

- Decide which muscle groups are important for your sport and choose exercises to develop them.
- Aim for at least three training sessions a week.
- Make sure you are thoroughly warmed up before starting.
- Breathe in when you lift the weight and breathe out as you lower it.
- Never hold your breath, as this could make you faint.
- Work the different muscle groups in turn, to give time for recovery.
- Increase the weights as your muscles grow stronger.

Why use weight training?

The aim of weight training is to improve your muscular strength – that is, muscular strength, power and muscular endurance.

- Muscular strength is improved by using at least three sets of six **repetitions** at near-maximum weight.

- Muscular endurance is improved by using at least three sets of 20–30 repetitions. The weight should be 40–60% of the weight which you can lift just once (your one repetition maximum, or 1 RM).
- Power is improved by at least three sets of 10–15 repetitions. These should be done at speed, using 60–80% of your 1 RM.

Who uses weight training?
Anyone who wants a basic health-related fitness level can benefit from a suitable weight training programme.

Sportspeople looking to improve their sporting performance can design their own weight training programme by comparing the physical demands of their sport with their own current level of fitness.

Weight training programmes are included in the training programmes of most sportspeople. They are of particular importance to power athletes such as jumpers, sprinters and throwers.

Plyometric training

Plyometric training involves a series of explosive movements including bounds, hops, jumps (on to and off boxes) leaps, skips, press-ups with claps, throwing and catching a medicine ball, all of which are designed to improve muscular power (explosive strength). The muscles can be stretched before they contract. This stores up elastic energy. When they next contract, they will produce extra power.

For example, in a vertical jump, you:

- bend at the knees, which stretches the thigh muscles
- immediately contract these muscles as you jump upwards.

This movement converts the stretch into an elastic recoil, and the extra power enables you to jump higher.

Plyometric training puts great stress on the muscles and joints, so it is vital to warm up thoroughly first. Beginners should take special care and should start by training on grass (if outdoors) or on mats if indoors.

Why use plyometric training?

The aim of plyometric training is to improve power by training the muscles to contract more strongly, and to improve sports performance by using your own body weight in movements similar to those found in your sport.

Who uses plyometric training?

This is a specialist training method for serious sportspeople who need to develop power and is not normally used for health-related fitness. It can be used to meet the needs of a variety of sportspeople, particularly jumpers, basketball and volleyball players. It is of benefit to all games and racket players.

Flexibility training

Flexibility training involves using a series of exercises to improve and extend the range of movement at a joint by stretching and moving the tendons and ligaments just beyond the point of resistance. A variety of exercises can used, involving static, passive, active and PNF stretching (see below).

Static stretching

In static stretching the limbs are extended beyond their normal range and the position is held for at least 10 seconds. After a few seconds the stretch is repeated. This is continued for at least five repetitions of 10 seconds, with the length of time the stretch is held being gradually increased.

Active stretching

In active stretching we extend a movement beyond our normal limit and repeat this rhythmically over a period of 20 seconds. It is very important that the muscles are warmed up before active stretching is started. Active stretches should be performed slowly at first, and bobs or bounces avoided.

Passive stretching

In passive stretching we increase the flexibility of our joints by using a partner to apply external force. He or she moves the limb being exercised to its end position and keeps it there for a few seconds. It is most important that this type of stretching is carried out carefully to avoid injury.

PNF stretching

PNF (proprioceptive neuromuscular facilitation) stretching is based on the principle that muscles are most relaxed (and therefore can most easily be stretched) immediately after contraction. The muscle is first contracted as hard as possible. It is then stretched fully and the stretch held for a few seconds. The muscle is then relaxed briefly before repeating.

Why use flexibility training?

The aim of all flexibility training is to improve flexibility and therefore performance. Good flexibility is important for most sports and can reduce the risk of joint injury as well as allowing us to use our strength more effectively through a full range of movement.

Who uses flexibility training?

Everyone who wants a basic health-related fitness level can benefit from a suitably designed flexibility programme. It is a valuable training activity for almost all sports and is particularly important for gymnasts, dancers, skaters and hurdlers.

Pressure training

Pressure training is a method for putting a technique or skill under stress. Pressure can be applied in a number of different ways, for example:

- You might make the performer work very hard for a period of time. This combines skill and fitness work. As the performer tires, the skill level will drop. The practice will increase fitness levels and help the performer to play better when tired. For example, in football you might alternate heading the ball and sprinting.
- A coach can also apply pressure by forcing a performer to react very quickly. In basketball the jump shooter could receive the ball from a player who is between him and the basket. As he receives it, the player runs at the shooter and attempts to block the shot. The pressure to receive the ball, and to prepare and execute the shot in a short period of time is similar to a competitive situation and will lead to improvement within the game itself.

Why use pressure training?

Pressure training is used to imitate the conditions experienced by sportspeople during competition. If performers can continue to reproduce a high level of skill when fatigued or mentally stressed they are far more likely to be successful in a game situation.

Who uses pressure training?

Pressure training should only be used when performers have developed their technique or skills to a high level. If the skill is not well learned the performers will repeatedly fail and lose motivation and confidence. This method is used with experienced performers in a wide range of games and sports.

Anaerobic and aerobic activity in training

Our bodies need energy so that our muscles can contract and make our body work. Our muscles can use energy only when it is in the form of a chemical compound called adenosine triphosphate, or ATP. Our muscles have only very small stores of this high-energy compound. As soon as it is used up we have to remake it. We can do this by using either of our two energy systems: the **anaerobic** or the **aerobic** system.

- **Anaerobic system**: our body works without oxygen as we cannot get enough to the muscles for them to work at the high rate demanded.
- **Aerobic system**: there is a constant supply of oxygen to the muscles enabling them to work hard, but not flat out.

The anaerobic system

The anaerobic system gives us both immediate energy and energy for the short term. In our muscles there are small stores of ATP which give enough energy for 5–8 seconds of hard work. This means that energy is available instantly, but will not last for long.

We can re-make ATP as quickly as we use up our muscle stores of ATP. To do this we use another chemical compound called creatine phosphate, which is stored in our muscles in small amounts. The extra energy we can gain from using up the creatine phosphate in our muscles will give us up to another 20 seconds of hard work.

When we work very hard the supplies of ATP and creatine phosphate in our muscles are quickly used up. As a result we breathe more quickly and deeply. This is in order to supply oxygen to the muscles to remake our ATP so that we can continue with the activity. Unfortunately, it takes some time for the oxygen to get into our bloodstream and to reach the working muscles. In the meantime, in order to keep our muscles working, our anaerobic system uses glycogen to remake the ATP.

We produce glycogen from the breakdown of carbohydrates in our food and we store it in our muscles and in our liver. Glycogen is carried in our blood and used to remake ATP in our muscles. However, if there is not enough oxygen available at the same time, then **lactic**

acid will be formed as well as ATP. If lactic acid builds up in the muscle it makes muscular contractions painful and we become tired. Therefore we cannot use the anaerobic system for very long. The energy from the anaerobic system will be enough for a maximum of about one minute of hard work.

Anaerobic respiration can be summarised as:

Glucose ⟶ energy + lactic acid

Oxygen debt and lactic acid
When we use the anaerobic system we produce an oxygen deficit – that is, our muscles need more oxygen than they can get at the time. As we saw above, we can continue the activity by using glycogen, but the disadvantage is that we also produce lactic acid.

A build-up of lactic acid causes muscle fatigue. This makes us feel tired and our working muscles start to stiffen and ache. This will force us to stop and rest eventually if no more oxygen is supplied.

If we are able to carry on, at the end of the exercise we have to rest and take in the extra oxygen we need to remove the lactic acid. This makes up our oxygen deficit.

The extra oxygen we have to take in at the end of the activity is called the **oxygen debt**.

activity

Feel the burn!
Feel the effects of lactic acid by straightening and curling your index finger as quickly as possible and for as long as possible. Discuss the effects as muscle fatigue begins to occur.

Taking in oxygen allows us to remove the lactic acid, replace the oxygen stores in our bodies and to build up ATP and creatine phosphate supplies.

The anaerobic system and sport
The anaerobic system is very important:

- for sprinters, throwers, gymnasts and judo players who need bursts of explosive speed

- for 100-metre swimmers, 200-metre runners or sprint cyclists who need to make a sustained effort over a short period of time
- for players of all games involving continuous short bursts of activity, including tennis, hockey, cricket and netball.

After activity, we need to rest to allow our bodies to refill their creatine phosphate stores. Some sportspeople take food supplements containing creatine which they believe will help them improve their performance.

The aerobic system

The function of the aerobic system is to give us long-term energy. It can be used only when enough oxygen reaches the working muscles. The aerobic system is used for all light exercise, including most of our daily activities. It gives us energy much more slowly than the anaerobic system.

During exercise or activity, the working muscles use up the ATP stores in the muscle and glycogen and oxygen together remake the ATP. But as enough oxygen is now available, lactic acid is not formed and the waste products are carbon dioxide and water, which do not cause tiredness. Therefore we can continue to use the aerobic system for a long time.

The energy provided by the aerobic system comes from using glucose, formed by the breakdown of carbohydrates and fats, combined with a plentiful supply of oxygen. Although this gives us energy much too slowly for intensive activity, it can supply energy for a very long time.

Aerobic respiration can be summarised as:

Glucose + Oxygen ⟶ Energy + Carbon dioxide + Water

Energy systems and sport

This aerobic system is important for nearly all sportspeople. It is very important for those who need energy over a long period of time – such as runners, cyclists, swimmers and games players. But the energy we need for different sports varies a great deal.

- A shot-putter uses one huge burst of energy lasting just a few seconds. This comes from the anaerobic system; energy from the aerobic system would take too long to arrive.
- A 100-metre sprint swimmer needs a longer, but still quite short burst of energy. The swim will take more than eight seconds so the creatine phosphate supplies would soon be exhausted. The aerobic system will not be able to supply oxygen fast enough. The swimmer will therefore rely on the anaerobic system to supply the energy needed. At the end of the swim there will be an oxygen debt.
- A marathon runner needs a continuous supply of energy over a long period and has no need of the anaerobic energy system. He or she must rely on a well developed aerobic system to send a steady stream of oxygen to the muscles over a long period of time.

In many sports the two energy systems work together at different times to supply the particular type of energy needed. For example, a hockey player will need the anaerobic system when shooting for goal and when repeatedly sprinting short distances, and the aerobic system when jogging into position when the ball is out of play.

% aerobic	Events		Primary energy sources
0	weight lifting 200 m	100 m	
10	wrestling 100 m swim	basket ball 400 m	Anaerobic system
20	tennis		
30		soccer	
40			
	800 m		
50	boxing		Anaerobic and aerobic system
60	rowing		
		1500 m	
70		800 m swim	
80	2 mile run		aerobic system
90	skating 10 km	cross country run	
100	jogging		

The anaerobic system works without oxygen and supplies our muscles with energy quickly. In contrast, the aerobic system must have oxygen to work and only supplies energy slowly to our muscles.

To train your energy systems for your particular sport you need to know to what extent you use each energy system. You can then decide, with your coach, what type of training is likely to improve your performance. You will also need to think about training thresholds and **training target zones**.

Training thresholds and target zones

To train effectively you must know:

- your present level of fitness
- the amount of anaerobic training you need for your sport
- the amount of aerobic training you need for your sport

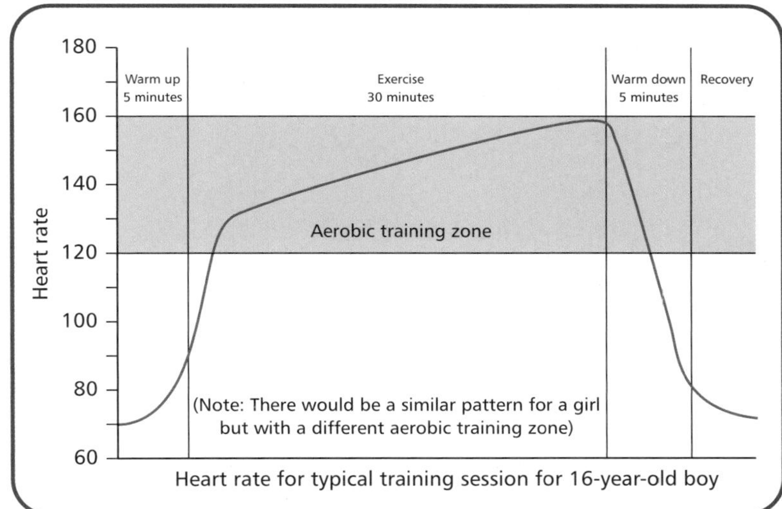

Heart rate for typical training session for 16-year-old boy

- your target, or training, zone. This refers to the range of heart rates within which you need to work in order to bring about a specific training result. For example, a runner may have an aerobic training zone of between 120 and 160 beats per minute. This means he or she must keep a pulse rate of between 120 and 160 beats per minute in order to have an effect on aerobic fitness.

Maximum heart rate

To work out our target zone, we need to know our maximum aerobic capacity (VO_2 Max), which involves scientific calculation. Fortunately there is a very close link between our VO_2 Max and our maximum heart rate (MHR), and we can use MHR instead.

As we saw earlier, maximum heart rate can be estimated in the following way:

- MHR males = 220 minus age
- MHR females = 226 minus age.

For example, a 16-year-old male has an MHR of 220 – 16 = 204 beats per minute. For a female of the same age, the MHR would be 210 beats per minute.

(Remember that the percentages of MHR which we give here are only approximate. Personal levels of activity and fitness will cause differences. The less fit we are the lower our training thresholds will be.)

Aerobic target zone

When we train in this zone we improve aerobic fitness. To achieve this we need to exercise above our aerobic threshold, which means keeping our heart rate between 60–80% of our MHR.

For a typical 16-year-old athlete, the aerobic target zone would therefore be:

- Male: 60–80% of 204 = 120–160 beats per minute
- Female: 60–80% of 210 = 125–170 beats per minute.

Anaerobic target zone

When we train in this zone we improve our anaerobic fitness. To achieve this we need to exercise above our anaerobic threshold, which means keeping our heart rate above 80% of MHR. For a typical 16-year-old athlete, the anaerobic target zone would therefore be:

- Male: 80%+ of 204 = over 160 beats per minute
- Female: 80%+ of 210 = over 170 beats per minute.

Recovery rates

Whenever we exercise, our heart rate increases to supply more oxygen to our working muscles. As a result our pulse rate increases from its resting level to a higher level depending on how hard we work. (Our pulse rate is simply our heart rate measured at the wrist or throat.)

A sportsperson's fitness can be estimated by checking their resting pulse rate. The fitter they are, the lower will be their resting pulse rate. A fit person will have a larger and stronger heart than an unfit

Resting pulse rates: comparative scores

85 and above	Poor
70–84	Average
56–69	Good
55 and under	Excellent

person. This means that a fit heart can supply the same amount of blood to the muscles but uses fewer beats than an unfit heart. Therefore the resting pulse for the fit heart is lower.

However, a better way of measuring fitness is to work out how long a person's pulse rate takes to return to normal after exercise. This is called the **recovery rate**.

During the recovery period the body deals with the oxygen debt. This is achieved by breathing deeply, transporting more oxygen from the lungs and removing the lactic acid. The recovery process is helped by gentle aerobic exercise immediately after the vigorous activity. This aids the removal of lactic acid, reduces the possible effect of muscle soreness and improves recovery time.

activity

Measuring recovery rate

You can estimate your recovery rate by comparing your heart rate before and after exercise.

Working in pairs, record your pulse rate at rest. Then run 400 metres as quickly as possible and after finishing, record your pulse every 30 seconds for the next five minutes. By recording and plotting your findings, you will be able to compare the results and discuss the reasons for any differences.

QUESTIONS

12 Methods of training

1 Training methods can be aerobic or anaerobic.

a Explain the difference between aerobic and anaerobic. *(2 marks)*

b Give an aerobic training method. Explain why it is aerobic. *(2 marks)*

c Give an anaerobic training method. Explain why it is anaerobic. *(2 marks)*

2 Weight training is often used to improve strength. Athletes vary the amount of weight and the number of sets and reps completed in order to train specifically.

a Describe a suitable programme to improve maximum strength. *(3 marks)*

b Describe a suitable programme to improve muscular power. *(3 marks)*

c Describe a suitable programme to improve muscular endurance. *(3 marks)*

3 Explain how recovery rates can be used to indicate fitness levels. *(3 marks)*

4 Knowledge of training thresholds and training zones helps us to plan effective training sessions. (AQA A only)

a Explain how knowledge of training thresholds helps us to train effectively. *(3 marks)*

b Explain how calculating training zones helps us to train effectively. *(3 marks)*

5 For each type of fitness listed, name a type of training and give an example of a training activity that would improve it.

a Stamina *(2 marks)*

b Muscular endurance *(2 marks)*

c Muscular power *(2 marks)*

d Agility. *(2 marks)*

6 There are a number of different types of training. Each is suitable for a number of sports. (AQA B only)

a Name two sports for which continuous training is suitable. *(2 marks)*

b Name two sports for which circuit training is suitable. *(2 marks)*

c Name two sports for which interval training is suitable. *(2 marks)*

d Name two sports for which flexibility training is suitable. *(2 marks)*

7 Choose a sport and describe four methods of training to include in a training programme. Explain why each method is suitable. *(8 marks)*

8 Explain how improvements in fitness can be brought about by monitoring exercise levels when training. *(8 marks)*

Factors affecting performance

13 Physiological factors

We are all born with ability. Some have more sporting ability than others, but ability alone does not guarantee success. Training, lifestyle, environment – these and many other factors can affect our sporting performance. As sports performers, we need to be aware of the importance of rest and of the potential dangers of alcohol and other social drugs.

Sometimes sporting performance is affected by influences that are difficult to control. All sportspeople are under pressure to do well, and in some cases the pressure to succeed can be destructive. We must all learn to recognise and cope with stress. We must also take account of our environment when performing if we are to be safe and competitive.

activity

Profile of a superstar

Working in pairs or a small group, make a list of five world-class sporting players/performers, past or present. Describe each player, considering especially:

- their age when at the peak of their career
- the length of their career
- their physique – size, body shape, etc.
- their personality – angry? calm? shy? confident? etc.
- their behaviour – any press reports that you have read, positive or negative.

Discuss your findings, comparing each of your superstars. Look for similarities and try to develop a profile of a highly successful sportsperson.

KEYWORDS

Ectomorph: a body type with little fat or muscle and a narrow shape

Endomorph: fat and pear-shaped body type

Environment: physical surroundings and conditions in which we play sport

Fatigue: tiredness as a result of physical activity, caused by a build-up of lactic acid in the muscles

Mesomorph: muscular and wedge-shaped body type

Physiological factors: factors which refer to the body

Somatotyping: method of classifying body types.

Key to Exam Success

For your GCSE you will need to know:

- how performance is affected by age
- the effect of lifestyle on sporting performance
- the effect of gender on sports performance
- why performance is affected by illness
- which body types are best for certain sports
- how and when fatigue occurs, and its effect on performance

how the environment affects performance

“ KEY THOUGHTS ”

‘Preparation is the key to success in sport.’

How does age affect our performance?

Childhood and adolescence

We grow very quickly in the first two years of our lives. Our rate of growth then slows down until we reach puberty. We then grow very rapidly, with girls reaching full height at about 16 and a half years, and boys reaching full height at about 18 years.

If we exercise regularly during childhood and adolescence, we are likely to establish a healthy pattern of activity for the rest of our life. Exercise also helps our bones to grow properly.

As our nervous system grows, our balance, agility and co-ordination improve. Children have much more control over their movements as their body systems develop. Their performances in most sports will improve as they approach physical maturity. However, in some sports, for example women's gymnastics, a mature body may not necessarily be an advantage.

Training can improve the strength, aerobic capacity and anaerobic capacity of young sportspeople. Training programmes must be designed for specific age groups. During childhood, strength can be increased by careful resistance training. But care must be taken not to damage the growth areas at the end of our long bones by, for example, heavy weight training before our bones are fully formed.

Physical maturity and beyond

Sports records suggest that we are in our prime for most sports during our twenties. After this age, our physical powers in both strength and endurance activities decline by about 1–2% a year.

From our mid-twenties:

- Our MHR decreases at about the rate of one beat per minute per year. As a result the training threshold is lowered.
- Our arteries gradually lose their elasticity. This increases our blood pressure and reduces the blood flow to our working muscles.
- Our maximum stroke volume, heart output and the vital capacity of our lungs all steadily decrease. These changes mean that less oxygen is carried to our working muscles and our VO_2 Max decreases.
- Our maximum strength decreases because our muscles reduce in size.
- Our muscle fibres change to slow-twitch rather than fast-twitch.

- Our body fat builds up steadily over the years, leading to increased weight. We exercise less, eat more and are less able to make use of fat for energy.

Our steady decline in physical ability is due mainly to a reduced amount of regular aerobic activity. However, we can slow down the effects of ageing on our cardiovascular and muscular systems by continuing to exercise.

How do gender differences affect performance?

Boys and girls mature at a similar rate and have similar body shapes and similar amounts of bone, muscle and fat until the age of about 9 or 10. Sporting competition between the sexes is quite fair at this stage.

Body size and shape

At puberty, boys develop larger bones and there is a big increase in their muscle size. This is due to the release of the hormone testosterone, an anabolic (growth-producing) steroid. Adolescent boys are larger and more muscular than girls.

For girls, the release of oestrogen results in breast development, broadening of the hips as well as increased body fat. Women have more fat in the hips and lower body, whilst men carry more fat in the abdomen and upper body.

Women have narrower shoulders, broader hips and smaller chest diameters. Women need wide hips for childbearing. As a result their legs are in a less mechanically efficient position for running.

None of these differences need affect the training programmes for girls and women, but they do have an effect on overall sporting performance.

Strength

Women are generally weaker than men. However, when their body size is taken into account, the differences are not significant. Men are much stronger in the upper body than women. When women train with weights, it is body tone which is increased rather than body size. With men, weight training helps muscles become larger and stronger because of their high levels of testosterone.

Aerobic capacity

Up to the age of 10, girls and boys have the same oxygen-carrying capacity. But while boys' capacity develops throughout puberty, girls stop improving after the age of 12. The best male competitors in endurance events are better than the best females by at least 30%. The differences are due to women's smaller lungs and hearts, as well as their smaller amount of blood. Women also have up to 30% less haemoglobin in their blood. This means that less oxygen reaches their working muscles.

None of these differences need affect the training programmes for girls and women. However, it is important that women take sufficient iron in their diet, as they lose iron in blood during menstruation.

The differences in times and distances achieved in sport between men and women are becoming smaller. It is vital that women have equal opportunity to take part in sporting activities and are given every encouragement to do so.

Body types

Using a method of body typing known as **somatotyping** it is possible to classify the enormous range of different body types into three main categories: **endomorphs**, **mesomorphs** and **ectomorphs**.

In practice, these extreme body types are rare. We are all part-endomorph, part-mesomorph and part-ectomorph. We can be given a score (from 1–7) for each of these basic body types. For example: 2, 6, 3 means: 2 (low endomorphy); 6 (high mesomorphy); 3 (low ectomorphy). In this way we can compare our body type with that of other people. Height is not taken into account in working out our body type.

Somatotyping is too lengthy and complicated a procedure to carry out in college and school. But it is interesting to look at – say – an athletics team and sort the athletes into approximate body types. The throwers are likely to be endomorphs, the long-distance runners ectomorphs and the sprinters mesomorphs.

Endomorphs are wider front to back than side to side and have:

- a pear-shaped body
- wide hips and wide shoulders
- a rounded head
- a lot of fat on the body, upper arms and thighs.

Mesomorphs are narrow from front to back and have:

- a wedge-shaped body
- wide shoulders and narrow hips
- a large cubical head
- broad shoulders and heavily muscled arms and legs
- a minimum amount of fat.

Ectomorphs have:

- narrow shoulders and hips
- a narrow chest and abdomen
- thin arms and legs
- a high forehead and receding chin
- little muscle and little fat.

Most successful sportspeople are high in mesomorphy. They are suited to sports requiring explosive strength and power. Their muscular bulk also helps them in contact sports.

Those who are high in endomorphy should work to develop their strength and control their diet. They are likely to do well in sports needing power but only limited movement, such as weight lifting and wrestling.

People who are high in ectomorphy could develop endurance and may be successful at long-distance events such

as running or cycling. By developing muscular strength they may also do well in many non-contact sports. Tall ectomorphs may find that they are suited to basketball and high jump.

The right lifestyle

We should keep our bodies healthy as part of our preparation for sport. This involves developing hygienic habits, such as showering and changing clothes after taking part in sport. Regular exercise will help us to maintain a level of general fitness that will keep us alert. It is also essential to get enough sleep and rest if we are to perform well.

The importance of sleep and rest

We will not be able to train or compete effectively if we do not get enough sleep. Most people need between seven and nine hours' sleep every night. If our pattern of sleep is disrupted, then our sporting performance suffers and we find it more difficult to make decisions and co-ordinate movements. Our sleep patterns can be disturbed by drinking alcohol or caffeine, smoking or eating high-protein meals shortly before going to bed.

Rest is essential for us to recover physically and mentally from the activities of the day. Rest is not the same as sleep. Rest is especially important for sports-people who train and compete at a high level. Lack of motivation and 'staleness' are direct results of a lack of rest.

How does fatigue affect our performance?

If we are tired from lack of sleep or rest between training sessions, we will not perform to our full potential. The major cause of fatigue in sport is playing or competing until we run out of energy. Fatigue causes us to slow down

activity

How much sleep and rest do you get?

List the number of hours you spent sleeping or resting each day last week. Add a comment if you wish to explain anything. Then analyse your sleep and rest pattern and explain the likely effect on your sporting performance.

Day	Hours of rest	Hours of sleep	Comment
Mon			
Tues			
Wed			
Thurs			
Fri			
Sat			
Sun			

considerably and it also affects our ability to perform certain techniques and skills. As fatigue develops, we make more mistakes and are more likely to suffer injury. When fatigued, we must rest and replenish our energy stores by eating carbohydrates.

The effects of illness

AQA B only

Although we may be fit for our sport our performance can be affected by short-term illness. Many of us carry on our everyday lives despite having a heavy cold, but we would not be able to play sport whilst sniffling.

Colds and 'flu

Colds are caused by viruses. The symptoms include raised temperature, headache and sore throat. The cold will also congest our nose and chest. As we fight the virus, our body feels fatigued and our heart rate is higher than normal. If we try to play sport we will find it difficult to get oxygen to the muscles and will be unable to continue at pace for a prolonged period. Our decision-making will also be slower and less clear when we have a cold.

Influenza ('flu) is also caused by a virus. It is often confused with a cold. In reality influenza does not begin with a sore throat as colds do. Its symptoms hit us very quickly and we are laid low with a high temperature and severe aches to our body. It is impossible to play sport when suffering from 'flu.

Hay fever

Hayfever is an allergic reaction to pollen. It leads to sneezing, itchy eyes and sometimes a wheezy chest. Sportspeople who suffer from hay fever will find it difficult to perform, especially out of doors where pollen levels are high. The sufferer will feel the same effects as someone with a cold. Although remedies exist, they only reduce the symptoms and cannot defeat the allergy completely.

Anaemia

Anaemia causes feelings of fatigue because the blood cannot carry enough oxygen to the muscles. A good supply of oxygen is vital for performance in most sports, and anaemia will dramatically reduce the performance of endurance athletes. An iron-rich diet, or iron supplements, can help to restore haemoglobin levels in the red blood cells and ensure that the sportsperson has enough energy to perform well.

Asthma

Asthma is not an illness, but a medical condition that appears to have a number of possible causes, including a reaction to exercise ('exercise asthma'). Asthma causes the air passages in the lungs to constrict, making it very difficult to breathe. Sportspeople need to be able to breathe freely to provide a supply of oxygen to the muscles. Asthma affects this process, but can be controlled through the use of inhalers before exercise and a large dose of determination.

Famous asthmatics in UK sport include footballers Paul Scholes and Ian Wright, cricketer Ian Botham and swimmer Nick Gillingham. We should always remember that the fitter we are, the better our lungs work. Asthma sufferers can only benefit by exercising regularly.

How does the environment affect performance?

The term **environment** is used to describe the physical surroundings and conditions in which we play sport. As sport is played around the world and throughout the year, sportspeople have to contend with a wide variety of different surroundings. Sometimes environmental factors can have a huge impact on performance.

Altitude

Many endurance athletes choose to train at high altitude as the lower oxygen level in the 'thin' air makes extra demands on the body. In time, the body adapts by producing extra red blood cells and improving the ability to carry oxygen to the muscles.

If we compete at altitude, the lack of oxygen causes fatigue to occur much more quickly than at sea-level. Mexico City has hosted the Olympic Games and a football World Cup, in spite of the fact that it lies at 2,300 m – higher than many mountain ski resorts! Footballers and athletes can spend time 'acclimatising' to conditions at these higher altitudes, but the pace of matches and the times of endurance events, such as the marathon and the 10,000 m, are still much slower than at lower altitudes.

Pollution

Mexico City also has a high level of pollution, caused by car exhausts and industrial fumes. As the pollutant gases, such as sulphur dioxide and carbon monoxide, are breathed into the body, there is less oxygen available to the muscles. This increases fatigue and reduces the ability of sportspeople to perform at a high level for a prolonged period of time. Pollution is also a factor in many other parts of the world. Some sportsmen and women pollute themselves by breathing in cigarette smoke, which has the same effect.

Humidity

Humidity refers to the dampness of the air. High humidity levels are a feature of tropical countries. When humidity levels are high, our sweat, which normally evaporates from our skin, cannot escape and our clothes become very wet. Sweating is the main way that we lose excess body heat when we play sport. If the air is humid, our bodies produce a lot of sweat to prevent us from overheating. However, we can still overheat very quickly. This leads to fatigue and, if we continue, can lead to heat exhaustion due to the large amount of water lost (dehydration).

In humid conditions sportspeople must drink small quantities continuously while performing, and pace themselves to avoid exhaustion.

Extreme weather conditions

The weather presents many difficulties for sportspeople. Skiers and snowboarders need snow on the ground, but cannot take part in their sport when snow is falling. Athletes cannot compete in extremely cold conditions. Footballers can continue in the rain, but cricketers cannot. Tennis players enjoy warm weather, but their performance is badly affected if the wind is high. Windsurfers look for strong winds to aid their performances. The risk of injury is greater when the weather is cold, skill levels drop in high wind and heat exhaustion becomes an issue when the temperature rises.

QUESTIONS

13 Physiological factors

1 Give three examples of the negative effects of age on sporting performance.

(3 marks)

2 Certain body types are more suitable for some sports than others.

a Name three different body types.

(3 marks)

b Name a sport which is most suitable for each body type.

(3 marks)

3 Lifestyle can have an effect on performance.

a How does a lack of sleep affect performance?

(2 marks)

b Why is rest essential when training?

(2 marks)

c Why does having a cold affect performance?

(2 marks)

d How should asthma sufferers view exercise?

(2 marks)

4 Using examples from sport, describe ways in which the environment affects performance.

(4 marks)

14 Drugs

Drugs are chemical substances that can affect our bodies. Medical drugs are made to fight illness and disease. The use of banned drugs in sport is known as doping. As sportspeople we need to know about the potential dangers of social and performance-enhancing drugs.

activity

Guilty or not guilty?

Name: Alain Baxter

Sport: Slalom skiing

Event: 2002 Winter Olympics (bronze medal)

Tested positive for: Methamphetamine, a banned stimulant

Defence claim: Baxter regularly uses a nasal inhaler which does not contain any banned substance. He bought the same brand of inhaler in the USA without realising that it contained the banned stimulant methamphetamine.

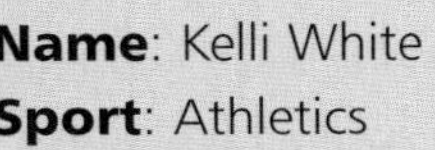

Name: Kelli White

Sport: Athletics

Event: 100 and 200 metres World Championships, Paris 2003 (gold medallist for 100 metres and 200 metres)

Tested positive for: Modafinil, a stimulant

Defence claim: Drug is not on the IAAF banned list. It was prescribed to her to treat sleepiness caused by narcolepsy (sleeping sickness).

Name: Mark Bosnich

Sport: Football

Event: Random testing

Tested positive for: Cocaine, an illegal banned stimulant

Defence claim: He took the drug unwittingly as his drink had been spiked on a night out.

Discuss the drug abuse cases above. Imagine you are one of the panel members meeting to decide whether or not the athlete should be banned from sport. In making your decision you should consider the effects on:

- the athlete who has tested positive
- other athletes in the same competition
- athletes in the sport worldwide
- young people who may see the athlete as a role model.

KEYWORDS

Doping: use of illegal drugs to obtain unfair advantage in sport

Social drugs: legal and widely used drugs such as alcohol and nicotine that are available within social situations

Performance-enhancing drugs: banned drugs used illegally by sportspeople to gain unfair advantage in competition.

Key to Exam Success

For your GCSE you will need to know:

- the effects of smoking, alcohol and social drugs on health and physical performance
- the effects of performance-enhancing drugs on sport.

Social drugs

When we play sport we often become part of a social group that meets after training and after competition. Adult sportspeople often meet in bars. Many sports clubs earn money from running a successful clubhouse bar. The drugs that are available within social situations are known as **social drugs**. Some are legal and are widely used. Other social drugs are illegal, but are still used by a number of people.

Name of drug	Type of drug	General effect
Alcohol	Depressant	Slows down how body works
Amphetamines	Stimulant	Speeds up nervous system. Fights fatigue
Caffeine	Stimulant	Increases heart rate. Increases alertness
Cannabis	Depressant	Reduces worry but slows down responses
Cocaine	Stimulant	Speeds up the nervous system. Creates feeling of well-being
Ecstasy	Stimulant	Increases confidence and sense of well-being
LSD	Hallucinogen	Changes the way we see and understand things
Nicotine (tobacco)	Stimulant	Increases heart rate. Increases concentration level

Social drugs and sport

Alcohol

Alcohol has a number of effects on our sports performance.

- **Reduced co-ordination, slower reaction time and poorer balance**: these changes affect our movements and skills, especially where catching and balance are involved, and reduce the steadiness needed in sports such as archery, gymnastics and shooting.
- **Dehydration**: alcohol is a diuretic and increases urine production. This leads to water loss from the body. Dehydration seriously affects performance in endurance events and on hot days.
- **Lower muscle glycogen levels and slower removal of lactic acid**: muscle glycogen is needed during endurance events. Lactic acid is produced during exercise and must be removed quickly. Drinking alcohol before any sport involving endurance will reduce performance and delay recovery afterwards.
- **Rapid loss of heat**: alcohol causes the blood vessels in the skin to open up. We lose heat quickly through our skin, which reduces our body temperature, although we feel warm. If we are in a cold environment, hypothermia can develop.
- **Longer injury recovery time**: RICE (see page 95) is used to reduce the blood flow to an injured area. Alcohol has the opposite effect. Recovery time will be increased. If you receive an injury during a match you should not drink alcohol afterwards.
- **Reduced size of arteries**: alcohol reduces the size of the arteries, so that less blood can flow along them. Heart rate and blood pressure both increase.

Alcohol also affects our:

- thinking, judgement, vision and hearing
- stomach (and can cause vomiting)
- liver, as it takes a long time to process
- weight, as it is very high in kilojoules.

Nicotine

Smoking has many effects on our sporting performance:

- **Reduced lung efficiency**: the smoke damages the hairs lining the bronchial tubes. Dust is not removed from the air so our lungs become clogged and do not work efficiently. We need efficient lungs for all sport.
- **Reduced oxygen-carrying ability**: carbon monoxide is taken into the lungs in cigarette smoke and passes into the blood. It attaches to red blood cells, reducing the amount of oxygen we can carry in our blood. This affects endurance activities.
- **Reduced fitness level**: even if we train hard, our fitness level will be reduced because of the damage to our lungs and circulatory system caused by smoking.
- **Lowered resistance to illness**: colds are caught more often and smokers take longer to recover from chest infections. Smoker's cough is a special hazard, as is bronchitis. Sportspeople need to keep well to train and compete.
- **Raised blood pressure**: nicotine causes our brain to release hormones which make the heart beat faster and the blood vessels in the skin to contract. This causes an increase in blood pressure and a feeling of being cold.

Smoking also affects our:

- **life expectancy**: smokers are at much higher risk of cancer and cardiovascular disease.
- **social standing**: we breathe harmful and unpleasant fumes on people around us. We also smell of stale tobacco.
- **senses**: by dulling our sense of taste and smell.
- **appetite**: by reducing it.

Other social drugs

- **Amphetamines** increase heart rate and blood pressure. They hide symptoms of fatigue and reduce feelings of pain. They are addictive and can cause anxiety and aggression.
- **Caffeine** is a mild stimulant found in tea, coffee and many soft drinks. It increases heart rate and blood pressure. This is not useful to endurance athletes.
- **Cannabis**, or **marijuana**, can result in lack of motivation and poor judgement. Since it is smoked in tobacco, it causes the same problems as cigarette smoking. It has no role to play in sport.
- **Cocaine** is a highly addictive stimulant. It encourages us to think that we are doing better than we are. This is no help in sport, where good judgement is essential.
- **Ecstasy** is a stimulant with mild hallucinogenic properties. It is not useful in sport because it affects our perceptions. Performance can also be affected the day after Ecstasy has been used, because of the negative effects of the 'come down'.
- **LSD** distorts reality and affects the ability to perceive situations and make decisions. The effects of LSD can often be felt in the form of 'flashbacks' long after the drug has been taken. This drug has no place in sport.

Performance-enhancing drugs

Types of performance-enhancing drug

Performance-enhancing drugs take many forms. In the table below, drugs that have similar effects are grouped together.

Some drugs are restricted in certain sports, but are not completely banned. These include all the illegal social drugs and alcohol.

Other proscribed methods of enhancing performance are:

- blood doping (see page 232)
- changing blood samples, or interfering with them in any way
- using masking agents to hide the use of a performance-enhancing drug.

Other restricted drugs

Drug	General effect
Beta blockers	Keep heart rate and blood pressure low, reduce tremble in hands; banned in archery and shooting
Corticosteroids (Cortisone)	Reduce inflammation and pain, masking effects of injury
Local anaesthetics	Reduce pain, masking effects of injury and allowing sports performance to continue

Dwain Chambers tested positive for the designer steroid THG and in February 2004 was banned from competition for two years.

Doping class	Examples	General effect
Anabolic agents	Nandrolone, Testosterone, Stanozolol, Clenbuterol, THG	Reduced recovery allows users to train harder and for longer. Increased muscle bulk and endurance when combined with regular exercise
Analgesics (narcotic)	Morphine, Methadone, Heroin	Pain-killing effect allows training and competing to continue even in times of injury
Diuretics	Frusemide, Probenecid	Rapid weight loss as result of reduction of fluid levels in body
Peptides, glycoprotein hormones and analogues	Human Growth Hormone (HGH), Erythropoietin (EPO)	Decreased fat mass. Thought to improve performance Increased number of red blood cells, more oxygen carried to body, endurance improved
Stimulants	Amphetamines, Cocaine, Ephedrine	Speeds up nervous system, quickening reactions. Masks fatigue and feelings of pain

Prohibited drugs in sport

All the performance-enhancing drugs and methods described on page 229 are banned throughout sport. Even nicotine and caffeine levels have to be below a prescribed limit in most sports.

The list of prohibited drugs contains over 1,000 substances and is regularly updated. Sportspeople must check the list before taking any medicine because some banned drugs are contained in standard medicines. These include the steroid clenbuterol, which is used in asthma treatment.

In January 2004 caffeine and pseudo-ephedrine (contained in many over-the-counter cold remedies) were removed from the banned substances list.

Sports performers must be aware that drugs can sometimes be found in the food supplements given to athletes by coaches. These include the steroids nandrolone and THG. A breakthrough in testing enabled the authorities to identify THG, and a number of athletes including world indoor 1,500 m champion Regina Jacobs and British sprinter Dwain Chambers tested positive for it.

As a result of a number of positive drugs tests in 2003, UK Sport issued the following statement:

> 'No guarantee can be given that any particular supplement is free from prohibited substances as these products are not licensed and are not subject to the same strict manufacturing and labelling requirements as licensed medicines.'

In May 2003 Czech tennis player Bohdan Ulihrach was suspended after testing positive for nandrolone, an anabolic steroid. He was the first of a number of professional tennis players to test positive during 2002/3. He has now had his punishment cancelled, as the food supplement was supplied to him by trainers belonging to the ATP (Association of Tennis Professionals).

UK Sport's Nandrolone Review Group have given this advice:

> 'Competitors are strongly advised that using dietary supplements carries the potential risk of unknowingly taking a banned substance.'

Michele Verroken, Director of Drug-Free Sport at UK Sport, commented: 'Athletes should look at suitable alternatives to taking supplements, the main one of course being to eat a balanced and healthy diet.'

Steroids

Anabolic agents, or steroids, can be taken orally or by injection. They have positive effects upon performance because, when combined with extra exercise, they increase strength, muscle growth, body weight and endurance. They enable sportspeople to train more often and harder. However, they have serious side-effects which, for men, include:

- increased aggression
- impotence
- kidney damage
- baldness
- development of breasts.

Disadvantages for women include:

- increased aggression
- development of male features including facial and body hair
- irregular periods.

Narcotic analgesics

Morphine, methadone and heroin are members of the opiate family. They have a positive effect on sporting performance by reducing the feeling of pain. By doing this they mask injury or illness and allow sportspeople to compete when they should not.

The dangers of taking narcotic analgesics are that:

- injuries can be made much worse and even permanent
- they are highly addictive.

Diuretics

Diuretics are mainly used by sportspeople in sports where they have to 'make the weight' – that is, to fit into a weight category. These include horse racing, boxing, weight lifting and martial arts. The diuretic works by removing fluid from the body as urine, so the result is rapid weight loss. They are also used to remove other drugs from the body in order to beat the drug-testers.

The side-effects of diuretics include:

- dehydration
- cramps
- dizziness
- headaches
- nausea.

These conditions seriously affect the ability to play sport.

Peptide and glycoprotein hormones and analogues

These hormones are produced naturally in the body. Analogues are the same hormones produced artificially.

Erythropoietin (EPO) improves endurance by increasing the number of oxygen-carrying red blood cells. The disadvantages of using this type of drug are that it may:

- thicken the blood, so increasing the risk of a stroke and heart problems
- cause oily skin, acne and muscle tremors.

Blood testing for EPO has been introduced, in addition to taking urine samples, at many endurance events as the authorities have sought to keep sport drug-free.

Human Growth Hormone (HGH) encourages muscle growth, increases the use of fat and improves the body's ability to cope with fatigue. The dangers of this type of drug are that it may cause:

- abnormal growth, including enlargement of internal organs
- atherosclerosis and high blood pressure
- diabetes, arthritis and impotence.

Stimulants

Drugs such as amphetamines, ephedrine and cocaine can lead to an improvement in performance because they give a 'lift', keeping us awake and competitive, speeding up reflexes and reducing feelings of fatigue.

The dangers are that they:

- increase heart rate and blood pressure
- hide symptoms of fatigue, putting high levels of strain on the body that can even be fatal
- reduce feelings of pain with the risk of making injuries worse

- can lead to acute anxiety and aggressiveness
- are addictive.

Blood doping
Blood doping does not involve the use of drugs, but requires blood to be injected into the body to increase the number of red blood cells. Athletes usually inject their own blood, which has been removed earlier and stored, but blood can also come from another person. Blood doping makes the blood able to carry more oxygen to the working muscles. This increases aerobic endurance, which is an effect that can also be gained by training at altitude. Blood doping has a similar effect to the use of EPO.

Blood doping has several dangers:

- overloading the circulatory system, increasing blood pressure and causing difficulties for the heart
- kidney failure
- risk of transmission of AIDS and other diseases.

The campaign against doping in sport

The desire to win is very high amongst competitive sportspeople. If they believe that a drug will help them achieve their goal, they may be tempted to use it – and the temptation is even higher when success will lead to great financial rewards. The pressure to succeed, from the media and public as well as from coaches and managers, can be very great.

Many sports performers rationalise their decision to use drugs by arguing that other competitors are using drugs, and that without them they will have no chance of winning. Some use anabolic agents while being treated for injury in order to speed up the recovery process. To them, the practice is risky but acceptable. Although out-of-competition testing may catch them and lead to a ban, they believe that they will not get caught and are prepared to cheat in order to win.

The case against doping
The International Olympic Committee (IOC) does not allow doping for three main reasons:

- to ensure that competition in sport is as fair as possible
- to protect the health of sportspeople
- to protect the wholesome image of sport.

Drug rules: who decides?
Each sport has its own international sports federation (ISF) which controls its activities worldwide. The ISFs make their rules own about doping. In the case of Olympic sport, the sport must also follow the drug code of the International Olympic Committee (IOC). Each governing body in a country has the responsibility for testing sportspeople in and out of competition. In Britain, drug-testing is co-ordinated at the London office of UK Sport, with the support of national administrators in England, Northern Ireland, Scotland and Wales.

What penalties do drug-takers face?
Competitors who are found guilty of taking banned drugs are often banned from competing in their sport for a minimum of two years. The competitor will also face a loss of earnings from competition and sponsorship and will have to live with the personal disgrace of being revealed as a cheat.

activity

Looking for doping offences

Imagine that you are a member of the UK Sport drug-testing team.

1 List all the banned and restricted types of drugs.
2 Make a list of sports in which you would be likely to encounter each type of drug. Conduct an Internet search to confirm that each of the drugs on your list has been found in the sports that you have indicated.

QUESTIONS

14 Drugs

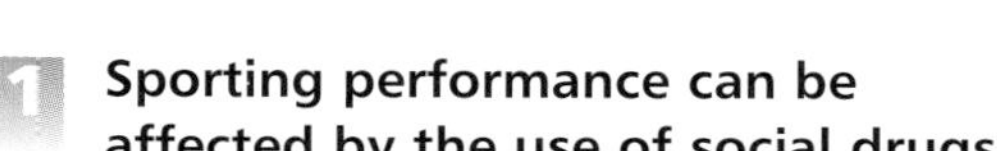

1 Sporting performance can be affected by the use of social drugs.

a Describe one general effect of smoking cigarettes and the effect this would have on sporting performance. *(2 marks)*

b Describe one general effect of drinking alcohol and the effect this would have on sporting performance. *(2 marks)*

c Describe one general effect of smoking cannabis and the effect this would have on sporting performance. *(2 marks)*

2 The use of banned drugs is a problem in many sports.

a Describe three reasons why sportspeople may be tempted to use banned drugs. *(3 marks)*

b Name and describe a banned performance-enhancing procedure that does not involve the use of drugs. *(3 marks)*

c EPO is now used by some endurance athletes and cyclists to gain an advantage. Describe the effects of EPO on the body and explain how this enhances performance in endurance events. *(3 marks)*

3 A number of performance-enhancing drugs are banned in sport. Describe the effect of each drug type and name one sport in which it is banned.

a Diuretics *(2 marks)*
b Amphetamines *(2 marks)*
c Steroids *(2 marks)*
d Narcotic analgesics. *(2 marks)*

4 How might drug use affect performance? *(8 marks)*

15 Psychological factors

Psychological factors are those which relate to the mind or mental processes. The three psychological factors which affect our sporting performance are closely linked. They are:

- **Personality**: our character and temperament
- **Motivation**: our determination to achieve success
- **Arousal**: the intensity of our motivation.

Our best performances are only possible when, with the help of our coach, we match our motivation level to our personality and achieve the right level of arousal.

KEYWORDS

Arousal: the intensity of our motivation

Extrovert: person who is carefree and socially outgoing

Feedback: information about the outcome of a performance

Introvert: person who is thoughtful and shy in company

Motivation: determination to achieve

Personality: our character and temperament

Psychological factors: factors which relate to the mind or mental processes

Skill: 'the learned ability to bring about a predetermined result with maximum certainty and efficiency; the ability to perform a physical task; the learned ability to choose and perform the right techniques at the right time' (AQA).

Key to Exam Success

For your GCSE you will need to know:

- how stress and anxiety affect performance
- AQA A only: which sports suit different personalities
- AQA A only: the importance of feedback
- AQA A only: the types of aggression seen in sport

How does our personality affect our performance?

Some researchers have described personalities called **extroverts** and **introverts**. In simple terms, we can say that extroverts are socially outgoing while introverts are shy in social situations. Research suggests that, although there are many exceptions to the rule, extroverts and introverts also prefer different types of sports.

Extroverts prefer:

- team sports
- activities involving the whole body
- activities involving much movement
- plenty of activity and unpredictability.

Introverts prefer:

- individual sports
- activities involving fine physical skills
- activities with limited movement
- routine and repetitive sports.

Extroverts seem to need high arousal levels to perform well. Introverts perform better at lower arousal levels.

What is arousal in sport?

In a sporting situation the intensity of our motivation is called **arousal**. The link between arousal and performance can be explained using the 'inverted U theory'. This theory suggests that our best performances come when we are moderately aroused. If our arousal

level is not high enough, we may feel bored and we will perform badly. This often happens when players or teams meet opposition of a supposedly lower standard. But if our arousal gets too high, we may become anxious and worried. This creates tension, which causes our performance to become less effective.

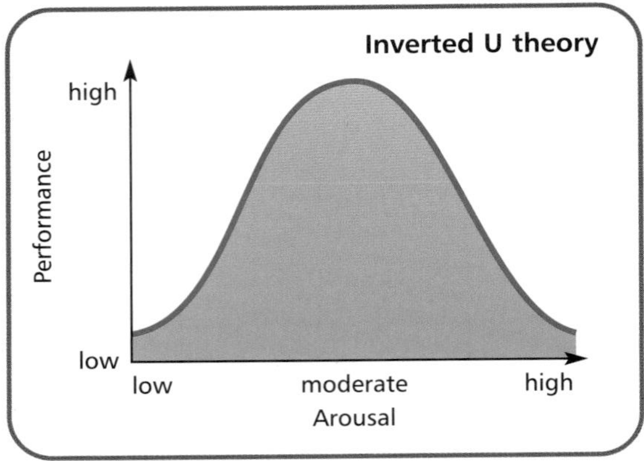

What are the different types of motivation?

- **Intrinsic (or self-) motivation** comes from our own inner drives. We may play for fun, for the satisfaction of performing well, for the pride in winning or for the enjoyment of taking part with others.
- **Extrinsic motivation** comes from rewards and outside pressures. We may play to win trophies, to please other people who are important to us or to avoid letting our team down.

Most motivation in sport is a mixture of both types. However, it is intrinsic motivation that will keep us interested in sport when extrinsic rewards are no longer there.

Coping with anxiety

It is natural to feel anxious about our performance before competition. Anxiety levels are often higher as the level of competition increases. An audience or crowd can also lift levels of anxiety, especially those of inexperienced players. However, as a coach or performer we must manage our level of anxiety, or stress, in order to perform to the best of our ability. Before performing we can help to do this by:

- **Thinking positively**: telling ourselves that we are good enough and that we will do well
- **Using mental rehearsal**: picturing ourselves carrying out successful movements and practising them in our mind
- **Relaxing**: through controlled breathing and by relaxing our body.

A good coach can also help us cope with anxiety by giving verbal reassurance, talking calmly to us and helping us to focus upon success.

activity

Looking at arousal

Working in groups of about 12, each player in turn attempts three free shots in netball or basketball under normal conditions. They then repeat the activity with a supportive audience, a totally silent audience and a hostile audience. The rest of the group provide the audience.

Discuss the results. Did the audience affect performance? How did the performer feel about each type of audience?

Aggression in sport

In sport we can compete against opponents, against standards of performance or pit ourselves against the natural environment. The amount and type of aggression involved varies from sport to sport.

- **Direct aggression** is a part of boxing, judo, rugby and many other sports. We have to be very aggressive to succeed at them. However, we must compete within their strict rules. Some sports require a limited amount of physical aggression. Players must be aggressive in hockey, football and basketball, but physical contact is limited by the rules of the games.
- **Indirect aggression** is used in sports such as volleyball and tennis. We hit the ball towards our opponents and the ball does the scoring rather than the player. In other words, the aggression is still aimed at the opponent but is directed through the ball. Aggressive players may find it difficult to mix both delicate and fierce shots.
- **Object aggression** is seen in some sports where an object rather than an opponent receives the aggression. For example, a golfer may hit the ball aggressively, but this does not guarantee success.

Some sports involve no aggression at all. For example, in ice skating, trampolining and archery there is no advantage in being aggressive.

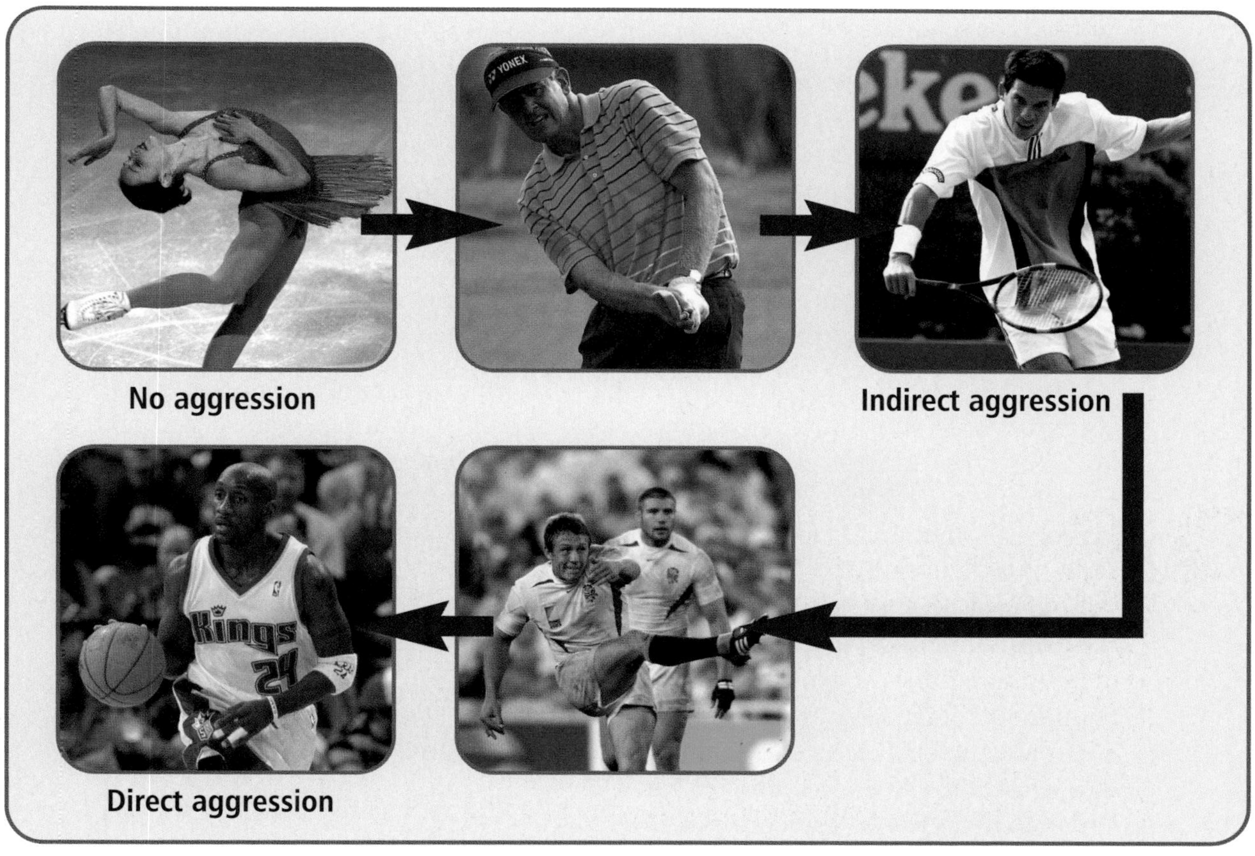

Psychology and sport

Successful coaching requires knowledge and understanding of players' personalities and the demands of the sport. Coaches have to know when to calm players down and when to 'psyche them up'. This is not always easy when dealing with a team which contains different personality types. Some team players can become over-aroused by the atmosphere created by their team-mates. The stress of being part of a team, or just partnering one other player, should not be underestimated. All team players must work together to ensure that everyone is performing at their optimum level.

How do we learn skills?

We all know that different sports involve an amazing variety of skills. Some people describe skills such as throwing a ball as **basic**, and more complicated skills, such as the spike in volleyball, as **complex**. Basic skills are often called **techniques**, with the term **skill** being reserved for complex combinations of movement. It is also possible to classify skills as being **open** or **closed**. We can place them on a continuum from 'open' at one end to 'closed' at the other.

- **Open** skills are skills that are affected by the whole sporting environment such as other players and the weather. An example of a sport involving open skills is lacrosse, which is played out of doors with a number of players. This gives it a lot of unpredictability. For example, each player must take account of opponents, team-mates, the speed of the ball, the surface of the pitch and the weather conditions. Players need open skills because they are not able to control what will happen next.
- **Closed** skills are used in a fixed environment where the performer has the situation under control. An example is a gymnast performing a vault, where the equipment is fixed and there are no influences from other people or the weather.

The skills continuum

We can place skills on a line (called a continuum) which goes from 'open' at one end to 'closed' at the other.

- **Judo** is placed towards the 'open' end, because the player must react to his or her opponent. However, the surface for competition is always the same, there is only opponent to consider and the weather has no effect. In this sense judo is not as 'open' as lacrosse.
- **Archery** is nearer to the 'closed' end, because the whole action is learned and repeated for competition. However, wind strength and direction will affect the flight of the arrow, so the skill involved is not completely closed.
- **High jump** could be placed near to the middle. The jump itself is a closed skill, but the run-up must take account of the weather, the runway surface and the height of the bar.

In some open sports, closed skills will be used. For example, squash and netball are open sports, but when players take a free serve or play a particular shot they are in control, and so the skill is a closed one.

Support for learning

We learn techniques and skills by practising. Our learning is affected by:

- the guidance given to us
- the type of practice we use
- the feedback we get

- the techniques we have already learned which can be transferred to the new skills.

Guidance

Guidance is given to us in three ways.

- **Visual**: demonstrations show us what we are required to do.
- **Verbal**: explanations must be brief and focus on the most important points.
- **Manual**: support will keep us safe and give us confidence.

All guidance must be easily understood and linked to our phase of skill learning.

Practice

Skills can be taught to us as a whole or broken down into parts (whole or part practice). If all the parts of the action take place at the same time we usually practise them as a whole – for example, cycling. Skills that use a number of techniques are usually practised in parts at first. For example, the basketball lay-up shot, which involves:

- footwork with the bounce
- the pick-up
- the jump
- the shot itself.

Massed practice means using long active sessions without rests. For example, a gymnast might spend an hour repeating the same vault.

Distributed (or **spaced**) **practice** means having rests between shorter practice periods. For example, a gymnast might have three sessions of vaulting practice in an hour, with other activities in between.

Long practice sessions can lead to tiredness and boredom, which may be dangerous for difficult activities.

Feedback

Feedback is vital information about our performance. By using feedback we are able to analyse and then improve our performance. We receive feedback from two sources:

- **Internal feedback** comes to us from our senses. The **proprioceptors** in our joints tell us how the shot felt and our eyes tell us whether or not we were successful.
- **External feedback** comes to us, for example, by watching ourselves on video, listening to our coach or being given our score.

There are two forms of external feedback. These are:

- **Knowledge of results**: these tell us the outcome of our performance – i.e. whether or not we scored the goal, how many points we were given or our position in the race.
- **Knowledge of performance**. This is about how well we performed and is partly internal. For example, skilled ice dancers will know how good their performance felt without needing to be told. They can also find out about the standard of their performance by talking to their coach or another observer.

Feedback is essential for skills learning. It is almost impossible to improve without knowledge of performance or knowledge of results. However, coaches must take care to give the right kind of feedback at the right time. A good coach will know what feedback to give, how much to give and when to give it. This will mainly depend upon the ability and experience of the performers (see Chapter 1, pages 00–00).

QUESTIONS

15 Psychological factors

1 Feedback helps us to learn skills.

a Explain what is meant by internal feedback.

(2 marks)

b Explain what is meant by external feedback.

(2 marks)

c List two types of external feedback.

(2 marks)

2 Performance can be affected by a number of psychological factors.

a Describe one type of personality and list two sports that these personalities prefer.

(3 marks)

b Explain how arousal levels affect performance.

(3 marks)

c Name two types of motivation and explain the difference between them.

(3 marks)

3 List three ways in which sports performers can manage anxiety levels.

(3 marks)

4 Skills can be classified as open and closed.

a List three sports or sporting actions that are examples of open skills.

(3 marks)

b List three sports or sporting actions that are examples of closed skills.

(3 marks)

5

a What do we mean by motivation in sport?

(2 marks)

b Suggest two sports that extroverts are likely to enjoy.

(2 marks)

c Give examples of two different types of aggression seen in sport.

(2 marks)

d How might performance be affected by too much or too little arousal?

(2 marks)

6 Stress and anxiety can affect performance in a number of ways. Describe some effects using a variety of sporting situations and player personalities in your answer.

(8 marks)

7 Some sports are preferred by specific personality types. Describe two types of personality and explain why some sports might suit them better than others.

(8 marks)

16 New technology

Sportspeople are always looking for new technology to help them improve their performance. Science makes advances all the time, and sports scientists are constantly watching the latest developments to apply the new ideas to sport.

In motor sports, racing cars, motorbikes and powerboats are now so powerful that rules have been introduced to keep top speeds down. In cycling, developments in frame design have revolutionised the sport. Modern materials keep racing bikes, hang gliders and sail boards both light and strong.

The greater speed of movement in many sports means that officials need help from new equipment in order to keep pace. In tennis the 'Cyclops' machine checks if a serve is in or out, and television replays are used to decide run-outs in cricket and tries in rugby.

Key to Exam Success

For your GCSE you will need to know:

- how technology can be used to improve performance.

In athletics, where races can be decided by very narrow margins, precision is essential. Gauges are used to measure wind speed and markers to record distances automatically. In sprint races, time-recording is electronically controlled. The gun and starting blocks are also linked in order to register false starts.

Equipment

New technology has improved sports equipment in many different ways.

- In tennis, players now hit the ball with much greater power, using tightly strung rackets with larger heads and graphite frames.
- Many years ago the introduction of the glass-fibre pole completely changed pole-vaulting. As heights increased, a need also arose for better landing areas.
- Highly aerodynamic javelins have had to be adapted to reduce the distance they can be thrown and ensure safety for spectators.
- In winter sports, changes to the design and materials for skis, bobsleighs and luges have led to increases in both speed and control.
- In archery, arrows of composite material travel further, faster and straighter.

Clothing

Improved technology means that clothing can now be adapted to meet the needs of a wide range of different sports.

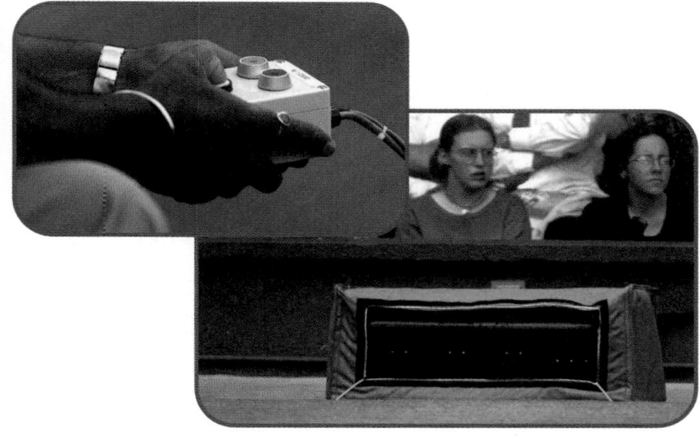

Materials can be:

- rain- and windproof, for adventurous activities
- heat-retaining, for sub-aqua sport
- heat-reducing, for distance athletes
- aerodynamic, for speed events
- hydrodynamic, for swimming events.

Sports shoes can also be specifically designed to improve performance, safety and comfort. Skiers need boots for skis, distance runners need shock-absorbing qualities and tennis players need grip for the different court surfaces. The use of light, impact-absorbing materials gives cricketers protection as well as mobility. At the Sydney Olympics, swimmers wore full-body suits based on the hydrodynamics of shark's skin in order to go faster in the water.

Facilities

All-weather artificial surfaces have helped many sports. Top-level athletics would be unthinkable today on any other surface. Hockey benefits from the speed and even bounce of articifial surfaces.

League football experimented with artificial pitches. Although the first pitches changed the game too much and were changed back to grass, Dunfermline Athletic FC has now installed a new type of pitch that looks and feels like grass. It stands up to wear and tear from studded boots and is in use in the Scottish Premier League.

Cricket still needs a natural surface for the complete game, but artificial surfaces are often used for practice. Of the top four tennis championships, only Wimbledon still uses grass. Most tennis at all levels is now played on a variety of synthetic surfaces.

Improvements in the design of specialist facilities have helped a number of sports. Gymnastics training has been made much safer by the use of landing areas placed below floor-level.

Modern all-glass squash courts have been built to make the game more suitable for showing on television.

ICT in training and coaching

Good coaches have always used their eyes to analyse performance. This is a very difficult task because of the speed of most sporting movements.

Using recent developments in ICT, it is possible to analyse performance much more accurately. Coaches can also collect and analyse information about performance in a variety of ways:

Technical information

Coaches can obtain technical information from many sources. Books and videos containing examples of technique and tactics are available in shops, but the Internet now enables coaches throughout the world to share their ideas. With a quick search, it is possible to find examples of good training practice and details of the latest developments in sports science within minutes.

Recording performance

Coaches can use digital camcorders to record sporting performance, then play it back at both normal speed and in slow motion to give immediate and valuable visual feedback.

Sportspeople can use similar methods to compare their actions with those of top performers, identifying, for example, differences in arm action, leg action, body position, speed of movement, etc.

Statistical analysis

Statistics can be used in various ways to analyse sporting performance. Many different aspects of performance can be recorded – for example, the number of shots, tackles and interceptions. A computer can then collate and analyse this information for immediate use.

Statistical analysis can be used to work out players' strengths and weaknesses. In a similar way, we can determine the strengths and weaknesses of our opponents and plan appropriate strategies and tactics.

Fitness monitoring and analysis equipment

Fitness clubs now have the latest electronic machines. Personalised exercise programmes can be created by inputting your details and requirements.

While you exercise, a constant stream of information, including heart rate and calories used, can give you useful feedback. Coaches can use this type of equipment to identify areas of weakness. When the data is fed into a computer, sophisticated software can suggest how weaknesses can be improved upon.

Tactics boards

Tactics boards enable a coach to explain tactical ideas and player positions. Interactive whiteboards can be used to show these ideas clearly – during training, at pre-match meetings and even during breaks in the game. These explanations ensure that every player is clear about his or her specific role.

QUESTIONS

16 New technology

1 **List two examples of the use of technology to improve performance under each of the following headings:**

- **a** Clothing *(2 marks)*
- **b** Facilities *(2 marks)*
- **c** Equipment *(2 marks)*
- **d** Training and coaching. *(2 marks)*

Factors affecting individual performance and participation

17 School

Sport is popular. Every weekend millions of us take part in sporting activities of one kind or another. Although we all realise that an active lifestyle will help to keep us fit and well, our reasons for taking part are many and varied. Why and how do we come to these decisions about sport? There are usually no simple answers. We are affected by many different factors in our lives.

However, sport is not for everyone. For some, sport is of no interest and plays no part in their life. Some decide not to take part but to enjoy watching sport instead. Society is made up of all sorts of people – men, women, different ethnic groups, able-bodied people, people with disabilities and people of all ages. Particular groups of people in society may encounter a number of barriers to taking part in sport. Not everybody enjoys equal access to sport. This is a complex issue. In order to be able to understand it properly, we need to understand why people take part in sports.

activity

Taking part in sport and physical activity

Our attitude to sport is often linked to our lifestyle and to the influence of our home, school and friends. Read the following pen pictures and then discuss why you think that each individual takes part in sport or physical activity.

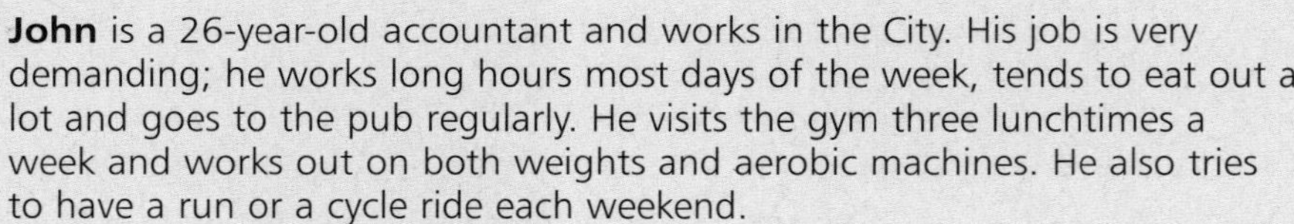

John is a 26-year-old accountant and works in the City. His job is very demanding; he works long hours most days of the week, tends to eat out a lot and goes to the pub regularly. He visits the gym three lunchtimes a week and works out on both weights and aerobic machines. He also tries to have a run or a cycle ride each weekend.

Nisha is a freelance graphic designer who works from home. She is single and in her late twenties and has little contact with the outside world during her working week. She tends to eat a lot, has problems controlling her weight and worries about her appearance. As a student she enjoyed dance and has recently joined a modern dance group which meets twice a week.

Martin is 17 years old and has returned to college after failing most of his recent exams. He gets frustrated with his lack of progress and loses his temper quite easily. He has always enjoyed sport without making the school teams, but his PE teacher recommended that on leaving school he joined the local rugby club. He now trains twice a week with the club and plays a match every weekend. He has also started serious weight training at a local gym.

Ellie (18) is quiet and shy and took little part in PE and sport at school. Through a friend at work she met a parascending group who eventually persuaded her to try the sport. To her surprise she not only enjoyed the thrill of the sport but realised that she was quite good. She is now group secretary, taking part every weekend and has also developed a growing interest in paragliding.

Can you think of any other reasons why people take part in sport? Think of your own experiences.

KEYWORDS

Extra-curricular activities: school activities that take place outside of lessons

ICT: information and communication technology, for example, computers, video cameras, etc.

National Curriculum: the basic subjects which schools are required to teach

Key to Exam Success

For your GCSE you will need to know:

- the importance of school in encouraging life-long participation in sport and physical activity
- how the attitudes of PE staff affect pupils
- reasons for participation in sport and physical recreation.

“ KEY THOUGHTS ”

‘Sporting success is built at school.’

Sport in school

We are all affected by our experiences of Physical Education (PE) and sport in school. Over the last twenty years very important changes have taken place in education and many of these have had an effect on PE.

PE has always been a foundation subject in the National Curriculum, enjoying equal status with other subjects. Targets for achievement are set for each age group. Particular sports are chosen by the school PE department, and checks are made to ensure all pupils achieve their targets. PE teachers decide on the best teaching methods.

Skill development is at the centre of a good PE programme. Within lessons pupils have the opportunity to take a variety of different sporting roles, including performer, official, observer, coach, captain, leader, organiser and choreographer. They learn that sport also needs administrators, instructors, teachers, trainers and spectators. Pupils learn how to take part in a number of different forms of competition, such as ladder, league and knockout. A wide variety of activities, well taught in a structured programme, develop skills and motivate pupils to continue taking part in sport beyond school.

PE and the curriculum

The PE department has overall responsibility for PE and sport in school. PE lessons are timetabled, and extra-curricular sporting activities take place at lunchtime, after school and at weekends.

Timetabled lessons include:

- practical PE lessons for all pupils
- examination courses, such as GCSE and A level
- cross-curricular links with other subjects, for example, respiration in science.

Extra-curricular activities include:

- team practices for different age-groups

- matches, competitions and tournaments for school teams
- clubs open to all abilities
- visits to sporting events, including international matches
- visits to specialist facilities, for example, indoor climbing walls
- visits to local sports clubs
- activities leading to sporting awards.

Why is PE taught in schools?

PE has the same aim as other subjects on the school curriculum. That is, it aims to help in the general education of children. As a National Curriculum subject which schools are legally required to teach, PE offers a wide range of educational benefits. It:

- educates children through physical activities
- helps to develop personal fitness and good health
- encourages a positive attitude towards health, fitness and life-long physical recreation
- teaches skills which enable pupils to take part in a variety of sports and physical recreation
- provides information about the world of sport, health and fitness.

Most pupils today have the opportunity to study PE at GCSE level and an increasing number can take PE at A level. Many continue with PE and sports studies at GNVQ, BTec and degree level. Within school, pupils usually have the opportunity to gain achievement, coaching and leadership awards in a variety of physical activities.

Although all schools are required to teach PE, the total amount of time given to PE and extra-curricular activities varies widely. The present government is aware of this and is trying to improve matters. It wants all children to have two hours of high-quality PE and school sport a week within and outside the curriculum.

Promoting PE in school

The government now encourages schools which have particularly high standards in sport to apply for sports college status. The creation of sports colleges and the establishment of the School Sports Co-ordinator Programme are at the heart of the government's plan to help talented young sportspeople and to increase sporting opportunities for all. The School Sports Co-ordinator Programme sends teachers into primary schools. It will eventually involve nearly every secondary school PE department working closely with its local feeder primary schools in order to develop and encourage quality physical education and sport.

Facilities in school

In recent years facilities for PE and sport in schools have greatly improved. Where facilities are lacking, pupils can often have access to local sports centres and specialist facilities. Many schools now have their own sports hall, and others have fitness rooms, dance studios and

swimming pools. In order to encourage pupils to continue with their sporting activities on leaving school, many schools have established close links with local sports clubs (see page 252).

The role of ICT in PE

Many schools are improving the way pupils learn by integrating ICT into the teaching of PE. ICT can help pupils evaluate their own work, as well as providing better access to information about the benefits of PE, health and sport to themselves and society in general. All students should be given the opportunity to use a variety of ICT applications such as computers, cameras and video cameras when taking part in PE in school.

The benefits of PE

Good PE lessons and enthusiastic teachers have an important part to play in encouraging pupils to take part in sport in later life. The following factors significantly affect pupils' motivation to continue with sporting activity after leaving school.

Skill levels

Through PE, pupils learn the basic skills of a variety of different sporting activities. These are developed during their time at school so that they can take part confidently in sporting activities as adults. While at school pupils also have the opportunity to:

- take on roles such as performer, coach, official, observer, captain, leader and choreographer
- improve their abilities through coaching and training during after-school practices
- visit local sports clubs or centres of excellence
- try for achievement awards in different sports.

Attitude

An important aim of PE is to develop a positive attitude towards health and fitness and make pupils aware of the advantages of life-long involvement in physical recreation. Teachers themselves often provide a positive **role model** for pupils by demonstrating the benefits of an active lifestyle.

Health
Through PE lessons, pupils can learn:

- the value of regular exercise for health and fitness
- the principles involved in training for different sports, both in theory and practice
- the importance of safety and safe practices in sport
- how to avoid and treat sporting injuries.

Bridging the school–community gap
Ideally, every pupil should leave school with a knowledge of the sporting opportunities that exist in their area.

There are many ways in which schools can establish sporting links with the wider community. These include:

activity

'In The Chair'
In small groups, prepare three questions to ask either your PE teacher, the head/director of PE, or the headteacher in your school, as part of an imaginary TV discussion programme.

To avoid repetition, each group should focus on one of the following areas:

- The amount of time given to PE and sport in schools
- The importance of PE and sport in the curriculum
- The range of sporting activities offered in your school and others
- Reasons for the government's interest in PE and sport
- The future of PE and sport in schools.

You have ten minutes to prepare your questions. Select one student to be the compére for the programme. He or she will invite the person selected to take the chair and then invite a representative from each group in turn to ask a question, allowing follow-up questions if appropriate.

One member of each group will act as a local reporter and make notes of the answers provided to each question.

- bringing club members, centre managers and others involved in community sport into the school to meet and talk to pupils
- arranging for pupils to visit clubs, centres and other facilities in the area
- explaining to pupils how to find out about sports not taught at school.

Similarly, clubs and centres can:

- run special introductory courses for young people at school
- ensure that clubs and centres are welcoming to young people
- provide special coaching and training for young people.

Why take part in sport?

Each of us makes a decision whether or not to take part in sport or physical activity. This can be based on a variety of different reasons, depending on our personal situation and all the other influences on our life. These reasons can be set out under the headings of health, vocation and leisure.

Health

We are very health-conscious today and know the benefits of regular physical activity and sport.

Lifestyle demands

In order to keep our bodies fit for the demands of daily life, we need minimum levels of strength, flexibility and stamina. We know that the more active we are, the better our health is likely to be and the more we can enjoy life.

Body shape

Combined with a healthy and balanced diet, regular exercise helps us control our weight and improve our body shape. If we are unfit and overweight, we know we are putting our health at risk.

Feeling and looking good

Physical activity helps us to feel and look good, improving our self-image and our confidence. Following a programme of activity helps us to increase our flexibility and to improve the strength and tone of our muscles.

Coping with stress

Stress is one of the greatest challenges to health today. Sport and physical activity may not solve our worries, but they can help us relax for a while, reduce our tension and take a fresh look at our problems. This can help us avoid stress-related illness.

Vocation

Most of us take part in sport as amateurs, purely for enjoyment. We train and compete in our own time and are not paid.

Professionals are paid to compete in sport. They train full-time and winning is all-important to them. Sport is their work and they are bound by contracts of employment. Only a very few people can earn a living as professional sportspeople.

Some are able to make money from sport as part-time professionals. This means that they have regular jobs, but earn income from sport in their spare time. However, they have to spend quite a lot of leisure time training and competing in order to maintain their fitness and ability.

Leisure

For most of us, enjoyment is the main reason why we take part in sport and physical activity. Sport is enjoyable for many different reasons.

Aesthetic

Sporting movement can be and often is beautiful. We can all appreciate the speed and elegance of a sprint hurdler in full flow or the controlled power of a gymnast in a tumbling routine. These activities appeal to our aesthetic sense. Dancers enjoy the experience of moving to the music and performing complex movement patterns.

Channelling aggression

Sport can provide an outlet for our natural aggression. Within the rules of sport it is possible for us to test our physical power against others in a controlled environment. We can see obvious examples of aggressive actions in sports such as rugby, judo and wrestling.

Accuracy

Many sports demand accurate movement, whether it is a pass in hockey, a shot in basketball or a volley in tennis. We all enjoy being accurate when taking part in sport. In a sport like archery, it is the central aim of the game, whilst in sports such as football it is just one aspect among many.

Speed

Most of us enjoy the thrill of travelling at speed over land, water or snow. This explains some of the attraction of sports such as horse racing, rally driving, white-water canoeing and downhill skiing. In some sports the fastest competitor is the winner, but in many, speed has to be combined with a number of other skills.

Achievement

Each of us has the potential to achieve in sport, at whatever level we take part. We may enjoy a successful climb, a low score in golf, completing a marathon, or going for an early morning swim. Those of us who are more competitive may gain a sense of achievement by winning a trophy, recording a personal best or representing our country.

Competition

Sport provides a perfect opportunity to test ourselves against others. We can compete directly in matches and tournaments in a variety of sports from lacrosse to water polo, and from basketball to sailing. Competition can take place at a variety of levels, from Sunday football in the park to the Olympic Games.

Physical challenge

Sport enables us to test our physical and mental strength and endurance to the limit. We can compete against our own best performance in running, swimming or cycling, or pit ourselves against the natural environment when climbing, caving or sky diving.

Friendship

We all need daily contact with other people. Sport and physical activity give us the opportunity to meet and talk to others. In clubs or classes, sport provides a common bond, helping to stimulate conversation and encouraging friendships and social mixing.

Co-operation

Many activities take place in sports centres and clubs. We may attend regularly and develop an interest in a group or a club. Many people like being part of a team and choose to play together. Others co-operate with one another to run the affairs of a club.

QUESTIONS

17 School

1 Give three reasons for teaching physical education in school.
(3 marks)

2 Describe five different ways in which your school provides for physical education.
(5 marks)

3 Explain why PE teachers are very important in encouraging young people to take part in life-long sport and physical activity.
(4 marks)

4 Suggest three ways in which school encourages the individual to take part in sport and physical activity.
(3 marks)

5 Give three different roles you are likely to play in your PE lesson. Give one reason why each is important.
(3 marks)

6 Suggest three different reasons why the School Sports Co-ordinators Programme is important.
(3 marks)

7 ICT is now used in many PE lessons. Suggest three ways in which it could be used.
(3 marks)

8 Helping pupils continue with sport after they have left school is important. Describe two ways in which schools can help and two ways in which clubs and centres can help.
(4 marks)

18 Changing attitudes

Overall, modern society shows a broadly positive attitude towards sport. It is widely accepted to be good for health, for weight control, for feeling good, for stress release and for enjoyment. Sport is undeniably an important part of the life of our country. Sports stars, with their successes and failures, regularly hit the headlines in our newspapers and on our televisions. Their achievements are praised or condemned and their private lives made public property.

But in spite of all this publicity and the popularity of major sports like football, cricket, tennis and athletics, we are not a nation of active sportspeople. Most people prefer to watch their favourite sport from the comfort of an armchair, rather than getting into their tracksuit and visiting their local sports centre. Research shows that young children today are less fit than the previous generation.

KEYWORDS

Role model: person who provides a good example for others to follow

Stereotyping: the holding of narrow or prejudiced views about a group or groups of people in society.

Key to Exam Success

For your GCSE you will need to know:

- how changing attitudes in society affect participation in sport
- the value of role models in sport

“ KEY THOUGHTS ”

‘Sports stars can inspire us all.’

The influence of role models

A **role model** is a person who is seen as a good example to follow. There are many sporting stars who are excellent role models, including Paula Radcliffe in athletics, Michael Owen in football, Tim Henman in tennis and Jonny Wilkinson in rugby. Their dedication to their sport, their talent and modesty are widely admired. However, there is little evidence that their example actually encourages more people to take part in sport. There are also well-publicised cases of sportspeople who have been unable to cope with fame, money and pressure from the media.

Fashions in sport

Society's attitude to physical recreation changes over time. Some activities become more popular and others less popular for a variety of reasons.

Jogging

Over the last twenty years jogging has greatly increased in popularity and is now widely seen as a healthy activity, helping with weight control and reducing stress levels. This has been due largely to the huge media coverage of mass events like the London Marathon.

Skiing

Skiing has become much more of a mass activity over recent years. This probably has much to do with the availability of cheap air flights. It is seen as a family sport in which all family members can take part.

Health and fitness centres

Many people, especially the young, are keen to be fit and have a well-toned body. Health and Fitness centres, with their rows of aerobic training machines and fully equipped weight lifting machines, enable these aims to be achieved indoors, without competing, and in the comfort of a fashionable environment.

Squash

Since the great boom in squash over ten years ago there has been a gradual decline in clubs and in the numbers of players. Squash was widely seen as the antidote to stress for office workers and as a way to improve both fitness and health in a minimum period of time. These benefits still apply, but fashions change in sport, and the squash court has been deserted for the fitness room.

Rugby

Prior to the success of the England team in winning the 2003 World Cup the number of rugby clubs was declining. It is hoped that the England win will stimulate interest in the sport and that many young people will wish to emulate players such as Jonny Wilkinson and Martin Johnson.

Disability and sport

In the not-too-distant past, people with disabilities were not expected to play a full part either in sport or in society in general. It was widely thought that people with disabilities were not able or motivated to take part in sport.

Today there is strong support for people with disabilities in society as a whole. This change has come about because of better understanding of disability and a determination to combat **stereotyping** – the holding of narrow or prejudiced views about groups of people in society.

In sport, great efforts have been made to give people with disabilities every opportunity to take part in sport. Wheelchair athletes have been given a high profile in major events such as the London Marathon, and the Olympic Games have shown the outstanding achievements of our paralympians.

Access for the disabled

It is now accepted that the benefits of sport apply to people with disabilities just as much as to able-bodied sportspeople. Sport allows everybody to be healthy and to mix socially. Equality of opportunity must be seen to apply to all citizens. The law now insists that buildings such as sports centres and swimming pools must provide access for people in wheelchairs. Many governing bodies of sport have formed sections for disabled sportspeople, and some sports have combined championships.

In practice, however, sportspeople with disabilities still face serious obstacles to taking part:

- It is not always possible for disabled competitors to get to events because of transport problems.
- Buildings still present problems. There may not be suitable doors and ramps at entrances.
- Staff at sports centres are not always trained to cope with sportspeople with disabilities.
- Sports centres do not always offer activities for sportspeople with disabilities.
- People with disabilities may not have had the opportunity to develop sports skills. They may not know of activities that are available and may not be able to afford them.

The organisation of sport

Since sport became organised in the nineteenth century, there have always been organisations encouraging people to take part in sport. Over the years this number has grown considerably. In the period before the establishment of the Sports Council in 1972, the government did not get involved in sport. Today it is encouraging us all to be involved with sport.

- Sport England pays for facilities and has development plans to encourage participation in sport.
- The Youth Sports Trust works with schools to increase participation.
- The Central Council for Physical Recreation runs the Sports Leaders' Awards with the British Sports Trust.
- The various sport national governing bodies develop schemes to encourage people into their own sports.
- SportscoachUK provides coaches to improve standards.
- The Women's Sports Association aims to encourage more women and girls to take part.
- Local authorities build leisure centres and other facilities for use by the community.

Full details of the work of these organisations can be found in Chapter 25.

activity

Sport for all?

Working in pairs, carry out a survey of your local sports centre. Find out which particular sporting activities are provided for people with disabilities and how many people with disabilities attend the centre.

Contact the manager before you visit and ask for permission to carry out the survey. Offer to give him or her a copy of the results.

Using your survey, draw up a number of proposals to make the sports centre even more helpful for people with disabilities. Remember it is often the small, simple and cheap modifications that provide the most benefits to the largest number of people. Also, remember that improvements for people with disabilities are often improvements for all users.

QUESTIONS

18 Changing attitudes

1 **Explain how attitudes to sport have changed over the years, making some sports more popular and some less popular. Give three examples.**

(3 marks)

2 **Many sporting organisations encourage participation in sport. Name one such organisation and explain what it is doing to achieve this.**

(4 marks)

3 **Explain what is meant by a role model in sport and describe the effect he or she might have on young people.**

(4 marks)

4 **Suggest four ways in which a leisure centre might ensure that people with disabilities are able to take part.**

(4 marks)

5 **Explain what is meant by stereotyping.**

(3 marks)

6 **Taking part in sport at local sports centres is not always easy for people with physical disabilities. Give four examples of possible problems they may experience.**

(4 marks)

19 Social groupings

People's attitudes to sport, and their decision whether or not to take an active part in sport, are influenced by many factors, including gender, family, friends and peers, ethnic background and socio-economic group.

KEYWORDS

Access: the different factors which affect our ability to take part in sport

Gender: being either male or female

Peers: people who are the same age as us and share the same social background

Peer pressure: the pressure to conform with what our peers are doing

Personal racism: racism directed at an individual by another person or persons

Racism: prejudice and discrimination directed at members of different ethnic groups

Socioeconomic group: factors including type of employment, income level and family background which affect our ability to take part in sport.

Key to Exam Success

For your GCSE you will need to know:

- how social grouping such as gender, family, peers and ethnic background affects sports participation
- (AQA B only) the influence of access, environment , age and politics on sports participation.

KEY THOUGHTS

'Sport for all is a goal, but not yet reality.'

The influence of gender, family and other social factors

It is now accepted that women should be able to take part in the sport of their choice without limitation. Social changes have given women more and more opportunity to control their own lives. But this is a relatively recent development, and the history of sport is mainly the history of men's sport.

Gender stereotyping

In the past girls were encouraged to play with dolls, to learn to cook and to keep themselves clean, while boys were encouraged to play ball games and allowed to climb trees and get covered in mud. Children were, and some still are, brought up to fit these gender stereotypes. As a result, girls have often had fewer opportunities to develop sports skills and to acquire the confidence which goes with them.

For boys, sport has high status, whilst many girls are turned off PE at school and do not consider sporting achievement to be important.

Some sports are still seen as unsuitable for women. Many young women think that playing sport makes them unattractive to men. Married women are often expected to take on the major responsibility for the home and children and to give a low priority to sporting activity. Coverage of sport on television and in the press focuses overwhelmingly on the activities and achievements of men.

Women and sport

However, women's participation in sport has increased over the years. Reasons include women's greater financial independence, improved childcare facilities at leisure centres, the availability of more women-friendly activities like aerobics, more female role models, and some increased media coverage.

Today women play rugby, throw the hammer and box – all activities that would have been unthinkable in the past. Women are also gradually moving into coaching, management and organisational roles in sport. This will give them more influence in the future development of sport. At present, however, there are still fewer opportunities for top sportswomen, with fewer events, smaller prize money and less media attention than for top sportsmen.

The influence of family

The family is a very important influence on us. If our parents play sport regularly, then the chances are that we will be brought up in a sporting atmosphere. Sporting parents and older brothers and sisters will give us role models to follow. Sporting parents will also be willing to provide transport and pay for sports equipment and sports clothing.

Sometimes children with famous sporting parents follow in their parents' footsteps (although many decide to do something completely different – for example Ian Botham's son is a professional rugby player, not a cricketer).

Friends and peers

Our **peers** are the people who are the same age as us and share the same social background. Our friends are often also our peers. What our friends do in their leisure time will usually affect us.

Friends often have similar interests. We all need friends, and if our friends are not interested in sport, we may drop out of sport too. On the other hand, if our friends enjoy taking part in sport, we may be encouraged to give it a try. In school, **peer pressure** – the pressure to conform with whatever our peers are doing – can be very strong.

Ethnic background

In our multicultural society, people of all races and ethnic backgrounds take part in sport at all levels. As a result of this, we often assume that they face no problems in sport. However, there is discrimination and disadvantage in sport, just as there is in everyday life.

Racism

Racism means not treating people of different races equally. Racists often hold stereotyped views about people from different ethnic backgrounds. Stereotypes lead to sporting myths about what different people can and cannot do. One example of a racist sporting myth is that 'Black people can't swim'. This is nonsense.

The most extreme example of racism in sport was seen under the apartheid system in South Africa prior to 1994, when people who were classified as non-whites were treated as second-class citizens both in society and in sport.

- **Personal racism** is seen when black and ethnic minority sportspeople are made to feel unwelcome by individuals at a sports club.
- **Institutional racism** is seen when an organisation lacks understanding or the willingness to understand and respond to the needs of black and ethnic minority sportspeople.

activity

Influences on my sporting life

Arrange to interview a man or woman aged over 60. Explain that you are investigating how access to sport has changed over the years and influences on people's choice of sports. Ask them if they would be prepared to answer some or all of the following questions, and either write down the answers as you talk, or use a tape recorder.

1 What did you do in your PE lessons when you were at:
  a primary school
  b secondary school?
2 Did you take part in sports or physical recreation after school or at the weekend?
3 Which sports have you tried during your life?
4 Which people have been the main influences on your choice of sport?
5 Has your ethnic background or socioeconomic group affected your choice of sport?
7 Which sports would you have like to have tried?
8 What were the reasons for you not being able to take part in them when you were younger?
9 Did you have any sporting heroes who were role models for you when you were young? Do you have any photos of them?

Work with two or three other students to analyse your results. Are opportunities to take part in sport better or worse than they were 30 to 50 years ago? Give reasons for your answer.

Using the information you have gathered, prepare and deliver a Microsoft Powerpoint presentation entitled 'Changing attitudes to sport'. You might like to include photographs of the person you have interviewed and any photos of their sporting past.

There are many different cultures in Britain, each with its own set of beliefs and practices. Amongst some groups, for example, women may not be able to take part in sport for religious reasons. Some people think this needs to change; others believe it is for individuals to decide.

Our socioeconomic group

Our **socioeconomic group** refers to a number of factors, including type of employment, income level and family background. These factors can affect the type of sporting activity which interests us. For example, a person who is well off, lives in the country and owns a horse is more likely to be involved in equestrian sports than someone who lives in a city and has a lower income.

Research shows that people from affluent socioeconomic groups are more likely to take part in sport than people from less well-off groups. This is because the amount of money coming into a family affects all the activities family members can take part in during their leisure time. Playing sport outside of school will involve costs of travelling, training and competition, as well as equipment, clothing, hire of facilities and club membership.

Other factors affecting participation

AQA B only

The term **access** refers to all the different factors which affect our ability to take part in sport, from the need to travel to facilities for training and competition, to the ability to pay for special sports clothing and equipment.

For example, equestrian sports are beyond the reach of most people because of the costs involved in buying, training and looking after horses – so access to such sports is limited.

In the case of sailing, we may live by the sea, but the cost of buying a boat will be prohibitive for many of us. However, sailing clubs encourage young people to join, and the boats belonging to the club as well as coaching are available to members.

Location

Where we live affects some of the sports we can take part in.

- If you live near the sea, a large lake or river, there will be greater opportunities to learn water sports.
- Country areas provide good opportunities for outdoor activities, but leisure centres and swimming pools may be hard to find.
- Inner-city areas are often short of open space, but indoor sports facilities are more likely to be within easy reach.
- Because of their high population, cities and towns can attract both commercial and private sports clubs.
- Particular parts of the country often have localised sporting traditions – for example, highland wrestling in parts of Scotland.

Depending on where we live, it is often necessary to arrange transport to get to and from sports facilities. If we do not have access to a car, this means finding money for public transport.

Climate

The climate can affect our participation in sport. For example, winter sports need low temperatures, and activities such as skiing depend on heavy snowfalls.

Many athletes like to train in a warm climate. Some British teams and individuals travel to training camps abroad, rather than train through the British winter.

Age

Children of all ages at school will follow a PE programme as part of the National Curriculum. They will learn the skills of a wide variety of sports. At secondary school they will be encouraged to join local clubs and to continue with their sport and physical recreation beyond their schooldays.

However, young people in their twenties have many demands on their time, and work and social pressures may squeeze sport out of their weekly routines.

Married people with young families often have to put their children before their own need to keep fit and healthy.

People who have not had the habit of physical activity may decide in middle age that the effort of getting into shape is simply too daunting.

Often, those who have managed to maintain their involvement in sport and physical recreation throughout their lives, find they can still enjoy sporting activity in retirement. However many older people lack the skills and physical health to have an active life.

Politics

As we have seen, good facilities are essential to encourage participation in sport. But the amount of money available for local authorities and national governing bodies to spend on sporting facilities is largely determined by the attitude and policies of central government.

Since the establishment of the National Lottery, vast sums of money have been available to top performers, for facilities for all and to fund developments throughout sport. This has encouraged participation at all levels.

However, research shows that there has not been an increase in adult participation in recent years. It is hoped that children currently benefiting from these extra funds will continue in sport longer than their parents.

QUESTIONS

19 Social grouping

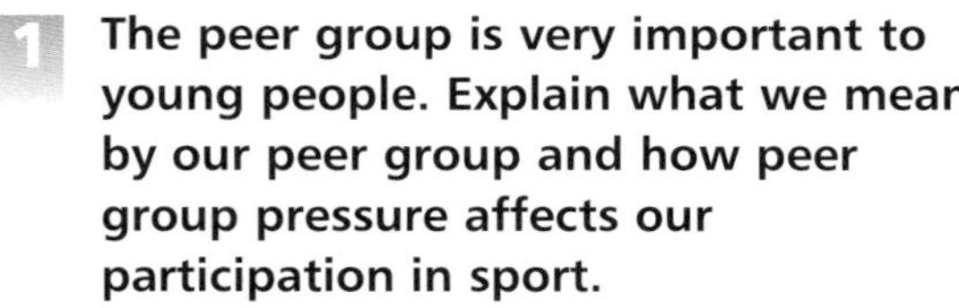

1 **The peer group is very important to young people. Explain what we mean by our peer group and how peer group pressure affects our participation in sport.**

(4 marks)

2 **Taking part in sport can be affected by many different factors. For each of the following factors suggest three ways in which our sports participation could be affected.**

a Family
b Gender
c Ethnic background

(3 marks each)

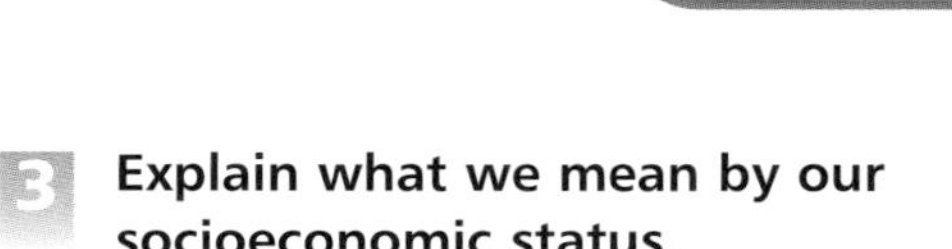

3 **Explain what we mean by our socioeconomic status.**

(3 marks)

4 **Give four reasons why our socioeconomic status is likely to affect our choice of sport.**

(4 marks)

5 **Give three ways in which our access to sport might be limited.**

(3 marks)

20 Leisure time

Most of our daily activities can be classified under the headings of bodily needs, work, duties and leisure time.

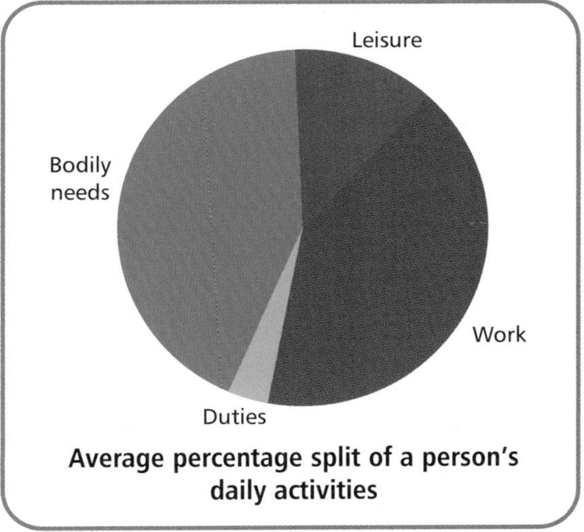

Average percentage split of a person's daily activities

- Our **bodily needs** consist of all the things we have to do to stay healthy, including sleeping, eating and washing.
- We also need to **work** to earn a living. Some unemployed people, mainly women, do not earn money but look after their home and children. This is also work. Pupils might consider time at school as work. Some activities are closely linked to work, such as travelling to work.

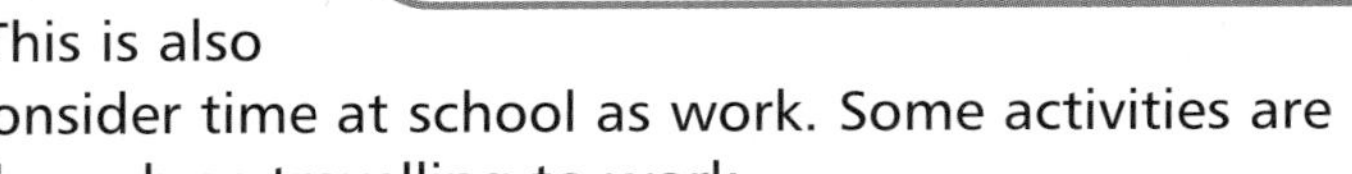

- There are also various things which we feel we have to do for our family or in the home – these are our **duties**. Many activities may be called duties, for example, washing up or taking the dog for a walk.

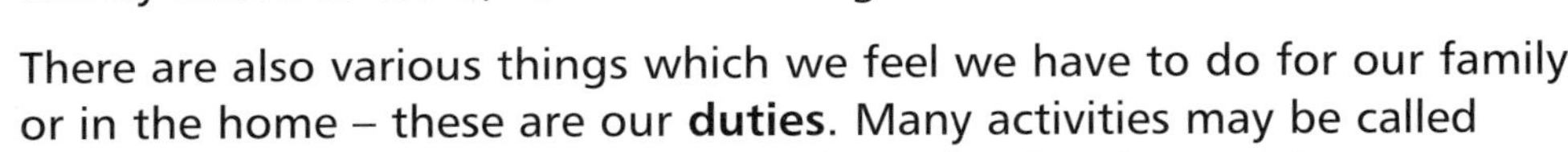

If we set aside the time used for bodily needs, duties, work and work-related activities, what we are left with is our **leisure time**. This is the time when we have the greatest choice about what we do. During leisure time we are free to take part in sport and physical recreation.

KEYWORDS

Leisure time: time that we can spend as we choose

Physical recreation: taking part in recreation involving physical activity

Recreation: the purposeful use of our leisure time

Key to Exam Success

For your GCSE you will need to know:

- the reasons why leisure time has increased over the years
- about user groups and their special needs
- (AQA B only) the value of good coaching and who can provide it.

KEY THOUGHTS

'Work hard, play hard.'

Work and leisure

Although changing work patterns have encouraged more weekend working, flexitime and working from home, most people still work regular hours, and fit their leisure activities into weekends, evenings and holidays.

People who work long hours or large amounts of overtime have little time for leisure. Those who work nights or on shifts may have to take their leisure time when other people are working. Despite this, over the last fifty years there has been a great increase in the amount of time people have available for leisure.

Leisure time will continue to grow for almost all of us. There are many reasons for this:

- Working careers have become shorter as we continue education for longer and retire earlier.
- Life expectancy has increased, meaning that we live longer in retirement.
- Paid holidays have increased.
- Working hours have become shorter.
- Jobsharing and part-time work have increased.
- Housework takes less time.

The way we spend our leisure time will depend on a number of factors, including our age, sex, culture, social class, financial situation, upbringing and the facilities available. Most people think it is a good thing to spend at least some leisure time being active and trying to follow a healthy lifestyle.

Leisure provision

As our leisure time has increased over the years, the leisure industry has responded by providing a variety of attractions and amenities, such as cinemas, theme parks and leisure centres. Some of these are provided by the local authority and others by private companies.

Local authorities have a responsibility to provide leisure services, including libraries, swimming pools, playing fields and sports centres. Facilities such as fitness clubs and racket centres may also be provided locally by private companies. However, commercially-run sports facilities must make a profit, and can only operate if there is a sufficient demand.

activity

Time for sport

It is recommended that all of us take part in some sport or physical recreation for at least 20 minutes at least three times a week. Using the survey sheet below, interview a working adult in order to calculate how much time he or she actually spent in sport or physical recreation over the last week.

Name and occupation	Total number of hours per day, to nearest half-hour					
	Work	Bodily needs	Duties	Leisure time		
				TV	Sport	Other (give details)
Monday						
Tuesday						
Wednesday						
Thursday						
Friday						
Saturday						
Sunday						
Total						

Collect all the information obtained by your group and create a database from which you can calculate how much time people actually spend on sport and other activities in their leisure time. From your results, make recommendations that you think would help people to develop a more active and healthy lifestyle.

User groups and their special needs

Local authorities aim to encourage a wide range of different groups of people to use their facilities. These include the elderly, active retired groups, people with disabilities, mothers with small children, ethnic minority groups and the unemployed. All these groups need different types of activities and special consideration if they are to be attracted into leisure centres.

The elderly

Many older people never had the opportunity to learn skills to take part in sport when they were younger. Others are not in the best of health or have lost a lot of their strength, flexibility and endurance over the years. They need to be shown exercises that gradually improve their physical fitness and help them maintain and improve their quality of life.

Active retired groups

These people may have skills which enable them to take part in activities at a variety of levels. Some will enjoy swimming, others indoor bowls or badminton. They need conveniently located facilities, staff to organise the activity and other people of a similar age and ability with whom they can take part and perhaps share transport.

People with disabilities

People with disabilities may have varying degrees of independence and sporting ability, depending on their needs.

If they are wheelchair-bound, they will need to be able to travel to and enter the facility easily. They will need staff trained to deal with their particular needs, and perhaps special equipment – for example, hoists to get into the pool. If they cannot take part with able-bodied sportspeople, they will need activities specially organised for their sport.

Mothers and toddlers

For many mothers, sport and physical recreation are low priorities, often because of lack of time, facilities and money. Their main need is for a crêche or similar childcare facility at their leisure centre so they can get on with their activity without worry. The activities need to be suitable, in pleasant surroundings and at a convenient time to fit in with the rest of the family's needs.

Ethnic minority groups

People from ethnic minority groups may need special encouragement to take part in organised activities. Sport and physical recreation may not play a very important part in their culture, and they may not have the skills, confidence or language skills necessary to make sport an attractive leisure option for them.

They need sympathetic staff who understand their culture and are prepared either to organise activities for them as a group or to help to integrate them into an established group. Women in particular may need special support if their culture does not encourage participation by women.

The unemployed

The main factor here is shortage of money, and so concessions can be an effective way help to increase participation. Unemployed people come from all sectors of society and so their sporting interests will vary greatly. Ideally they should be able to join other groups, at reduced, or no, cost.

Coaching

AQA B only

The provision of coaching, facilities and finance can make a difference both to the number of people taking part and the standards of performance.

It is essential that young children and other beginners are taught correctly at the start. Incorrect techniques and skills can be quickly ingrained and may be very difficult to correct in the future. Coaching can be provided by a variety of people:

- **School staff**: all PE teachers have a general qualification to teach the skills of the major sports and physical activities taught in the school PE curriculum. They may also have specialist qualifications to coach individuals and groups to a higher level in particular sports. Other members of the teaching staff may also have a particular interest or experience in a sport, and be willing to help coach school groups.
- **Coaches or instructors**: teachers are concerned with the whole development of the child, whilst coaches concentrate on improving the skills in a particular sport. Instructors are usually very skilful and pass on their skill to others. Coaches and instructors may not necessarily have passed formal examinations in their sports.
- **Family or friends**; when children are young, parents or family friends who have had some experience of a sport may be able to pass on their enthusiasm and expertise. But as the children get older and develop, they will need good teaching and coaching to avoid picking up incorrect techniques and skills. Parents and friends may not be able to provide this level of help.

SportscoachUK

SportscoachUK supports and develops all aspects of coaching. The organisation offers courses to coaches to improve their knowledge and skills and the opportunity to take formal examinations. A network of coaching has been developed throughout the country.

Depending on the ability of the sportsperson, it should be possible for coaching to be made available locally, in the region or at the national level for the very best performers. Coaching starts with introductory and elementary activities for beginners, and continues right through to the training of world-class performers at national sports centres and other centres of excellence.

QUESTIONS

20 Leisure time

1 **Our daily activities can be put under a number of headings. Name these headings and explain what we mean by leisure time.**

(3 marks)

2 **Leisure time has greatly increased in recent years. Give four reasons for this change.**

(4 marks)

3 **Coaching encourages people to stay in sport. Explain who might provide coaching.**

(3 marks)

4 **Explain what is meant by a user group at a leisure facility. Give three examples of user groups, together with details of ways in which their particular needs can be met.**

(7 marks)

5 **Give three examples of leisure facilities likely to be provided by the local authority and three likely to be provided by private enterprise.**

(3 marks)

6 **The way we spend our leisure time is affected by many factors. Give four examples.**

(4 marks)

21 Facilities available

Most sport involves the use of equipment or facilities of some kind, and often these are shared between a number of different users or user groups. This chapter looks at the issues surrounding the provision of sports facilities by the public sector (government and local authorities), the private sector and the voluntary sector.

KEYWORDS

Public sector: the part of the economy that is run by government and local authorities

Private sector: part of the economy that is run by business for profit

Voluntary sector: part of the economy run by volunteers on behalf of the community.

Key to Exam Success

For your GCSE you will need to know:

- the importance of providing leisure facilities, both indoor and outdoor
- the issues related to outdoor adventurous activities.

“ KEY THOUGHTS ”

‘Sport: available to all, chosen by many.’

activity

Planning a sports facility

In groups of 6–8, study the following extract from a local newspaper. Imagine this is your town. Find out what facilities already exist before you decide on new and improved facilities. Use the information from your survey to complete each of the tasks below.

Local Sports Council scoops the jackpot

Glenwood's sports centre manager, Brian Blake, received the shock of his life when he heard on Friday that the centre had taken first prize in Sport England's 'Centre Management' national competition. This means that the local Sports Council will receive a grant of £2 million to improve the town of Glenwood's sports facilities. The only condition is that the plans are acceptable to Sport England.

1 Use maps of your town and surrounding area to produce a radial chart showing the direction and distance of sporting facilities from the centre of town.

2 Use a separate map to shade in housing areas, playing fields, parks and recreation grounds.

3 List the major sports facilities in your town and comment on the ease of access using a chart like the one below:

Facility	Travel by car including parking facilities	Travel by public transport	Proximity to town centre	Access (easy–difficult, scale 1–5)
Swimming pool	On the main road. A large car park.	Regular bus service. 5 minutes walk from station.	15 minutes walk.	1
Squash club	Minor roads, long queues in early evening. No car park; difficult to find parking in early evening.	10 minutes walk from nearest bus stop. 30 minutes walk from station.	45 minutes walk.	4

4 Compile a summary of the sports facilities in the town and comment on the standard of each facility and possible improvements as in the chart below. Take photographs, video, or make sketches of the facility if possible.

Facility	Number	Comments	Possible development
Tennis courts	20	6 in good condition at private club, 14 in two recreation grounds in poor repair.	Improve facilities at one site, convert other courts to all-weather surfaces for 5-a-side football, etc., in association with local youth club.

5 Prepare a presentation to explain your recommendations, preferably using Microsoft Powerpoint and including drawings, photographs, video, etc. Your teacher may be able to arrange a representative from your local Sports Council to attend your presentation.

The public sector

The government gives grants to the regional sports councils to run the national sports centres. Sport England runs five national sports centres, each equipped with special facilities for particular sports:

- **Crystal Palace**: athletics, swimming and diving
- **Bisham Abbey**: judo, powerlifting and tennis
- **Lilleshall Hall**: football and gymnastics
- **Holme Pierrepont**: water sports
- **Plas-y-Brenin:** outdoor activities.

Each centre has facilities and support services for top sports performers and aims to provide them with the best possible training environment. Priority is given to:

- sportspeople participating in the World Class Programme
- national team training and competition
- training of leaders and officials.

The national sports centres form main sites within the English Institute of Sport regional network. Funding, primarily through the Sport England Lottery Fund, is available to enhance existing facilities so as to provide the best possible training environment for world-class athletes.

The National Lottery Fund

The government distributes National Lottery funds to the five sports councils for a variety of projects, including facilities. Through Sport England, the National Lottery fund has provided money for a large number of schemes throughout the country. A total of £13 bn has been raised and 150,000 projects supported to date. Sport is one of the six 'good causes' to receive money. There is also a small grants programme set up to help local groups apply.

The new English National Stadium at Wembley

The site of the former Wembley football stadium was bought by Sport England from Wembley plc and has received £120 million of National Lottery money. With 90,000 seats, the new Wembley will be the largest football stadium in the world, with no obstructed views and every seat under cover. It is scheduled to open in 2006.

The Countryside Agency

The government funds the Countryside Agency, which is responsible for the eight national parks of England – the Broads, Dartmoor, Exmoor, the Lake District, the North Yorkshire Moors, Northumberland, the Peak District and the Yorkshire Dales. The New Forest has a similar status. These areas provide a wide range of opportunities for outdoor recreation.

The new English National Stadium at Wembley: facts and figures

- With 90,000 seats, the new English National Stadium at Wembley will be the largest football stadium in the world, with every seat under cover. There will be no obstructed views. There will be more leg room in each seat than in the Royal Box of the old stadium.
- The stadium roof will rise to a height of 52 m above the pitch. (The famous twin towers of the old stadium were just 35 m tall.) The roof will form an area of more than 11 acres, 4 acres of which will be movable. It will weigh almost 7,000 tonnes.
- The new Wembley will have a circumference of 1 km. The rows of seating, if placed end to end, would stretch 54 kms.
- With a span of 315 m, the arch will be the longest single-span roof structure in the world. The London Eye could fit between the top of it and the pitch. With a diameter of 7.4 m, it will be wide enough for a Channel Tunnel train to run through.
- The foundations of the new stadium will consist of 3,700 separate piles. The deepest of these, at 35 m, will be as deep as the Twin Towers were tall. A total of 90,000 cu m of concrete, 23,000 tonnes of steel and 35 miles of heavy-duty power cables will be used in the stadium's construction.
- At peak construction there will be 1,500 people working on site.
- Each of the two giant screens in the new stadium will be the size of 600 domestic television sets.
- There will be 2,000 toilets – more than any other building in the world!

Local authorities

Local authorities provide a variety of services such as education, street-cleaning and leisure. In large cities, these services are usually provided by a single authority, but in other areas a county council may be responsible for major services such as education, with district or town councils providing leisure and recreation services.

In all areas there are small town or parish councils which are responsible for halls, play areas and open spaces.

Leisure and recreation departments

Each local authority has separate departments to deal with their services, including leisure and recreation. Facilities for general leisure are not compulsory, although sports centres, swimming pools and recreation grounds are usually provided, as well as halls, play areas and open spaces. All facilities need qualified staff, good equipment and regular maintenance.

Leisure and recreation departments provide facilities for all sections of the community and costs must be kept as low as possible so that programmes are attractive, accessible and affordable. Local authorities usually employ sports development officers whose job is to develop local sport and to encourage links between schools and local sports clubs.

Sport in schools and colleges

- Schools and colleges are required by law to provide facilities for sport and physical education.

- Local authorities also provide sports facilities for colleges, youth clubs and adult education.
- Some schools have dual-use sports facilities which are shared by the school and the local community.

The private sector

Specialist facilities

Where there is a need that is not met by the public sector, specialist sports facilities may be provided on a commercial basis. Commercial sports facilities can be expensive, but are usually friendly and welcoming and offer good value for money, combining social activities with up-to-date facilities and equipment.

Examples include health and fitness centres, golf driving ranges, riding centres, tenpin bowling halls, ice-rinks and tennis courts. Purpose-built activity holiday centres are often well-equipped for sport, and some hotels and country clubs offer high-class sports facilities as an extra attraction for members.

Company sports and social clubs

In the past, large companies had social clubs which provided a range of sports and social facilities for employees and their families. This not only helped to create a healthy and contented workforce, but encouraged employees to be loyal to the company.

Although sports facilities were provided free of charge to employees, the cost of upkeep of the buildings, courts, pitches and greens was considerable. Today companies are more likely to make arrangements with sports centres to offer special rates or introductory fitness courses for employees.

The voluntary sector

Sports clubs

For many adults, taking part in sport means belonging to a local club. Most towns have their own sports clubs, which are usually run by enthusiasts and concentrate on one sport.

Those that are well established may own their own facilities – for example, golf, tennis and cricket clubs. Clubs that are new or do not have the money often have to hire facilities from the local sports centre, school, playing field or church hall.

Community associations

Sometimes groups of people in a village or neighbourhood get together to provide forms of physical recreation for the local community.

In rural areas, the village green may be available for cricket in the summer and hockey in the winter. Village and church halls can also provide facilities for a number of indoor sports, such as table tennis and badminton. Other facilities may be available for hire if necessary.

National governing bodies

Some national governing bodies (NGBs) have magnificent facilities – for example, the Rugby Football Union's ground at Twickenham. Most of the newer NGBs have no facilities of their own and have to use the facilities provided by the national sports centres.

Some NGBs have close historical links with an established club and use their facilities for major events – for example, the Marylebone Cricket Club (MCC) uses Lords cricket ground. The Football Association does not own its own ground and has used Wembley Stadium, which used to be owned by a private company before it was acquired for redevelopment by Sport England.

Athletics and swimming do not have their own national facilities, and neither do many other major sports.

Types of sports provision

Sports facilities vary greatly. A local badminton club might play in a church hall with one court, faded markings and a low ceiling. In the past, swimming pools were usually built as facilities on their own, but are now more often part of modern leisure centres. Running tracks were originally used only for running, with other field events neglected. Nowadays they may include a stand, changing rooms and indoor training facilities such as a weights room or fitness suite, with a range of equipment to monitor fitness.

Many playing fields, especially for Sunday football, still have very poor changing facilities – and little

else. Teams that are able to use school playing fields may benefit from the use of the school's facilities on match day and also for training.

Sports facilities can be grouped into two main categories:

- **Indoor facilities**: these include general-purpose facilities such as sports and leisure centres together with specialist facilities, such as swimming pools, squash centres, fitness suites or ice rinks.
- **Outdoor facilities**: these include pitches for major games, golf courses, hard areas for tennis, netball and five-a-side football, water sport centres and parts of the countryside used for sport, such as climbing areas, stretches of river, sea or lakes, walking or jogging trails.

User needs

Sports centres must be able to cope with the needs of a variety of different user groups. including the elderly, active retired groups, people with disabilities, mothers with small children, ethnic minority groups and the unemployed. They must also meet the needs of individuals, teams, clubs and advanced groups.

- **Individuals**: many people will use the centre on a casual or regular basis, for example, to train in the fitness room, take part in aerobics sessions or play squash.
- **Teams**: there may be teams who want to train or compete at the centre. These may include squash teams who need courts, footballers who need pitches and changing rooms, and netball teams who need a court inside or outside.
- **Clubs**: sports clubs will need a wide range of facilities, both for players who wish to compete seriously and for those who simply enjoy the social aspect of club membership. For example, a karate club might have competitors from beginner to international level, while a badminton club might be happy to have club nights only, with friendly matches between members.
- **Advanced groups**: these groups may be of regional or national standard and will need top-class coaches. They may require specialist facilities and high-quality equipment which can only be provided at centres of excellence. Top sportspeople will usually be involved in one of the World Class Programmes and will be able to use facilities at the national centres of excellence.

These different user groups may include different ages, including junior groups, single or mixed-sex groups, able-bodied people or people with disabilities. The groups and individuals may want facilities for training or to compete at a variety of levels.

Location

Voluntary clubs and private businesses will make their own decisions about where to locate their facilities. For voluntary clubs the decision will centre around the money available to buy or rent a facility and the everyday costs of running the club. Unless a club can find a wealthy backer, the money required will have to be raised by members.

A business will only set up a club if it is confident of making a profit. It will study the project, call in experts and assess the demand for the activity in the area. It will then usually need permission from the local authority to go ahead.

If the local authority decides to provide a facility for the local community it has to consider many factors including the following:

- **Local need**: the support of local people is necessary for the local authority to go ahead with projects, especially if they are expensive and involve a lot of new planning.
- **Planning**: the local authority must be sure that the facility is really needed and fits into their future plans for leisure facilities in the area.
- **Funding**: the local authority must spend its money wisely as it will not usually wish to increase the council tax to fund recreational projects. Costs of major facilities are very high and will include the cost of land as well as any building work.
- **Running costs**: the cost of running a sports facility can be very high and the facility should therefore be in an area where local people will use it and make it pay.
- **Access**: local people must be able to get to the facility relatively easily by public transport, including road and rail. Adequate parking must also be provided. Elderly people and people with disabilities must be able to use the facility easily. Facilities should not be sited in areas where the roads are already congested.
- **Expected use**: the local authority must be sure that the facility will be used throughout the week and at weekends. This is particularly important if it is a specialist facility such as a swimming pool. Facilities should be available to the elderly, to people with disabilities and to mothers with small children.

- **Environment**: new buildings will require planning permission and should be constructed with sensitivity to the surrounding buildings or countryside.
- **Activities**: Multi-purpose facilities such as leisure centres have the flexibility to offer a wide variety of activities, depending on demand. If a specialist centre such as an ice rink is built and interest in ice-skating declines, the facility may be underused and will not pay its way.
- **Dual use**: In recent years many schools have been built with sports facilities which can be also be used by the local community. The school has the use of the facilities during the school day, with the community taking over at evenings and weekends. This ensures that maximum use can be made of all the facilities, although it can also present problems of over-use.

Outdoor and adventurous sports

Some outdoor activities like sailing and canoeing have always been popular with people living near water, and many people enjoy rambling and hill walking on a regular basis. However, in recent years there has been an upsurge of interest in more demanding activities such as surfing, board sailing, free-fall parachuting, snowboarding, bungee jumping and hang gliding. In these more extreme activities, the challenge is not only to grapple with the forces of nature but also to conquer the fear inside ourselves.

Risk

All sport carries some risk of injury, although the chances of getting injured in rugby are obviously greater than in badminton. In more challenging outdoor and adventurous activities, however, the risk is very much greater. Most people are not willing to consider taking such a risk, but those who do find the stress involved to be enjoyable. They talk enthusiastically of the 'adrenaline rush' as they overcome their fear by scaling rock faces, launching themselves out of planes or challenging the waves. For them, the risks are worth taking.

Issues

The rise of interest in extreme outdoor sports raises some important issues:

- **Acceptability**: some activities may be too risky or dangerous to be considered sports. Whilst climbing mountains and rocks in natural areas is acceptable, climbing high buildings in city areas is not.

- **Access**: Relatively few people live within easy reach of mountains, waves and fast-flowing water, so the majority could not easily take part in these activities even if they wanted to. Sports such as hang gliding also involve a great deal of expense in terms of equipment and travel.
- **Environment**: the countryside and seaside are there to be enjoyed by everyone and must be looked after. Large numbers of people taking part in mountain-climbing, for example, can cause erosion and damage the land.

QUESTIONS

21 Facilities available

1 **Make a list of eight different sports facilities and put them under the heading of indoor or outdoor facilities.**
(8 marks)

2 **When planning a local sports facility many factors must be taken into account. Give four factors and explain why each is important.**
(8 marks)

3 **User groups take part in sport at a number of different levels of ability. Explain how the different needs of three different groups might be met in a leisure centre.**
(3 marks)

4 **List the three main ways in which the government provides for sport.**
(3 marks)

5 **Name three of the five national sports centres run by Sport England and give one of the main sports in which they each specialise.**
(6 marks)

6 **Describe three ways in which the local authority provides for sport.**
(3 marks)

7 **Explain why some people like outdoor and adventurous sports.**
(3 marks)

Social and cultural factors affecting participation

Sponsorship

In the past, individual sportspeople, groups and clubs developed sport in their own way and sports clubs and governing bodies operated largely independently. This freedom meant that there was no overall pattern for the development of sport. Today clubs and national governing bodies are still at the heart of sport in England. However, the government now provides much funding – and it strongly influences the direction of the development of sport.

At the highest levels, sponsorship and television have combined to transform sport and its performers into a product to be sold. Sport is no longer important for its own sake – it has become big business. Control of sport has moved away from the people taking part and towards the managers of sport, the sponsoring companies and television networks. This is called the **commercialisation** of sport.

activity

What's the issue?

Working in groups of four, look at the photos on this page and try to link them to the various issues in sport listed below. Some photos may involve more than one link.

Be prepared to say why you have made the links.

Issues in sport

- The power of sponsorship on sport
- The influence of television on sport
- The importance of sport for national morale
- The importance of success in sport
- Funding for sport
- Technological advances in sport.

KEYWORDS

Commercialisation: the domination of sport by big business and the media

Donation: a gift

Publicity: using the media to attract attention

Sponsorship: when a company gives financial help to a sport in return for linking their name with an individual, team, sport or sporting event.

Key to Exam Success

For your GCSE examination you will need to know:

- what sponsorship is and the many forms it can take
- who provides and who receives sponsorship
- the advantages and disadvantages of sponsorship.

“ KEY THOUGHTS ”

‘Sponsorship and sport depend upon each other.’

What is sponsorship?

Sports **sponsorship** takes place when a company gives financial help in return for linking the company's name with an individual or team, or a sport in general.

Sponsorship is a form of investment. Companies exist in order to make profits. They do not have to make donations to charity or to sponsor sport, although many do so. When sponsoring a team or individual, the company expects to get something in return. The return is that sponsorship helps a company to sell its products. The company wants to have an impact on likely customers. This impact comes through the link between the sporting activity and the product.

Donations are different from sponsorship: a donation is a gift, usually of money. The company chooses to give money to sport, and benefits by being seen to care about the community. There is no direct commercial advantage in giving money in this way.

Promoting a sales message

At its simplest, sponsorship gives a company a chance to put over a sales message – such as 'Buy our product':

- Sports stars are linked with a particular company's product.
- A team wears shirts with the company's name for all to see.
- Advertising hoardings at a televised sports event are caught by the cameras.
- A competition may carry the sponsor's name, for example the 'Barclaycard Premiership'.

Sponsorship aims to put the company's name in front of the public so that it is remembered.

Promoting an image

At another level, selling a product can be a more subtle process. Sponsorship is not necessarily linked directly to sales. Instead the aim is to make the potential customer feel happy about the sponsoring company and its product. For example, if the name of the company is worn by our favourite player, we may, without realising it, also start to feel warmly towards the company.

In this way, a company can transfer some of the values of the team or player to its own products. If the player or team is successful, then this success also reflects on the sponsoring company.

High-level sport is played, in general, by young people. They bring energy, enthusiasm, excitement and skill to the activity. These qualities make very helpful partners when marketing a product.

Sponsorship is about getting spectators to enjoy the sporting event and – by extension – to take a positive view of the sponsor. This makes them more likely to buy the sponsor's product.

For example, O2 has tried to maintain its place as a leading mobile phone supplier by sponsoring the England Rugby team. The company hoped that the excellence and achievement of the team would be linked with its products. By winning the World Cup, both the team and the sponsor have achieved their goal!

Factors in sponsorship

When a company looks at sports sponsorship, it must consider many factors.

- It must ask questions about the **sports organisation**:
  - Is it a respectable partner with the right image?
  - Has it received sponsorship before?
  - Is it run in a professional way?
  - Will it offer value for money?
  - Will the product go well with the sport?
  - Will the company reach its target audience?
  - Will it be possible to extend the sponsorship?
- It must also ask questions about **publicity**:
  - How 'visible' will the event be?
  - Will the company's name be given a high profile?
  - Is the public interested in the sport?
  - Will the individual, team or event be seen on television?
  - Will there be publicity on radio or in the papers?
  - Will the event be well attended?
  - What type of people will attend (age, sex, social group, income)?
  - Will the team or individual win?

Types of sponsorship

Today sponsorship money is usually provided by companies for sportspeople and sporting organisations to spend as they wish. In the past, when amateur players could not be given money, they were helped in a whole range of other ways.

- **Equipment**: companies who make sports equipment want to see the equipment used by the sportspeople they sponsor. When we see players using golf clubs, cricket bats and tennis rackets, the maker's name is usually prominently displayed.
- **Clothing and shoes**: companies manufacturing sports clothing and shoes expect their sportspeople to wear their products. Baseball caps, sunglasses, sun visors and watches are also used to keep the manufacturer's name in front of us.
- **Transport and travel**: companies are always keen for sportspeople to use their flights, coaches, cars, travel companies and hotels – usually free or at a greatly reduced rate.
- **Food and drink**: most sportspeople need a specialised diet because of their particular training. Sports drinks companies sponsor top sportspeople to advertise the special advantages they claim their drinks bring to sporting performance.

Who receives sponsorship in sport?

Today, sponsorship is available throughout the sporting world, and it is not only star performers who are sponsored. Local teams and individuals can also find sponsors, often among the local business community.

Individual sportspeople

For professional sportspeople, sponsorship is an important way of adding to their income from sport. World champions and Olympic gold medallists can usually take their pick of sponsors. Successful sportspeople are in great demand because sponsors want the name of their product to be associated with sporting excellence. We forget sometimes that players advertise one product rather than another because of the money they are paid. For younger up-and-coming sportspeople, sponsorship is a means to buy the best equipment and to meet all the costs of training, competition and travelling.

Top amateurs rely on sponsorship to pay their living expenses so that they can give up work or only work part-time. Money is also available for equipment, clothing and travel, accommodation and the expenses of training and competition.

Successful sports teams attract a lot of sponsorship. Sponsorship received by a team is used by the organisation responsible for the team.

Amateur teams who are sponsored may have their equipment, clothing, training and travelling expenses paid for by the sponsor.

Sometimes sponsorship is given to teams at different age levels. Sponsorship of junior teams usually results in very favourable publicity for the sponsor.

National governing bodies

The national sport governing bodies receive various forms of sponsorship, both to develop their sport generally, and to pay for events and special projects.

Coaching and achievement schemes

Most children are very happy to win a competition or achieve a standard in

sport, and many sponsors support achievement schemes for young people.

Sponsors pay the costs of running the scheme, including badges and certificates, and receive publicity when the children take their badges and certificates home. Their aim is to get credit for encouraging young people to take part in sport and to improve their ability.

Sporting events

International matches and championship finals are very popular with sponsors. These events are televised and the sponsor is guaranteed good publicity. Sponsors pay for the administration, organisation and expenses of the event and the sport keeps any profit from television fees or gate money.

Sometimes companies sponsor a league or a cup competition which takes place over a period of time.

Most major events depend on sponsorship to take place.

Local events are also sponsored, with companies benefiting from local publicity.

Sports sponsorship organisations

SportsAid

Established in 1998, SportsAid is a charity.

SportsAid aims to educate young people through sport, especially those disadvantaged. It supports talented young sportspeople and is a major supporter of sportspeople with disabilities.

activity

Link the sponsor

Below you will find details of four companies who are considering sponsoring sport in some form or another. You will also find information about a number of sporting individuals and groups who are seeking sponsorship.

Your task is to see if you can match the sponsors to these individuals or groups. You should consider:

- whether the company and the individual or sport will make good partners
- what will be the advantages and disadvantages of a sponsorship agreement between them.

Companies considering sponsorship

1 The **Coopersale Brewery** is a long established company providing a range of popular beers and lagers. The company is trying to increase sales, particularly to younger adults, and believe that sponsoring sport or sportspeople could improve their image and raise awareness of the brand.

2 **Future** is a clothing company which specialises in selling fashionable clothes to people within the 15–25 age range. It currently has 20 shops, mainly in the south east of England. It has had a very good year for sales and is now looking to expand its business throughout England. It is looking at sponsoring sport and its team of designers gain much of their inspiration from sportswear.

3 **WH Jones** is a bookseller and stationer known throughout the country. The company is facing fierce competition from other similar stores. Its last venture into sponsorship was a disaster as it involved professional footballers whose careers were shortened because of involvement in a drink and drugs scandal. The company wishes to be involved in sport but is looking at a different form of sponsorship.

4 **Peabody & Nurden** are traditional cricket bat manufacturers who have recently taken over a smaller company making a range of cricket goods, including clothing. They are based in Berkshire and are looking to link their name with sport in general and cricket in particular.

activity

Sporting individuals and groups seeking sponsorship

A **Carlos** is an 18-year-old skateboarder who has represented Great Britain in the World Junior Championships. He is a full-time student and finds it difficult to fit in his heavy training schedule with his studies. His coach lives 50 miles away, near the skateboarding training facilities, and he does not have a car. He does not have time to take a part-time job and finds it difficult to make ends meet.

B **Pieta** has had a very successful career as a speed skater. She has won a bronze medal at the European championships and looks destined for even greater things at the next Olympics. Her partner, who is a top swimmer, has recently been found guilty of taking a performance-enhancing drug and has been banned from competition for two years. He has retired from the sport in order to coach Pieta. Her sponsorship contract with a well-known cosmetics company has just come to an end and the company has taken the decision not to renew it.

C **Carlton** is director of a charity which helps people with learning disabilities to take part in competitive sport. The charity is based in a major city and organises evening classes at sports centres, swimming pools and other venues. The charity has decided to hold an international event in their city and Carlton has been given the task of raising funds through sponsorship. The event will feature athletics, swimming and gymnastics. It is expected that 2,000 competitors will take part ,and up to 10,000 carers and spectators will attend. It is hoped that full television coverage will be available.

D **The Old Swan** football club in the village of Appledom, in Berkshire, has entered a team in the local Sunday football league. The new owner of the pub is an ex-professional footballer who is not only enthusiastic about the team, but is also a very good coach. The team are very keen but of mixed age, experience and ability. In the past, they have raised a great deal of money for local charities.

E The **county organisers for archery** have decided to launch an achievement scheme to promote archery in schools. The scheme will give badges and certificates to children who achieve set standards when shooting at a target from different distances. At present only 50 schools take part, but the organisers hope to double this number within two years. If sufficient sponsorship is available, they would hope to subsidise the cost to schools when buying archery equipment.

The Institute of Sports Sponsorship (ISS)

The Institute of Sports Sponsorship is a national non-profitmaking organisation founded in 1985 in order to promote sports sponsorship by bringing together sponsors and sports. It consists of a group of companies who support sport and is run by a committee made up of member companies. Affiliated to the European Sponsorship Association, the ISS aims to:

- protect the traditional nature of sport
- help companies get a fair return on their sponsorship.

The ISS has strong links with Sport England, the Central Council for Physical Recreation (CCPR), and the national governing bodies. It runs the Sportsmatch scheme for the government and the Sports Sponsorship Advisory Service with the CCPR.

The advantages and disadvantages of sports sponsorship

There are advantages and disadvantages to sports sponsorship for both the sports and the sponsoring companies.

Advantages for sport

- For professional sportspeople and organisations, sponsorship is another source of income.
- For amateur sportspeople, sponsorship may:
  - allow them to give up their jobs and train full-time
  - pay day-to-day living expenses
  - pay for clothing and equipment
  - pay for costs of training and competition
  - remove financial worries.
- For amateur organisations, sponsorship money can be used to:
  - fund the running of events
  - improve facilities
  - organise coaching and training schemes
  - promote the sport and encourage participation
  - improve the image of the sport
  - run and advertise award schemes.

Disadvantages for sport

- Once sponsorship is accepted, the sport comes to rely on it. If sponsorship is removed, there may be financial problems for sport. This gives the sponsor a powerful hold on the sport.
- Sponsors may be able to change the sport. For example, professional rugby league has been changed to a summer game and completely reorganised.
- Some sports have little television appeal and so attract little sponsorship. They may find it hard to develop their sport without money from sponsorship.

- The national governing bodies make agreements with sponsors without necessarily consulting their sportspeople. As a result players may find themselves forced to wear their sponsor's clothing or use the sponsor's equipment, and have their name linked to the sponsor without their agreement.

Advantages for the sponsor

Sponsorship:

- advertises the name of the company's product, linking it with a popular activity or person
- provides exposure on television whenever the sport is seen
- ensures the use of the sponsor's name in the media
- improves a company's reputation because the company is supporting British sport
- transfers the spectators' good feelings about the sport to the sponsoring company's product
- can reduce the company's tax liability, depending how they give the money to sport.

Disadvantages for the sponsor

Sponsorship does not always represent good value for money for the sponsoring company. Having embarked on a sponsorship deal, a company must ask itself:

- Has the sportsperson, team or event been successful?
- Has the publicity been good in the media, especially television?
- Does the public link our company with the sport?
- Does the public feel good about our company?
- Have sales increased or business improved?

Sponsorship agreements sometimes last for years, and sponsors cannot immediately pull out if things go wrong. From time to time the action of a sportsperson or a team on or off the pitch brings bad publicity, and the sponsor may want to withdraw its sponsorship. This is not always possible.

Sponsors need success. Regular losers and weak teams attract few sponsors.

Unacceptable sponsorship

Although sport has undoubtedly benefited from sponsorship in many ways over the years, the issue of sponsorship remains controversial. For example:

- Tobacco companies sponsor sport, yet smoking is a proven health risk. Sport keeps us healthy, so smoking and sport cannot go together. Young people should not be encouraged to smoke.
- Companies making alcoholic drinks sponsor sport, yet alcohol is known to cause both health problems and problems involving anti-social behaviour. Alcohol and sport do not go together. Young people should not be encouraged to drink alcohol.

A similar argument is now being used about high-fat products such as chocolate, biscuits and cakes which may raise cholesterol levels and contribute to obesity. Young people should not be encouraged to eat unhealthy foods.

In 1998, the European Union voted to ban all sponsorship of sport by tobacco companies in magazines and newspapers by 2002, at normal cultural and sporting events by 2003, and at 'world level' sporting events, including Formula One, by 2006.

QUESTIONS

22 Sponsorship

1. **Explain what is meant by sponsorship in sport today.**
   (2 marks)
2. **Sports sponsorship is very important. Explain who and what may be sponsored.**
   (4 marks)
3. **Sports sponsorship can take many forms. Describe six different forms of sponsorship available to individuals and different sports.**
   (6 marks)
4. **Give three advantages and three disadvantages of sports sponsorship for an individual amateur sportsperson.**
   (6 marks)
5. **Companies give a lot of thought before sponsoring sport. Give three advantages and three disadvantages of sports sponsorship from the company's point of view.**
   (6 marks)
6. **Suggest three things a company might look for in a sport before signing up to a sponsorship deal.**
   (3 marks)

23 The media

When we talk about the **media**, we are referring to all the different channels of communication that are used to bring us stories, coverage of sports events, news, comment and information. Examples include magazines, books, newspapers, radio, the Internet and ICT, television, film, video and DVD. Newspapers and magazines are known collectively as the **press**.

KEYWORDS

Media: the different channels of communication that are used to bring us stories, news, action and information

Press: print media such as newspapers and magazines

Listed events: nationally significant sporting fixtures which cannot be sold exclusively to one TV company.

Key to Exam Success

For your GCSE you will need to know:

- what is meant by the media
- the positive and negative effects of media coverage of sport.

“ KEY THOUGHTS ”

'We see our sport through the eyes of the media.'

Media categories

Magazines

If you walk into any newsagent you will find dozens of magazines about individual sports, from major activities like tennis to minority sports like the triathlon. Within the covers are pages packed with pictures, stories and news about particular sports. General sports magazines are very much rarer, although a number focus on health and fitness.

Books

Successful books on sport usually consist of biographies of current sports stars. At regular intervals, the histories of individual sports or their clubs are published in great detail. Coaching and training books help us to improve our sporting performance. There are now many textbooks at all levels to help pupils and students studying sport – like this one! Novels based on sport are much harder to find.

Newspapers

Although there is no national daily newspaper solely devoted to sport in Britain, all the national newspapers devote several pages to sport and employ a large number of sports journalists. Sunday newspapers even have separate sports sections.

The aim of editors is to sell more newspapers. This is reflected in the sports pages. Some carry more details about the private lives of the sports stars than they do about the sport itself. Newspapers are good at building up stars when they are successful. However, they are even better at knocking them down when they fail. Today, newspapers play a major part in forming our views about sport. The way sports writers present sport, and the pictures they use, have a key influence on the way we think about sport.

Radio

Before television, the great advantage of radio was that it reported events live. The commentator described the action as it happened and listeners felt they were there. In spite of television, radio still has its place. From the broadcasters' point of view, it is much cheaper to report on radio, and it uses a much smaller team of people.

Radio Five Live is a national radio station which concentrates on news and sport. There are also many local radio stations serving particular areas which are more likely to report local sports news and developments.

From the listener's point of view, radio is a much cheaper and more mobile medium than television. It also allows us to do other things while we listen to the match, race or competition, and to keep in touch with the action, particularly when the events take some time to complete, for example, in cricket matches and tennis championships.

Film, video and DVD

Sport, being dramatic, full of heroic triumph and tragic tears, should make fabulous material for films. However, successful fims about sport are relatively rare. Examples include: Hoop Dreams (1995) about basketball; True Blue (1996) about rowing; Fever Pitch (1997) about the experiences of a football supporter, and Bend it like Beckham, about a young British Asian girl who wants to play football.

Video and DVD collections of great sporting occasions and outstanding individual performances are very popular, as are instructional videos for improving our sporting performances and to help coaches. No doubt the England Rugby World Cup victory will make a popular video and DVD, allowing viewers to relive past glories in the comfort of their own home.

CD-ROMs and the Internet

CD-ROMs contain a wealth of information about a whole range of sporting subjects. For example, we can find out every detail about the modern Olympic Games from just one disc. Much of the information in this book is also available on CD-ROM, together with interactive tests and animated diagrams of the body in action.

Through the Internet we can get information on sporting subjects almost instantly from around the world. Sports organisations from Sport England to local hockey clubs have their own websites which provide visitors with all the information they need.

activity

Sport interactive

As one of a team of four journalists, you have been given the task of creating a new TV sports channel.

The new channel must:

- provide news and information about a wide range of popular sports
- cater for minority sports interests
- aim to attract 16–30-year-olds
- appeal to both men and women
- meet the sporting needs of people from different ethnic groups and people with disabilities
- satisfy the needs of sports performers as well as spectators
- provide links to viewers' favourite sports, teams, players, etc.
- Include a 24-hour sports news service
- make it easy for viewers to influence future programmes and how they are shown
- be at the cutting edge of technology by using links between mobile phones, televisions, computers and future ICT developments.

continued on page 300

activity

You have one week to prepare a presentation which will be shown to the management group of the television company (your PE class). You will need to use a variety of sources of information. For example, check the sport currently available on television and radio, research the sports coverage in newspapers, use the Internet for further information. Do not limit yourself to what is currently on offer. Try to be creative and think ahead. Technology is moving very quickly.

Make sure that your presentation is lively and persuasive. Try to use music and pictures, perhaps even video to enhance your delivery.

Online booking also means that sports events can be advertised on websites and tickets booked in advance. By using e-mails we can communicate with other people very quickly and easily. This is the future for both sports fans and those interested in sports knowledge.

(In fact, you can contact the authors of this book with your sporting queries through our website. From The World of Sport Examined website at www.worldofsportexamined.com, you can also go directly to a number of other sport-related websites.)

Sport and television

Whether you love sport or hate it, you certainly cannot get away from it on television! An ever-increasing number of hours are devoted to sports of many different kinds. This is because sport is immensely popular and relatively cheap to produce for television. Sport also transcends language barriers, making it easier for sporting events to be screened in other countries.

Sport on television can be seen on terrestrial channels and satellite channels, some of which are now also available via cable. The five terrestrial channels include BBC1 and BBC2, which are funded by the television licence fee, and the independent companies who rely on money from advertising in the same way as the satellite companies. The BBC and these companies must all bid for the right to show sport on television – that is, they must negotiate with the national governing bodies of the individual sports or the organisers of specific events. This has led to fierce competition for the rights to televise popular events such as Premier League football matches.

Major events

The government decided many years ago that a number of events were too important to the nation to be sold exclusively to one company. These are called **listed events** and in 1999, they were put into two groups. In the first group are events such as the Olympics, the FA Cup Final, the FIFA World Cup, the Derby, the Grand National, the Rugby World Cup final and Wimbledon finals. This group has to be available free to terrestrial television.

In the other group are events including the Commonwealth Games, the World Athletics Championship, the Ryder Cup and cricket test matches played in

England. These can receive live coverage on pay TV, as long as arrangements have been made for highlights to be available free on terrestrial television.

Satellite television

Satellite television has had a great impact on sport, allowing us to watch a wide variety of sports events in this country and live from around the world. It also gives us the choice of a large number of channels, including Sky Sports and Eurosport. This has resulted in many minor sports being seen regularly on television. Satellite sport is, however, not free. It is only available if you can afford to buy the equipment and make monthly payments to the satellite network.

Sports programming

Sport is televised in many different ways.

- We can watch live events as they take place and then see edited highlights later. Some major live events, such as major boxing tournaments, can only be seen on a 'pay-per-view' system.
- News programmes bring the results of major events like the Olympic finals, as well as the latest stories.
- Sports quizzes, documentaries and magazine programmes are also popular.
- Dedicated sport channels are also available on subscription; for example, Manchester United FC have their own subscription channel.
- Educational sports programmes can show how to get started in a sport or how skill can be developed in a coaching series.

There seems to be no limit to the amount of analysis, discussion and interviewing we can see on some sporting subjects.

Television also supplies sports information such as results and reports throughout the day and night on Ceefax, Teletext and Skytext.

When watching a match on digital television, interactive technology now enables us to choose a particular camera angle, see the highlights, access extra facts through on-screen menus or home

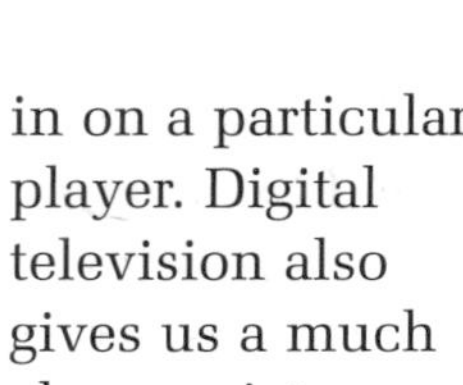

in on a particular player. Digital television also gives us a much clearer picture and better sound.

How does television affect sport?

Television benefits sport in a number of ways.

- Sport increases in popularity through exposure on television. This is especially true when a national team or individual does well in international sport. Minor sports may also become more popular when covered on television.
- Large amounts of money come into sport from the sponsors and television companies. This can be used to pay sports performers and to help develop the sport.
- Some sports have been saved from economic collapse by money from sponsors and television companies. These sports have needed money because their costs have increased but crowds have decreased.
- Television increases the rewards for both individuals and teams. This in turn raises the standards of performance.

Undeniably sport has been changed by television – and not everyone has welcomed the changes. Television has also caused the following problems for sport:

- Rule changes have been introduced to make sports more exciting for TV

audiences. Examples include one-day cricket, tie-breaks in tennis and penalty shoot-outs in football.

- Changes have been made in clothing. For example, in some competitions cricketers wear multicoloured clothes instead of the traditional white.
- Starting times of events have been altered to increase the number of viewers – for example, Premier League football matches now take place on Sunday and Monday.
- Complete control and reorganisation of rugby league has passed to the sponsors, with the sponsoring company forming new league teams and arranging for the game to be played in the summer.
- The authority of officials can be undermined when their decisions are examined in detail. Umpires and referees have to make decisions instantly without the help of replays and different camera angles. Constant criticism of officials is not good for sport. Ways need to be found to help them make good decisions.
- Domination of television by a few of the most popular sports can lead to the impression that others are of little importance.
- The emphasis on winning has produced sportspeople and teams who are desperate for success. This can encourage sportspeople to take part too often, to play when injured, to resort to unsporting play or to cheat by using drugs.

- Some sports have great difficulty in making their sport attractive for television. For example, squash is popular at club level but is rarely seen on television. Television has tried to cover squash through using all-glass courts, special balls for the cameras to pick up and different scoring.
- Loss of television coverage has had disastrous effects on some sports in the past, for example, table tennis and darts.
- There will be bad publicity for sport when violence, drug abuse or personal problems make all the headlines.
- Spectators may be discouraged from attending live matches and events if they can see it all on television from the comfort of their living room.

Sport, sponsorship and television

Today, television, sport and sponsorship are very closely linked. What brings them together is money. Television companies want to show major events because they are popular with the public and are prepared to pay vast sums of money to win exclusive rights. This money is usually paid to the national governing bodies of the sport or the organisers of major events such as the Olympics.

Who controls what we watch?

In theory the national sport governing bodies are responsible for everything to do with their sport. However, the money paid by the television and sponsoring companies is so great that the sponsors can exert undue influence. This is because the NGBs have come to rely on money from television coverage and sponsorship to run their sport. Without it, they would be in financial trouble.

Many people believe that decisions are often made in the interests of sponsors and television producers rather than of the sport. The NGBs have been willing to change their sports to meet the new requirements. Sport on television is now an important part of the entertainment industry and has to respond to influences outside sport itself.

How does televised sport affect viewers?

The vast amount of sport available through the media means that we know far more than we used to about what is going on in the world of sport. We have more detailed knowledge about our favourite sports and a better understanding of all the new and less popular sports.

Sports stars can act as an inspiration for us all and as role models for young people. We hope that they will combine the highest skill with good behaviour, but this is not always the case.

The gap between top sportspeople and the viewers is getting wider. Their level of skill is now far beyond that of the casual performer. The financial rewards and lifestyles of top sportspeople are also far removed from ordinary people.

How do sports programmes influence our opinions about sport?

Our opinions about the world of sport are heavily influenced by what we see on television. The responsibility for the programmes lies with presenters, commentators, producers and editors. They are in a powerful position to influence us.

The domination of sport on television by football and a few other sports reinforces their popularity. This makes it difficult for other sports to be presented as being of equal value.

The way sport is presented on television affects our views about it. For example, a team may play well in a match, but if the presenters concentrate on poor decisions by officials or bad behaviour by players they can change the emphasis dramatically.

So-called experts may praise a particular player or highlight a skill, but we must remember that these are only their opinions.

Sport on television can also reinforce stereotypes. In the past, sport on

television was dominated by young, able-bodied male sportspeople. Today, older performers, sportspeople with disabilities and sportswomen are seen much more often. However, some commentators still focus on the appearance of women performers and whether or not they are married, rather than on their sporting achievements.

How does television influence us to watch or take part in sport?

The answer is: we are not sure. We can claim that television increases our interest in sport of all types. This has been true of sports such as snooker and show jumping. Sports from abroad, for example, American football and Sumo wrestling, have also become popular. Major events like world championships attract huge television audiences.

On the other hand, many people would rather watch sport in the comfort of their homes than go to an event. Good television coverage of sports means that there is little reason to go and watch it as a spectator. This has been accepted in football: part of the television payment to televise the matches live goes to compensate the clubs outside the Premiership for reduced gate money.

Television certainly encourages us to be a national of sports watchers. It seems less likely that it will inspire us to put on our sports kit and take part.

QUESTIONS

23 The media

1 **Television is part of the media. Describe what is meant by the media.**
(4 marks)

2 **Sport on television is covered by the channels in many varied ways. Give six different examples.**
(6 marks)

3 **Televised sport can bring both benefits and negative effects to sport. List three benefits and three negative effects, with examples for each.**
(6 marks)

4 **Give two ways in which sport has been influenced by coverage on satellite and cable television.**
(2 marks)

5 **Television can change sport. List six examples to show how sport has been changed because of the demands of television.**
(6 marks)

6 **Give three advantages of listening to sport on the radio.**
(3 marks)

24 Social and cultural factors

Although sport involves competition, it also requires a high degree of co-operation: players must co-operate in obeying the rules and regulations; officials must enforce the rules fairly, and spectators also must obey certain codes of behaviour in order to make sport an exciting spectacle and enjoyable activity in which all three groups can take part. This chapter looks at some of the codes of behaviour, written and unwritten, which underpin our national sporting life.

activity

What's the score?

Complete the following charts to show your knowledge of the rules and regulations of a variety of different sports. You may need to do some research using the Internet.

Who's in charge?

Sport	Number of officials and details
Rugby league	Referee, two touch judges, video referee (professional matches only)
Synchronised swimming	
Tennis	
Diving	
Trampoline	
Netball	
Orienteering	
Ultimate Frisbee	

activity

Making up the numbers

Sport	Number of players	Number of substitutes
Soccer	11	3
Water polo		
Hockey		
Baseball		
Basketball		
Australian rules football		
Volleyball		
Lacrosse (men's)		

Sport and duration

Sport	Duration
Rugby union	Two halves of 40 minutes
Test cricket	
Gaelic football	
Polo	
American football	
Netball	
Handball	
Judo	

How do I win?

Sport	Method of deciding who is the winner in cup or knockout competitions
Tennis (men's)	Tie-break in the first four sets of a five set match
High jump	
Table tennis	
Basketball	
Squash	
Golf (match play)	
Rugby union	
Slalom skiing	

KEYWORDS

Amateur: someone who takes part in sport purely for enjoyment and is not paid

Conduct: the way people behave

Etiquette: the special ways we are expected to behave in our sport

Professional: someone who takes part in sport for payment

Open events: sporting events in which distinctions between amateurs and professionals are no longer recognised.

Key to Exam Success

For your GCSE you will need to know:

- the importance of the conduct of players, officials and spectators
- the differences between amature and professional sport.

KEY THOUGHTS

'The spirit of sport is the responsibility of all.'

People in sport

Players

All sports and most physical activities have rules and regulations which set out how we should take part in the activity. These rules are the responsibility of the national governing body for the sport. For example, in tennis it is the Lawn Tennis Association. Outside the UK, the International Tennis Federation controls all aspects of the game and makes the rules.

We all need to know and understand the rules of our sport. The purpose of rules for games is:

- to set out how the game is to be organised
- to explain the responsibilities of players and officials
- to protect players from injury
- to encourage good sporting behaviour
- to help the game to flow
- to promote enjoyment for all.

Rules must be followed and players punished if they are broken. Injury causes pain and stops us from playing. In high-risk collision sports such as rugby, injuries are inevitable. However, players who break rules and harm opponents must be dealt with severely. In recent years some players have been taken to court when their deliberate foul play has led to serious injury.

Rule changes

Rule changes are made in sport from time to time in order to:

- make the activity safer. For example, no tackling from behind in football

- make the event more exciting for players and spectators. For example, the tie-break in tennis
- keep up with technical developments in equipment in sport. For example, the gun linked to starting blocks in athletics to prevent false starts.

Rule enforcement can take place in different ways. In most major sports the player can be given a card warning or have to sit out from the action, temporarily or permanently. If the offence is more serious, action may be taken by the club or association resulting in a lengthy or permanent ban from the sport.

Etiquette

Etiquette means the special ways we are expected to behave in our sport. Etiquette is not a set of written rules, but an unwritten code of behaviour which has become part of each sport over a long period. Etiquette allows players to demonstrate fair play, sportsmanship, sporting spirit and respect for their opponents; it also helps to encourage fair play and reduce violence. Although it is not enforceable, players will make themselves very unpopular if they do not meet these expectations.

Officials

The official's central task is to enable sportspeople to take part in sport fairly and safely. Administrators organise events, but officials control the sporting action. The number and type of officials varies from sport to sport, and they can be referred to variously as referees, judges and umpires. Some sports also have different levels of officials (e.g. senior, minor). All officials have to work together to make sure everything runs smoothly. For example, in athletics, the starter works closely with the marksmen and timekeepers. Officials:

- have an excellent knowledge of the sport and its rules, laws and regulations
- apply the rules fairly to all
- maintain control by making decisions firmly
- check the equipment to be used beforehand
- keep the time for the match or event
- check that the correct number of people are taking part
- look after the safety of all those involved
- be patient, good with people and have a sense of humour
- be in good physical condition.

In most sports, officials are volunteers, possibly receiving expenses for helping to control the event. Often teams have to manage with a very small number of officials. For football matches in the local

park, substitute players will often act as referee's assistants; similarly, cricket players will take it in turn to be umpire.

In professional tennis, football, cricket and rugby today officials are paid professionals. It was realised that it was not possible to rely on amateur officials because the standards of play and the financial rewards were so great. Only the best officials could cope with the demands of the game and command the respect of players, managers and spectators alike.

Training as an official

To qualify as an official takes time. Often former players take on the role. They will already have a good knowledge of the game, but will need to take formal examinations and gradually work their way up through the different levels.

Being an official is often a thankless task. However, we should always respect officials and never take them for granted: without them, sport would not be possible.

Spectators

Spectators are welcome at all sporting events, from mums and dads at school sports days to the thousands of paying spectators at World Cup finals.

Spectator needs

Spectators pay to watch sport live at stadiums, halls or grounds. In the case of top Premier League football clubs or the finals of the Olympic Games track events, the income they provide is considerable.

Good facilities must be provided for the spectators, including comfortable seats with an uninterrupted view, clean toilets, food and drink available at reasonable prices and a range of souvenir merchandise. Special provision must also be made for people with disabilities, children and family groups.

Spectators must be able to get in and out of the stadium easily, with entrance and exit routes having good lighting. There must be no overcrowding, and emergency procedures must be ready in

place should they be needed. To ensure the comfort and safety of all, there must be enough stewards and marshals, backed up by the police.

Home team advantage

Supporters undoubtedly can affect the outcome of a match in certain circumstances. Home teams in all sports are thought to have an advantage. When England won the rugby World Cup in Australia, the presence of so many supporters in their white shirts, singing and cheering on their team, is said to have lifted the team considerably.

Professional football has suffered from hooliganism amongst a small group of so-called supporters for many years. The problem has been very hard to remove completely. In particular, trouble caused by a few supporters at matches and tournaments around Europe has resulted in England fans gaining a very bad reputation. After problems playing Turkey at home in 2003, England supporters were not allowed to the away game.

The Hillsborough tragedy

In 1989, 95 fans were crushed to death during an FA Cup semi-final at the Hillsborough stadium in Sheffield. The report into the causes of the tragedy suggested ways to improve the safety at football grounds. It recommended that football league grounds should become all-seaters; that fencing should be made safer; and that policing and medical facilities be improved. Clubs were forced to make these changes, and football grounds today are considerably safer and more welcoming as a result.

Amateur and professional sport

AQA A only

The difference between amateurs and professionals in sport can be summarised as follows:

- **Amateurs** take part in sport because of the enjoyment and satisfaction they get from the activity. Taking part is more important than the result of the game or competition. Amateurs train and compete in their own time, usually after work or at weekends. They are not paid. Above all, amateurs make their own decisions about sport. They choose to play. No one can force them to take part. Sport is quite separate from their work. It is strictly a leisure activity.
- **Professionals** are paid to compete in sport. Winning is all-important to them. The more successful they are, the more money they earn. Professionals usually train full-time and devote themselves completely to their sport. Sport is their work. They sign contracts and must take part in competitions.

The 'gentleman amateur'

Labelling sportspeople as amateurs or professionals lasted for most of the last century. It originated in the nineteenth century when 'gentlemen amateurs' who did not need to be paid for playing were contrasted with professionals for whom sport was a means of livelihood. The modern Olympics were based on the ideal of the true amateur sportsman.

However, after 1945, it became extremely difficult for amateurs training in their spare time to reach the high standard required for international sport.

To get around this difficulty, countries found their own solutions. These included sports scholarships in the USA, trust funds and sponsorship in the UK and state-sponsored schemes for athletes in communist countries. Eventually, the International Olympic Committee (IOC) changed its rules by abandoning the term amateur and allowing sportspeople to receive payment. This resulted in open Olympics with full-time professionals taking part.

The status of sportspeople today

Throughout the UK, thousands of people take part in sport in the traditional way without financial reward of any kind. At the same time, a small group of professional sportspeople earn their living by playing sport. Between these two extremes are many people who get help in playing sport or receive rewards for playing sport. This group includes **part-time professionals**, who are paid for playing but still earn a living outside sport. Sponsorship of all kinds helps both amateur and professional sportspeople.

Most sports today are **open**, meaning that distinctions between amateurs and professionals are no longer recognised. But a few sports maintain the traditional differences. For example, in boxing there are the Amateur Boxing Association and the Boxing Board of Control for professionals. The two parts of the sport function quite separately and operate under different rules.

A career in sport?

For most of us, sport seems a very attractive career. To spend all day playing sport and get paid for it seems an ideal life.

The advantages of being a professional sportsperson might include:

- high earnings
- luxurious living
- the attention of the media
- high-profile success
- popularity with the general public
- opportunities to travel round the world
- eventual retirement to a life of comfort!

However, this is not the typical lifestyle of a professional sportsperson. The reality is that many fail to make it to the top for a number of reasons:

- failure to fulfil early promise
- the effect of serious illness or injury
- personal problems reducing performance

- pressure from younger players
- difficulties in handling the media
- lack of determination in training
- age
- pressure to win leading to cheating or taking of banned drugs.

For those who do achieve star status, success is often short-lived. Even the most successful sportspeople may find themselves having to look for a new career when they are only halfway through their working life.

There are a limited number of sports in the UK where professional sportspeople can earn a living. Opportunities in professional sport are mainly for men. Only in tennis, golf and athletics are women, in any numbers, able to earn a living.

QUESTIONS

24 Social and cultural factors

1 **Officials are essential for all sporting events. Suggest three qualities they must have.**

(3 marks)

2 **List the officials needed for four different sporting activities.**

(4 marks)

3 **Explain the meaning of etiquette in sport and give three examples of sporting etiquette.**

(5 marks)

4 **Spectators are essential to professional sport. Suggest two ways in which they must be looked after and two ways in which they may affect a sporting contest.**

(4 marks)

5 **Explain the differences between amateur and professional sportspeople.**

(6 marks)

25 Influence of local and national providers

The huge range and variety of sporting opportunities in the UK today exists thanks to the work of a large number of different sporting bodies. These organisations provide facilities, training, education, funding and many other support services without which sport would not be possible. This chapter looks at the work of the local and national bodies which provide the infrastructure of sport in the UK.

KEYWORDS

Funding: the way finance (money) is provided

National Governing Bodies (NGBs): the organisation responsible for a particular sport throughout the country

World Class Programme: the way top sportspeople receive funding from the National Lottery to achieve success.

Key to Exam Success

For your GCSE you will need to know:

- about the importance of national sports organisations
- how sport is funded
- how local clubs are organised.

KEY THOUGHTS

'Start, stay and suceed in sport.'

activity

Under new management

Reat the report from the Daltringham Echo *which gives the background to the problems being faced by Daltringham Sports club. Then read the letter from Mr. Sweetingham to Trevor Woodhouse (both supplied by your teacher). For the purpose of this activity, in your groups of four, you must imagine you are Trevor Woodhouse. Draft your reply agreeing to become Chairman. Set out any conditions which are necessary for you to take up the post and give your plans for reorganising the club.*

You might like to use the following headings:

Immediate action:
- Finance
- Fixtures
- Clubhouse
- Pitches

Proposals for improvement for next season:
- Meetings
- Committees
- Publicity
- Fundraising
- Clubhouse
- Social events.

Sport at local level

Local sports clubs exist because enthusiastic people have met together in the past to enjoy their sport. However, enthusiasm is not enough to keep a club going. To be successful, a club needs members, a committee, a constitution, facilities and finance.

Members should be:

- enthusiastic about their sport
- happy to take part with others
- willing to pay their share of the costs
- able to accept club rules
- available to play, organise, coach or officiate at competitions.

Committee members should be:

- willing to take on jobs
- ready to work as a team
- able to make decisions for the club
- elected by the club's Annual General Meeting (AGM).

There are three essential jobs:

- **Chairperson**: controls committee meetings and acts as the club's representative
- **Secretary**: deals with the day-to-day business, arranges meetings
- **Treasurer**: deals with all the club's finances.

The **constitution** sets out the rules of the club. It explains:

- how the club is organised
- how to become a member
- how people are elected to jobs
- how fees can be charged
- what happens if members break the rules
- how the club can be changed.

Facilities are needed for playing, training, as well as for meetings and social events. The needs of the club will depend on the type of activity and the number of members. Facilities might be hired or owned.

A club will need to pay for:

- hire or upkeep of facilities
- team clothing and equipment
- training and competition costs
- office expenses.

It can raise money through:

- fees and subscriptions
- fundraising
- grants and sponsorship.

Club and school links

Schools want their pupils to continue playing sport when they leave school. The clubs need a steady stream of young members to improve the standard of sport and to replace those retiring. For these reasons, schools and clubs both benefit from strong links.

Funding of sport

To understand the funding of sport, we need to look at why sport needs money and where the money comes from.

Why does sport need money?

Sportspeople need clothing, equipment, facilities and opportunities to take part in sport. They also need teaching, training, coaching and competition. At school, many of these things are provided free of charge, but as adults we have to pay for them.

- **Professional sportspeople** expect to be able to pay their living, training and competition expenses. In addition they expect payment and rewards for performing.
- **Clubs and governing bodies** need to pay for running costs, facilities, events, competitions and development projects.
- **Local authorities** need to provide sports facilities for schools and leisure facilities for the community.

Sources of funding for sport

As with the financing of sports facilities, funding for sport is provided by the public, private and voluntary sector. The total government and lottery money spent on sport and physical activity is about £2.2 billion a year.

The public sector

- The **government** raises money through taxes. It also receives money from the National Lottery. The government gives grants to local authorities to help provide services, including education and leisure services. Some of the National Lottery money is passed on to Sport England for distribution to various sports organisations. The government also funds the Countryside Agency and the Sportsmatch scheme, in which it doubles the value of any new grassroots sponsorship money.
- **Local authorities** raise money through local council tax and business rates. They also receive grants from the government, the National Lottery, the Foundation for Sport and the Arts, and by forming partnerships with local businesses. Some of the money is used for education, to provide sports facilities, equipment and staff for schools, youth clubs and adult education. The local authority also pays for local sports facilities such as pools, leisure centres and playing fields.

The private sector

- **Companies and businesses** make profits. Some companies use this money to sponsor sport directly with individual sportspeople and also through national governing bodies. Others support SportsAid, which distributes sponsorship money for them. The football pools companies support the Foundation for Sport and the Arts.
- **The National Lottery** was established by the government in 1994 and is run by a commercial company. It is now the central source of money for sport. This money is distributed by Sport England.

- **The Foundation for Sport and the Arts** was established by the football pools companies and the government in 1991 to support grassroots sport.

The voluntary sector

- **Local sports clubs** can raise money through membership subscriptions, fees, fundraising and organising sponsored events. They can also apply for financial help to improve facilities from the Sportsmatch scheme, local authorities, Sport England, the sports national governing bodies, the National Lottery, the Foundation for Sport and the Arts and companies (through sponsorship).
- **Individual sportspeople** can apply for grants from the World Class Programme. This is funded by the National Lottery and organised by the various sport national governing bodies. Grants and other forms of funding are also available from SportsAid, the sports national governing bodies, the Foundation for Sport and the Arts, sports trusts, charities and businesses. Individual sportspeople often also receive financial support from their families.
- **National governing bodies (NGBs)** receive regular income in the form of membership fees from sports clubs to cover the basic running costs of organising events, competitions, training, coaching and achievement schemes. They can also apply for grants from Sport England, the National Lottery, the Foundation for Sport and the Arts and charitable trusts, or seek sponsorship from companies in order to build new sports facilities or launch new schemes. Some NGBs run major events which are very popular; they can also raise large sums of money by selling television rights to major events such as the Wimbledon tennis championships.

Organisations which support sport

England has a history of strongly independent sports clubs and national governing bodies going back more than a century. However, since the setting up of the first Sports Council in 1972, government influence over sport has steadily grown. The original Sports Council was the first sporting body to receive a government grant. Today the separate sport councils receive annual grants from the government and also distribute vast amounts of National Lottery money.

What are the government's plans for sport?

In 2002, the government published Game Plan, a strategy for delivering its sport and physical activity objectives. One aim is to greatly increase the

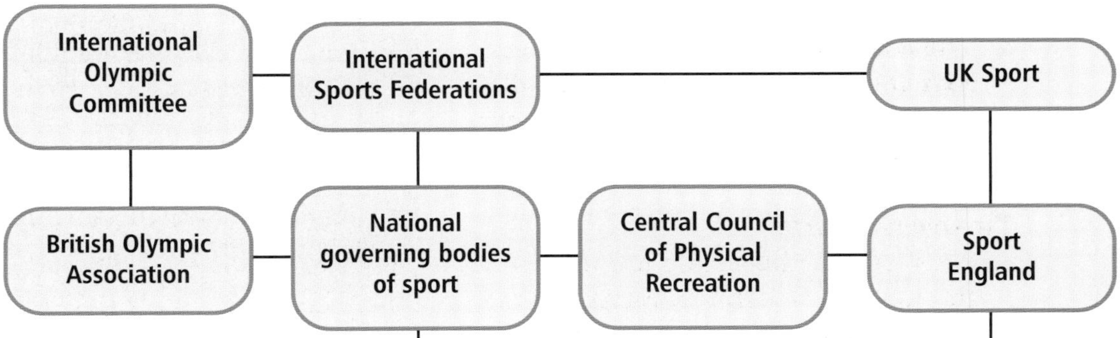

International Olympic Committee
International Sports Federations
UK Sport
British Olympic Association
National governing bodies of sport
Central Council of Physical Recreation
Sport England
Area associations
Regional offices of Sport England
Sports clubs
Local sports councils
Individual members

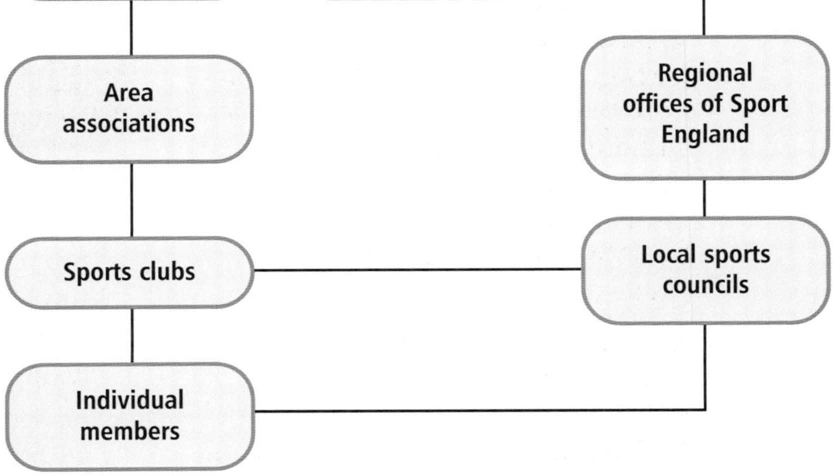

number of people taking part in sport. The target is for 70% of the population to be 'reasonably active' – i.e. taking part in 30 minutes of moderate exercise five times a week – by 2020.

The government is committed to sport, especially to the sporting needs of young people. Sport is seen not just as a good thing in itself but is increasingly linked to aspects of social policy, such as health, crime prevention, social cohesion and community problems.

The sports councils

As we have seen, the original Sports Council was founded in 1972. The sports councils which developed later were themselves reorganised in 1997. Today we have five independent sports councils:

- The UK sports council, now known as **UK Sport**, looks after issues at UK level.
- The four councils of England, Scotland, Wales and Northern Ireland are each responsible for sport in their own countries.

What is UK Sport?

UK Sport consists of a council of members appointed by the Secretary of State for Culture, Media and Sport, a chief executive and a full-time staff. It is funded by an annual government grant for UK-wide sporting projects.

UK Sport deals with high-performance sport at the UK level and aims to achieve sporting excellence for Britain. In order to do this, it:

- gives full support to top performers through the World Class Performance Programme and the UK Sports Institute
- distributes National Lottery money to projects which promote and support sporting excellence
- extends the UK's international sporting influence
- encourages the world's major sporting events to come to the UK
- promotes ethical standards of behaviour
- is the UK's national anti-doping agency.

What is Sport England?

Sport England is the brand name of the English sports council. It is funded by the government (currently £35 million) and acts as a distributor of National Lottery money (currently £200 million). The sports councils for Scotland, Wales and Northern Ireland work in a similar way.

Sport England is responsible for putting into action the government's plans for sport.

Members of the Sport England council are appointed by the Secretary of State for Culture, Media and Sport. Sport England has a London head office with full-time staff and nine regional offices across England.

The regional offices:

- promote Sport England policy through regional sports boards
- keep Sport England in touch with needs at grassroots level
- have close links with local authorities, local sports councils, national governing bodies and other organisations involved with sport, education, recreation and the environment.

The local sports councils are supported by Sport England but act independently. Their role is to:

- bring together local people, clubs and groups interested in sport
- discuss problems, exchange views and plan for the future
- to promote developments in local sports in the best interests of the community.

Sport England is also responsible for a network of ten centres run by the English Institute of Sport (EIS). These help the national governing bodies and their elite sportspeople on World Class programmes to reach their medal-winning targets.

The Sport England Strategy

Vision: to make England an active and successful sporting nation

Mission: to work with others to create opportunities for people to get involved in sport, to stay in sport, and to excel and succeed in sport at every level.

Objectives

1. **Opportunities to play sport**: to increase participation in sport in order to improve the health of the nation, with a focus on priority groups.
2. **Opportunities to stay in sport**: to retain people in sport and active recreation through an effective network of clubs, sports facilities, coaches, volunteers and competitive opportunities.
3. **Opportunities to achieve success in sport**: to make sporting success happen at the highest level.

'Start, stay and succeed in sport.'

The aims of Sport England

The role of Sport England is to lead the development of sport in England.

Its aims are:

- to make England more active
- to influence decision makers on sport
- to distribute funding.

Sports England uses its money to start, stay and succeed in sport.

Funding

In 2003, Sport England changed the way it funded sport. Its money is now used for:

- Community investment – the money is distributed through the regional sports board. They provide the money for the active England campaign. The money comes from both the National Lottery and the Government grant. The aim is to develop sporting facilities and activity projects in local communities across England.
- National investment – the money is distributed through the national governing bodies of sport. There are 30 sports that receive priority for support and development.

Active England Campaign

An ambitious new campaign, based on the Government's plans to get 70% of the population doing 30 minutes activity a day by 2020. This is intended to improve the health and happiness of the nation.

The UK Sports Institute (UKSI)

The UKSI provides sports science, medicine, coaching, first-class facilities, expert advice and support for elite sportspeople, teams and their coaches. A central services team is based in the London offices of UK Sport.

The Youth Sport Trust

The Youth Sport Trust (YST) is a registered charity, founded in 1994. The trust has a mission 'to develop and implement, in close partnership with other organisations, quality physical education and sport programmes for all young people aged 18 months to 18 years in schools and the community'. It receives funding from a number of sources, including the DfEE, companies, other charitable trusts and individuals.

The YST has developed a variety of programmes for schools and the community. It also:

- runs the TOP programmes (see below) jointly with Sport England
- works on a programme for young disabled people called Sportsability
- was appointed by the DfEE to work with schools interested in becoming sports colleges
- works with established sports colleges to assist their development
- carries out research – for example, the Nike project to explore new ways to involve girls in PE and sport.

The TOP programmes

These are a series of linked schemes, started in 1996, to promote young people's sports development. All the programmes provide equipment, activity resources and training.

- **TOP Tots**: aimed at helping children aged 18 months to 3 years to experience physical activity
- **TOP Start**: aimed at helping children aged 3–5 years to learn through physical activity
- **TOP Play**: aimed at helping children aged 4–9 years to learn core skills and fun sports
- **TOP Sport**: an introduction to sports and games for children 7–11 years
- **TOP Skills**: aimed at helping children aged 11–14 years to extend their sporting skill and knowledge
- **TOP Link**: aimed at helping children aged 14–16 years to take a lead in organising sport
- **Millennium Volunteers**: encouraging 16–19-year-olds to volunteer through sport
- **Sportsability**: creating opportunities for young people with disabilities
- **Dreams and Teams**: enabling young people to travel abroad and help to spread the Tops programme worldwide.

The national governing bodies of sport

The national governing bodies of sport (NGBs) are voluntary organisations with democratic constitutions which are independent of the government and exist in order to promote development of individual sports. They are made up of members who are elected by clubs to make decisions and represent them at national level.

Although the NGBs use mainly unpaid volunteers, they are run by full-time paid officials.

The role of the NGBs is to:

- organise competitions and events
- select teams at all levels
- arrange coaching and training
- organise award schemes
- enforce rules and laws, including the rules of the international federation
- negotiate with television and sponsoring companies
- distribute funds for the World Class programmes
- produce detailed plans with clear targets for participation and excellence
- work through their area organisations.

The NGBs are financed by members' subscriptions, sponsorship by companies, sale of television rights, profits from spectator events, grants from Sport England, the National Lottery, the Foundation for Sport and the Arts and partnerships with central government and local authorities.

The World Class programme

Under the World Class programme, the NGBs select outstanding sportspeople to receive funding from the National Lottery to support their training for international competition. It gives them the opportunity to be successful on the world sporting stage. Only sportspeople selected by their NGB will receive help.

Individual schemes are:

- **World Class Start**: for promising young sportspeople
- **World Class Potential**: for talented sportspeople with the potential to represent their country
- **World Class Performance**: for elite sportspeople with the potential to succeed in international competition.

The Central Council of Physical Recreation

Founded in 1935, the Central Council of Physical Recreation (CCPR) is a voluntary body that acts as the independent voice of UK sport and recreation. It is composed mainly of national governing bodies of sport and is split into six divisions: movement and dance, games and sports, major spectator sports, outdoor pursuits, water recreation and interested organisations.

The CCPR has two main objectives:

- to improve and develop sport and physical recreation at all levels
- to support the work of the NGBs.

Acting as a forum, the CCPR enables NGBs to meet to discuss common problems and the best way to develop their sports. It also:

- runs campaigns, for example, against the loss of school playing fields
- advises government, local authorities and Sport England on sporting matters
- gives advice on sports sponsorship through the Sports Sponsorship Advisory Service
- helps professional sport through the Institute of Professional Sport
- runs the Sports Leader Award scheme with the British Sports Trust
- encourages and supports volunteers who administer sport.

The CCPR is funded by Sport England, donations from NGB members, sale of publications and other services.

The Sports Leaders Award Scheme

This scheme was started in 1982 in order to train young people as voluntary sports leaders. It aims to give young people the opportunity to become purposeful, positive and employable and offers awards at four levels – junior sports leader, community sports leader, and basic and higher expedition leader. The scheme is financed by the British Sports Trust and by donations from companies.

SportscoachUK

SportscoachUK (formerly the National Coaching Foundation) is an independent charity founded in 1983 in order to co-ordinate sports coaching and coach education. It is funded by grants from UK Sport and Sport England and earns income from trading.

SportscoachUK improves the skill and knowledge of coaches by offering courses at all levels and providing a network of Coaching Development Officers. It also works closely with Sport England, national governing bodies, the British Olympic Association, local authorities and education.

The Women's Sports Foundation

The Women's Sports Foundation (WSF) is a national charity funded by Sport England and through subscriptions and sponsorship. Its aims are to:

- increase awareness of the problems for women and girls in sport
- support the involvement of women and girls in sport at all levels
- encourage better access to sport for women and girls
- challenge and redress inequality in sport
- raise the profile of all British sportswomen
- advise sports organisations about women's issues in sport.

The Countryside Agency

The Countryside Agency (CA) is a government-funded public agency established in 1999 through the merger of the Countryside Agency and the Rural Development Commission. The role of the CA is to look after and improve the countryside in England, to run the National Parks of England and to develop access for outdoor activities. It also works with organisations such as the Ramblers' Association and advises the government on all countryside matters.

The National Playing Fields Association

The National Playing Fields Association (NPFA) is a national independent charity, founded in 1925. It is open to membership by both individuals and organisation and is run by a council and trustees.

The NPFA:

- acquires, protects and improves playing fields, playgrounds and play spaces
- works for those who need play areas most, especially children of all ages and people with disabilities
- protects around 2000 playing fields across the UK.

The NPFA is paid for by the public (through appeals), by supporters (through donations) and through sales of publications and technical advice.

QUESTIONS

25 Influence of local and national providers

1. **Name the two different sources of finance for local sports facilities.** *(2 marks)*
2. **Local sports clubs need to be organised to survive. Explain how a typical club might be organised by naming the different officials and describing their roles.** *(12 marks)*
3. **Suggest six different ways in which schools might develop links with local sports clubs.** *(6 marks)*
4. **Sport is funded in many different ways. Give five ways a local club might obtain financial support.** *(5 marks)*
5. **The National Lottery provides money for sport. Explain how this is organised.** *(6 marks)*

International sport

s chapter

In today's world, winning is sometimes seen as all-important. As Clive Woodward said at the Rugby World Cup, 'We're not here to score marks for style; we're here to win.' However, many people still believe that there is more to international sport than the result. In fact, the slogan for the 2006 Football World Cup is 'A time to make friends'.

KEYWORDS

Hosting: providing the venue and organisation for a sporting event

International Sports Federation: organisation responsible for all aspects of the Olympic Games

International Olympic Committee: organisation responsible for all aspects of the Olympic Games.

Key to Exam Success

For your GCSE you will need to know:

- the advantages and disadvantages of holding international events
- the major controversial issues as past Olympic Games.

KEY THOUGHTS

'Sport is war without weapons.'

Why international sport?

All sportspeople dream of one day representing their country in an international competition. It is natural for the best sportspeople in a country to want to compare themselves with those in other countries.

Many good things can come out of international sport:

- Players and spectators have the opportunity to travel to other countries, to have new experiences in other cultures and to develop new friendships.
- Sport can help to bring together people from different backgrounds, ethnic groups, religions and cultures in a shared activity.
- Although people always want their national team to do well, they are usually realistic about the outcome. Playing other national teams can stimulate interest in sport in the countries involved.

International sporting events

The international sports federations (see below) are responsible for arranging their international fixtures for their sport. In the case of major games, this may mean matches spread throughout the sporting year and World or European championships every two or more years. World championships for football, cricket and rugby are well-established events. Winning is the ultimate aim, not just for the players, but for the whole nation.

Sports such as swimming and athletics have their own world championships but are also included in the Olympic Games and Commonwealth Games every four years. Tennis does not have one World Championship event, but four. These are the Australian, French, American and Wimbledon championships, which, together with results in other tournaments, decide who is the number one player in the world.

The Olympic Games are organised by the International Olympic Committee (IOC) and take place every four years, featuring a very wide range of sports.

Following the success of the Olympics, the Commonwealth Games were started in 1930 and are open to all member countries of the Commonwealth. Known as the 'Friendly Games', they follow the Olympic pattern, taking place every four years in between the Olympics. The Asian Games and Pan-American Games (for countries in North and South America) follow the same pattern.

Who controls international sport?

International sport is controlled by the international sports federations and the International Olympic Committee (IOC). The British Olympic Association promotes the Olympics in Britain.

What are the international sports federations?

The international sports federations (ISFs) are independent organisations which are responsible for their sport worldwide. Their membership is made up of representatives of the national governing bodies in all countries where the sport is played.

The role of the ISFs is to:

- encourage the worldwide development of their sport
- control international fixtures and competitions
- enforce and change the rules of their sport
- make sure the rules agree with those of the International Olympic Committee.

The ISFs are financed by the sale of rights to televise major championships and international events; by sponsorship of events, and by payments by national governing bodies.

The International Olympic Committee (IOC)

Working through national Olympic committees, the 125-member strong IOC has responsibility for all aspects of the Olympic Games. It strongly encourages the participation of women in sport and is actively opposed to doping in sport.

The IOC is funded through the sale of television rights and by sponsorship deals with companies acting as official sponsors of the Games.

The British Olympic Association

The British Olympic Association (BOA) is an independent organisation, founded in 1905 as the National Olympic Committee of Great Britain. It is made up of representatives from all Olympic sports and is totally independent of government and politics.

Its mission is to:

- develop interest throughout the UK in the Olympic Games and the Olympic Movement
- run the British Olympic Medical Centre, which offers medical help and sports science expertise to Olympic sportspeople
- help the NGBs of sport to prepare their teams by, for example, providing warm-weather training facilities

- organise the British Olympic team, arranging travel, transport, insurance, healthcare, accommodation, food, training and publicity.

The BOA is paid for by the public (through the British Olympic appeal), by companies (through sponsorship) and through the sale of merchandise licences.

Hosting the Olympics

The IOC chooses the Olympic host city through the votes of its members. Only cities, and not countries, are eligible to apply. Following a number of bribery scandals, new rules were introduced in 1999. Cities cannot now be accepted as official candidates until the IOC is satisfied that they are properly prepared in accordance with IOC guidelines. IOC member visits to such cities and gifts to IOC members are now banned.

All summer Olympics since 1984 have made a healthy profit. This has been because they have taken advantage of commercialisation. Although there are some problems to overcome, there are many benefits in hosting the Games and consequently fierce competition between cities to be chosen.

Advantages include:

- **Improved status**: all great cities and their countries want the high profile and prestige of being an Olympic host.
- **Publicity**: the enormous amount of media coverage ensures that the city becomes famous worldwide.
- **Tourists** spend large amounts of money not just at the Games themselves but throughout their visit to the host country.
- **Improved infrastructure**: roads, transport system and visitor accommodation can all be built or improved to meet the needs of the Games.
- **Sporting facilities**: new or improved sports facilities are essential for the huge range of sporting activities which take place during the Games. These remain afterwards as a permanent part of the city infrastructure.
- **Profit**: commercialisation has meant that all recent Games have made profits through sponsorship, sale of television rights, merchandise and gate receipts.

The key drawback of hosting the Games is that any failure in planning or organisation reflects badly on the city and on the host nation. Other drawbacks include:

The Olympic Games – ancient and modern

The earliest known Olympic Games were held at Olympia in Greece in 776 BC in honour of the God Zeus. From this time onwards they were held every four years without a break for over a thousand years. This was remarkable because the Greek city states were often at war. However, during the period of the Games there was a sacred truce. The events consisted of athletics, boxing, wrestling and chariot racing. The athletics included sprints, a distance race, long jump, discus, javelin and pentathlon, all of which still take place at the Olympics today.

In the early Games the competition was friendly and fair. As they became more important, so did winning. Athletes found trainers, specialised in one event and were well rewarded by their city if they won. The Christian emperor Theodosius stopped the Games in AD 393, claiming they were a pagan festival. Eventually the sacred site at Olympia was destroyed by invaders and by a later flood. It was not until 1896 that the Olympic spirit was brought back to life again.

The modern Olympic Games

The modern Olympic Games were revived in 1896, by Baron Pierre de Coubertin, a French aristocrat who had become interested in sport and recreation. Following a visit to England where he was impressed by the sport he saw in the public schools, de Coubertin organised a conference in 1894 with 79 members from 12 countries, at which it was agreed to revive the Olympic Games.

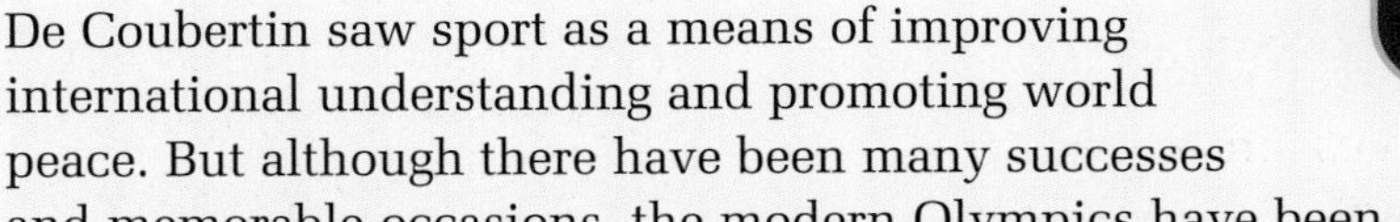

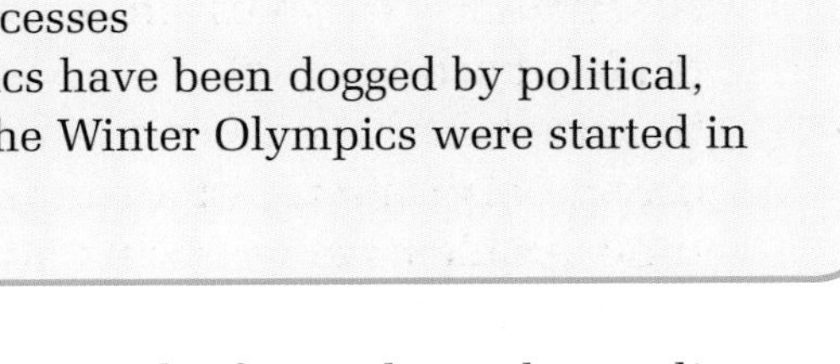

De Coubertin saw sport as a means of improving international understanding and promoting world peace. But although there have been many successes and memorable occasions, the modern Olympics have been dogged by political, financial and other problems over the years. The Winter Olympics were started in 1924 at Chamonix in France.

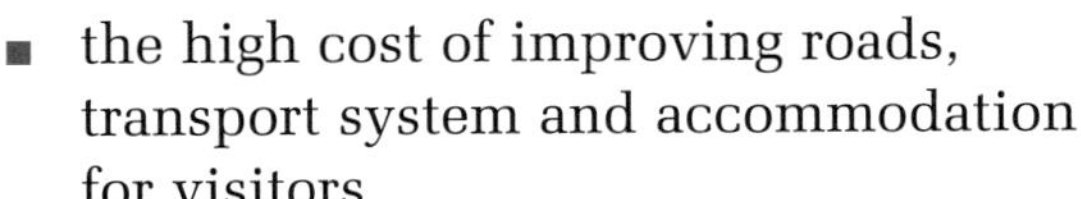

- the high cost of improving roads, transport system and accommodation for visitors
- the huge difficulty of guaranteeing the security of sportspeople, spectators and venues
- the vulnerability of the Games to political protest, terrorist attacks and natural disaster
- the risk of complaints by media, competitors, officials or others about inadequacies in the organisation
- the huge level of financial expertise needed to ensure the event makes a profit.

THE OLYMPIC GAMES 1896–2008

1896 Athens
The Greek government was unable to pay for the Games but they were saved by a wealthy businessman. Thirteen countries took part: Australia, Austria, Britain, Bulgaria, Chile, Denmark, France, Germany, Hungary, Sweden, Switzerland, USA and Greece. Most competitors made their way to the Games at their own expense. There were nine sports and 311 male competitors.

1900 Paris
Coinciding with the Paris Universal Exhibition, the Games were a near-disaster, poorly organised and largely ignored. There were many new sports and women competed in golf and tennis.

1904 St Louis
Held at the same time as the World Fair, the Games made little impression beside the main event. Few countries took part and most competitors were American.

1908 London
Some pride returned to the Games when proper rules were followed. However, there were arguments because all the judges were British.

1912 Stockholm
This was a very well organised event without any major problems. The number of competitors nearly doubled.

1916 Berlin
The Games were cancelled because of the First World War.

1920 Antwerp
Europe had only just recovered from the war and many competitors had suffered during it. Germany, Austria, Hungary, Bulgaria and Turkey were barred from competing.

1924 Paris
The number of participant countries rose to 44, with over 3,000 competitors. Germany and its war allies were still absent. The Winter Games were launched in Chamonix, France.

1928 Amsterdam
De Coubertin, the founder of the modern Games, who was ill, sent a message of farewell, calling on the athletes to keep alive the Olympic spirit. Women took part in athletics and a number collapsed at the end of the 800 metres.

1932 Los Angeles
Travelling costs reduced the number of competitors. There were high spectator numbers, with 100,000 attending the opening ceremony. The first Olympic village was built for competitors.

1936 Berlin
Hitler's Nazi party was in power and persecution of the Jews and others had already begun. However, the IOC insisted that the Games should take place. Hitler used the Games for propaganda purposes to show the superiority of the German people. The black American athlete Jesse Owens defeated Hitler's aim by winning four gold medals. Hitler congratulated the German winners but not Owens.

1940 Tokyo/Helsinki and **1944 London** was cancelled because of the Second World War.

1948 London
This was held in a blitzed city, by a nation exhausted by war. Fifty-nine countries and 4,500 competitors took part, but Germany, Japan and the Soviet Union were absent.

1952 Helsinki
Though known as the 'Friendly Games', these Games saw the start of East–West rivalry. Germany was still absent. The Soviet Union took part again after 40 years.

1956 Melbourne
East and West Germany combined into one team. Spain and Holland withdrew in protest at the Soviet invasion of Hungary. Egypt and the Lebanon withdrew because of fighting over the Suez Canal. China withdrew in protest against the presence of Taiwan, which it considers to be part of China and not a separate country. China only returned to the Olympics in 1984.

1960 Rome
There were no political problems at the Games, which were televised worldwide. A Danish cyclist died after using drugs. South Africa was represented by an all-white team and was subsequently expelled from the Olympic Movement because of the system of apartheid, which discriminated against the black majority. However, some non-Olympic sports, like rugby, maintained their contacts with South Africa.

1964 Tokyo
South Africa was banned because of apartheid, as were Indonesia and North Korea for taking part in an unofficial competition. A total of 94 other countries took part. The Games were expensive but successful.

1968 Mexico City
The Games were overshadowed by the brutal breaking-up of a demonstration against poverty, during which many people were killed. East and West Germany entered as separate teams. There were drug tests for the first time. Mexico's high altitude caused problems for distance athletes. During the medal ceremonies, Black American athletes staged a protest at inequality and injustice in the treatment of black people in the USA by raising black-gloved clenched fists during the medal ceremony. All the athletes involved were sent home.

1972 Munich
The Games were technically brilliant. The all-white Rhodesian team was sent home amid allegations of racist selection. Black American athletes again protested during the medal ceremonies. Against a background of Arab–Israeli conflict, Palestinian terrorists captured and held hostage Israeli athletes and officials in a bid to bring publicity to their cause and to secure the release of Arab prisoners. Following a failed police rescue attempt, all the hostages were killed. After a memorial service, the Games continued, although some teams and individual competitors left early.

1976 Montreal
These Games were enormously costly. French Canadians were angered when the Queen was chosen to open the Games, and Taiwan was forced to withdraw because Canada only recognised China. Black African countries staged a boycott, arguing that New Zealand should have been expelled for playing rugby against South Africa. The IOC refused because rugby was not an Olympic sport.

1980 Moscow
These Olympics were successfully organised but with high security. Western countries, led by the USA and including Canada, Japan and West Germany staged a

boycott in protest at the Soviet invasion of Afghanistan. The British government supported the boycott but would not withdraw passports. A large British team decided to compete.

1984 Los Angeles
These Games were highly commercialised and made a huge profit. Libya withdrew after two of its journalists were refused entry. The Soviet Union, Cuba and most East European countries boycotted the Games following threats of violence by American anti-Soviet groups, claiming that the security of their teams could not be guaranteed. They also complained that the commercial nature of the Games went against Olympic principles. Others saw this as a riposte to countries which had boycotted the Moscow Olympics four years earlier.

1988 Seoul
These Olympics were superbly organised and made large profits. South Korea had no diplomatic links with communist countries and there were no boycotts or disruptions. Ben Johnson won the 100 metres but was disqualified for using drugs. Professional tennis players took part for the first time.

1992 Barcelona
This was a peaceful Olympic Games without incident. South Africa took part again after the release of Nelson Mandela from prison and the collapse of apartheid. Germany took part again as one country following the unification of East and West in 1990. The Soviet team was replaced by a 'Unified' team, and other newly independent countries took part for the first time. Following the break-up of Yugoslavia, former citizens competed as Croatians or independents.

1996 Atlanta
Nearly all countries took part – 197 in all. Competitors numbered 10,788. The Soviet Union was replaced by the Russian Federation and a number of newly independent countries took part for the first time. Full professionals competed, including the USA basketball 'Dream team'. There were problems with high temperatures, the transportation system, overcrowding and computer failures. A mysterious bomb shattered the peace in spite of high security.

2000 Sydney
The Games saw 199 countries take part, with East Timor competing under the Olympic flag. North and South Korea had a combined team for the first time. Women competed in all events except boxing and wrestling. Testing for drugs was made more effective by the introduction of blood tests. A number of Chinese sportspeople and officials withdrew just before the Games. There were ten positive tests for drugs. The Games were said to be the most successful ever.

2004 Athens
These Games are currently giving cause for concern. Some argue that Athens was a poor choice to host the Olympics, given its problems of congestion and air pollution. Construction has not gone smoothly, and there are fears that the work may not be completed on time. In view of the worldwide terrorist threats, security will be a major problem. It is estimated that 201 countries will take part with 10,500 sportspeople and 5,500 team officials.

2008 Bejing
With China's abysmal human rights record, many believed Bejing should not have been awarded the Games. Others argued this would be an opportunity to pressurise China to make improvements. The Chinese have promised that the Games will be highly organised and peaceful.

activity

What's going on?

For each of the following newsflashes about the Olympic Games, write down the year and city in which the Games were held, together with full details of the incident reported.

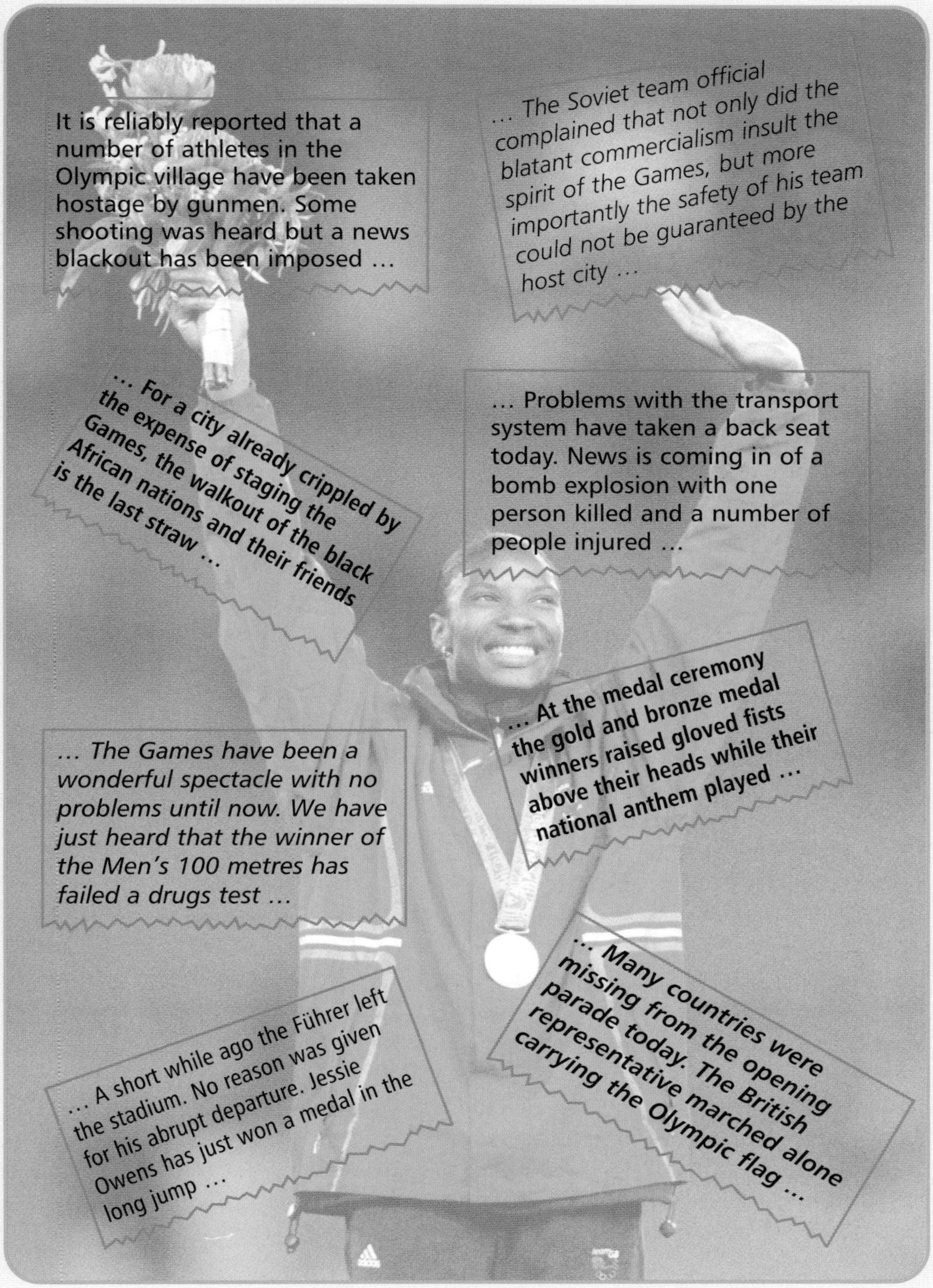

It is reliably reported that a number of athletes in the Olympic village have been taken hostage by gunmen. Some shooting was heard but a news blackout has been imposed …

… The Soviet team official complained that not only did the blatant commercialism insult the spirit of the Games, but more importantly the safety of his team could not be guaranteed by the host city …

… For a city already crippled by the expense of staging the Games, the walkout of the black African nations and their friends is the last straw …

… Problems with the transport system have taken a back seat today. News is coming in of a bomb explosion with one person killed and a number of people injured …

… At the medal ceremony the gold and bronze medal winners raised gloved fists above their heads while their national anthem played …

… The Games have been a wonderful spectacle with no problems until now. We have just heard that the winner of the Men's 100 metres has failed a drugs test …

… A short while ago the Führer left the stadium. No reason was given for his abrupt departure. Jessie Owens has just won a medal in the long jump …

… Many countries were missing from the opening parade today. The British representative marched alone carrying the Olympic flag …

QUESTIONS

26 International sport

1 **The Olympic Games have always been a focus of controversy. For each of the following issues, give the name and date of one of the Games involved together with details of the issue:**

- a Drugs scandal
- b Terrorist attack
- c Financial problems
- d Race issue: Black Power
- e Race issue: apartheid
- f Race issue: nazism
- g Boycott

(3 marks each)

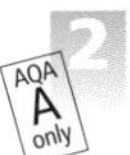

2 **Cities compete to host the Olympic Games. Suggest three benefits and three negative effects of hosting the Games for the city involved.**

(6 marks)

INDEX